# Psychological Assessment
# of Adult Posttraumatic States

# Psychological Assessment
## of
# Adult Posttraumatic States

### PHENOMENOLOGY, DIAGNOSIS, AND MEASUREMENT

#### SECOND EDITION

## John Briere

AMERICAN PSYCHOLOGICAL ASSOCIATION
WASHINGTON, DC

Published by
American Psychological Association
750 First Street, NE
Washington, DC 20002
www.apa.org

To order
APA Order Department
P.O. Box 92984
Washington, DC 20090-2984
Tel: (800) 374-2721
Direct: (202) 336-5510
Fax: (202) 336-5502
TDD/TTY: (202) 336-6123
Online: www.apa.org/books/
E-mail: order@apa.org

In the U.K., Europe, Africa, and the Middle East, copies may be ordered from
American Psychological Association
3 Henrietta Street
Covent Garden, London
WC2E 8LU England

Typeset in Palatino by World Composition Services, Inc., Sterling, VA

Printer: Victor Graphics, Baltimore, MD
Cover Designer: Berg Design, Albany, NY
Project Manager: Debbie Hardin, Carlsbad, CA

The opinions and statements published are the responsibility of the authors, and such opinions and statements do not necessarily represent the policies of the American Psychological Association.

**Library of Congress Cataloging-in-Publication Data**

Briere, John.
    Psychological assessment of adult posttraumatic states : phenomenology, diagnosis, and measurement / John Briere.—2nd ed.
        p. cm.
    Includes bibliographical references.
    ISBN 1-59147-144-3
    1. Post-traumatic stress disorder—Diagnosis. 2. Stress (Psychology)—Testing. I. Title.

RC552.P67B75   2004
616.85′21—dc22                                                    2003028287

**British Library Cataloguing-in-Publication Data**
A CIP record is available from the British Library.

*Printed in the United States of America*
*Second Edition*

This book is dedicated to Murray Wexler, PhD, Chief of Psychological Services at Los Angeles County–University of Southern California Medical Center from 1960 to 1993. Although he liked to tell young psychologists that "the business of life is trouble," he was, and is, an inspiration far beyond that partial truth.

# Contents

# Acknowledgments

Many thanks to those who helped me with the writing and editing of this book or who provided feedback on a specific measure, area of traumatic stress, or assessment issue. These include Judith Armstrong, Megan Berthold, Richard Bryant, Eve Carlson, Connie Dalenberg, Elaine Eaton, Catherine Ehrlich, Diana Elliott, Melissa Farley, James High, Carol Jordan, Laurie Pearlman, Holly Prigerson, Shannae Rickards, Joseph Spinazzola, Frank Weathers, and Onno van der Hart. Thanks also to Judy Nemes and Debbie Hardin for editorial and production assistance. As always, I am indebted to Cheryl Lanktree for sustaining and supporting me and my work over these many years.

# Introduction

Professional awareness of posttraumatic psychological disturbance is relatively new, especially when compared with more
traditional areas of psychological research and clinical practice.
Although there have been anecdotal reports of the psychological
effects of wars and natural disasters throughout recorded history,
much of the empirically validated information on the impact of
interpersonal violence, disasters, and other traumatic events has
been published only since the early to mid–1980s. As a result,
mental health professionals have had less access to clinical data
regarding posttraumatic stress than, for example, similar information on anxiety, depression, or psychosis. Fortunately, our
knowledge of psychological trauma, as well as the availability of
validated trauma-specific assessment devices, has dramatically
increased during the past decade.

The first edition of this book was written in response to this
proliferation of research on psychological trauma, along with the
growing need for scientifically based evaluation of posttraumatic
disturbance and its assessment. The second edition updates and
expands on this endeavor. It reviews in detail a number of new
trauma-relevant tests that have become available since the last
edition and discusses a variety of critical issues associated with
trauma-relevant *DSM–IV* (American Psychiatric Association,
2000) diagnoses. Also included in this second edition is information on additional forms of trauma (e.g., mass violence against
noncombatants, including the terrorist attacks of September 2001;
life-threatening illness and medical procedures; stalking; and sex
trafficking), as well as added material on acute stress responses,
complicated grief reactions, adjustment disorders, posttraumatic
depression, panic disorder, trauma-related psychosis, "culture-
bound" stress responses, peritraumatic dissociation and other
dissociative responses, and complex posttraumatic syndromes.
In addition, this edition includes a brief analysis of "assault
syndromes" (e.g., rape trauma syndrome and battered woman

syndrome) as they relate to trauma assessment in forensic contexts.

This book devotes considerable attention to different forms of trauma exposure and describes in detail the full range of potential posttraumatic responses. In addition, the reference section is relatively extensive. This focus reflects my belief that accurate trauma assessment requires not only knowledge of clinical diagnosis and psychometrics but also a relatively detailed understanding of the etiology and phenomenology of posttraumatic distress. This approach includes not only attention to symptoms and disorders but also some understanding of the various ways and contexts in which people can be traumatized in Western culture. Without such knowledge, the clinician may overlook important traumatic events while taking a history or may not consider certain symptoms or syndromes because he or she is not aware of their potential relevance. For this reason, this book is intended to be a reference on trauma and posttraumatic response as much as a discussion of diagnoses, tests, and interviews.

Although children also experience a variety of difficulties in response to major stressors, this book is limited to adult posttraumatic responses. The interested reader is referred to Friedrich (1994, 2002) and Nader (in press) for information specific to the assessment of traumatized children.

# Psychological Assessment
# of Adult Posttraumatic States

# I

# Etiology and
Phenomenology of
Posttraumatic Stress

# 1

# Trauma Types
# and Characteristics

**B**efore the mid-1980s, individuals in the United States and other English-speaking countries suffering from the sustained effects of overwhelming stressors were either seen as not experiencing a psychological disorder or were given diagnoses of "Adjustment Reaction to Adult Life" or "Transient Situational Reaction" (*Diagnostic and Statistical Manual of Mental Disorders;* 2nd ed.; *DSM–II;* American Psychiatric Association, 1968), or, earlier in diagnostic history, "Gross Stress Reaction" (*DSM–I;* American Psychiatric Association, 1952). As it turns out, the original "Gross Stress Reaction" diagnosis was, in many ways, more in agreement with modern trauma theory than the diagnoses that replaced it. *DSM–II's* "Adjustment Reaction," for example, did much to blur the boundary between posttraumatic responses to an acute trauma and generalized distress associated with conflicts or unwanted (but not necessarily traumatic) life experiences. All of these diagnoses, however, referred to transient responses that could be expected to diminish rapidly when the stressor was terminated. As a result, any individual who experienced significant symptomatology that endured well beyond the traumatic event was thought to have some other, often preexisting, mental condition.

It was not until *DSM–III* (American Psychiatric Association, 1980) that the diagnosis of *posttraumatic stress disorder* (PTSD) appeared, wherein a potentially sustained symptomatic response to a previous trauma was seen as primarily the result of a stressor—not as a reflection of premorbid psychopathology. As noted in chapters 1 and 2, this view of traumatic stress as the result of trauma exposure, alone, was flawed as well. Nevertheless, the formalization of PTSD as a psychiatric diagnosis represented a turning point in the field, codifying as it did the growing awareness of trauma-related distress and disorder.

Interestingly, although formal professional awareness of posttraumatic stress is quite recent, on another level it has been acknowledged by clinicians and lay people for centuries, often with reference to the effects of war. For example, some version of posttraumatic stress has been variously described since World War I as "shell shock," "combat fatigue," "soldier's heart," and "combat neurosis" (Davidson & Foa, 1993). In fact, Trimble (1981) noted that posttraumatic syndromes arising from natural and human-caused events were acknowledged as early as in the 1600s.

## Definition of Trauma

Beyond the substance abuse and "organic mental" disorders, most *DSM–IV*[1] diagnostic categories do not make specific reference to causation. In contrast, a determination of posttraumatic stress requires a specific evaluation of etiology as well as symptomatology. Because *DSM–III, DSM–III–R* (American Psychiatric Association, 1987), and *DSM–IV* (American Psychiatric Association, 2000), require the presence of a major stressor (referred to as "Criterion A") before a diagnosis of PTSD can be made, the clinician must not only assess symptoms of stress but also the nature of the stressor. Although this might appear to be a simple matter of listing those events known to produce posttraumatic stress, the wide variety of adverse circumstances to be found in North American culture defies easy categorization. In addition, it is now clear that an event that produces posttraumatic stress in one individual may not do so for another. For this

---

[1]Throughout this book, the term *DSM–IV* will refer to the final "Text Revision" version (that is, *DSM–IV–TR*) of that manual.

reason, the last three *DSMs* (*DSM–III, DSM–III–R,* and *DSM–IV*) have defined more broadly and parametrically the minimal requirements for a PTSD-level stressor. This definition has changed with each *DSM* edition, theoretically as a result of increasing knowledge about trauma and posttraumatic conditions.

In the spirit of acknowledging the importance of the precipitating stressor, as opposed to solely a pathologic predisposition in the individual, *DSM–III* required only that the trauma satisfy two conditions: (a) that it be of sufficient severity that it would evoke "significant symptoms of distress in most people," and (b) that it be "outside the range of normal human experience" (American Psychiatric Association, 1980, pp. 236–238). *DSM–III–R* added to this definition the notion that the stressor is "usually experienced with intense fear, terror, and helplessness" (American Psychiatric Association, 1987, p. 247), although the *DSM–III–R* did not require one of these responses to categorized the stressor as a trauma. It also noted that a trauma could involve hearing about or witnessing (as opposed to solely experiencing) stressful events. *DSM–III–R* criteria were modified again in *DSM–IV* where trauma is defined as the following:

> Direct personal experience of an event that involves actual or threatened death or serious injury, or other threat to one's physical integrity; or witnessing an event that involves death, injury, or a threat to the physical integrity of another person; or learning about unexpected or violent death, serious harm, or threat of death or injury experienced by a family member or other close associate (Criterion A1). The person's response to the event must involve intense fear, helplessness, or horror (or in children, the response must involve disorganized or agitated behavior) (Criterion A2). (p. 463)

*DSM–IV* provides a nonexhaustive list of representative stressors, including combat, sexual and physical assault, robbery, being kidnapped, being taken hostage, terrorist attacks, torture, disasters, severe automobile accidents, and life-threatening illnesses, as well as witnessing death or serious injury by violent assault, accidents, war, or disaster. Also included is childhood sexual abuse, even if it does not involve threatened or actual violence or injury—an exception to the general A1 requirement.

Although not fully appreciated by some clinicians, *DSM–IV* criteria require that all of the symptoms of PTSD be linked to the same, single traumatic event. In other words, one cannot have PTSD whereby some of one's symptoms are associated with one stressor and others arise from one or more other stressors—the symptoms must all occur in response to a single incident. This is a tenuous proposition, logically. Torture, rape, war, and other severe traumas often consist of a number of discrete events (e.g., being pursued, threatened, expecting injury or death, and the process of being assaulted or being actually physically or psychologically hurt, which may last for minutes, hours, days, or even years), each of which may occur multiple times within a given "trauma," and all of which may be associated with different posttraumatic effects. Yet, although PTSD symptoms can be linked to these "single" mega-traumas under *DSM–IV*, they cannot be combined in other instances where similar—but less connected—multiple traumas have occurred. For example, extended exposure to "the Vietnam war" or "childhood sexual abuse" is an acceptable trauma with which to link PTSD symptoms, yet associating PTSD symptoms to the combined effects of multiple but unrelated physical or sexual assaults experienced over the same time duration (e.g., "raped twice this year on dates" or "attacked three times by gang members since August") is not supported in *DSM–IV*.

In addition to logical problems with the "single stressor" requirement of A1, many traumatized individuals are hard-pressed to describe their various posttraumatic symptoms (especially, for example, psychic numbing or feelings of a foreshortened future) as arising from a single aversive moment. As well, in many cases these individuals have experienced a variety of traumas or an ongoing traumatic process (e.g., terrorization during a physically abusive childhood), the chronology of which may be difficult to link to the specific symptoms of a stress disorder. In fact, despite the expectations of *DSM–IV*, it is not clear what proportion of those diagnosed with PTSD in the "real world" actually developed that syndrome based on a single event. As noted by Carlson (1997), the notion of what constitutes a trauma—and whether it is appropriate to constrain all symptoms to that single traumatic experience—is the subject of ongoing debate in the field.

An additional problem with trauma determination is the notion of threat or injury. A major change in *DSM–IV*'s Criterion A1 was the decision to remove the *DSM–III–R* notion of threats to psychological integrity as a valid trauma. *DSM–IV* considers only events that threaten life or physical injury to be traumatic, no longer including events that were very upsetting but not life-threatening, such as severe emotional abuse, especially humiliating events, major losses, and coerced (but not physically threatening) sexual experiences. Because not all forms of victimization involve physical threat, this change necessarily underestimates the extent of "valid" trauma in the general population and—because Criterion A is required for a PTSD or acute stress disorder (ASD) diagnosis—may inappropriately reduce the availability of a stress disorder diagnosis in some individuals who would otherwise meet all other criteria for ASD or PTSD.

A final issue is that of the individual's subjective response to the potentially traumatic event (Criterion A2). Although generally supported by the *DSM–IV* field trials, the addition of this criterion may be problematic. First, the criterion is, in fact, subjective, in the sense that both client and clinician may have difficulty determining if the fear, horror, or helplessness was sufficiently intense to qualify. Second, there is insufficient research available to determine whether a stressor must evoke these specific responses to be traumatic or PTSD-producing (March, 1993). For example, other negative emotional or cognitive states at the time of a trauma (e.g., humiliation, extreme guilt, disgust) also may be sufficient to produce the symptoms associated with PTSD. Third, reports of subjective distress are easily affected by emotional avoidance, including dissociation, as well as social, gender, or occupational roles regarding denial of emotional distress. It is not at all uncommon, for example, to encounter trauma victims who initially report few negative responses to a traumatic event, only to later acknowledge, as their numbing or denial wanes, that the event actually was quite upsetting. Ironically, the posttraumatic avoidance symptoms of such individuals may cause them to miss the Criterion A2 and be categorized, at least on first evaluation, as nontraumatized by *DSM–IV*.

At minimum, it is likely that the rate of PTSD in the general population has decreased under Criterion A2 (see, for example,

Blanchard & Hickling, 2004), because only more extreme stressors (and more expressive or vulnerable individuals) qualify for the diagnosis—regardless of the existing level of reexperiencing, avoidance, and hyperarousal symptoms associated with a traumatic event.

When the various problems associated with *DSM–IV* trauma specification are considered together, it is clear that mental health professionals have yet to agree on what is a traumatic event and what is not. This poses potential difficulties for the assessor, who may see an individual who has what appears to be a full-blown case of PTSD but who denies any of the three A2 criteria, whose stressor—although highly traumatic—did not include fear of injury or death, or who cannot discriminate which symptoms are linked to which of several traumatic events. In such cases, the diagnostic criteria for PTSD or ASD are not met, and another, less specific diagnosis (e.g., anxiety disorder, not otherwise specified) must be substituted.

## Specific Stressors Known to Produce Posttraumatic States

Although there are many potentially traumatic events, a smaller subset of these is cited regularly in the literature as producing posttraumatic states. Several of these more common stressors are described briefly in terms of their incidence and potential posttraumatic effects. It is important to reiterate that these (and other) traumatic events are often well within the range of normal human experience, in contrast to earlier *DSM* conceptualizations. In fact, surveys suggest that 39% to 75% of people in the general population have experienced at least one major traumatic stressor (Breslau, Davis, Andreski, & Peterson, 1991; Elliott, 1997; Kessler, Sonnega, Bromet, Hughes, & Nelson, 1995; Norris, 1992; Resnick, Kilpatrick, Dansky, Saunders, & Best, 1993).

Although such stressors are common, their ability to produce significant posttraumatic disturbance varies as a function of a wide variety of other variables, as will be discussed later in this chapter. Perhaps one of the most significant of these variables is whether the event was due to nonhuman factors (e.g., earthquakes, floods, tornadoes), unintended acts (e.g., motor vehicle accidents), or arose from intended interpersonal violence (e.g., rape or physical assault). In general, assault or abuse by another person is associated with substantially more posttraumatic disturbance than are natural disasters or unintended acts. In a study directly comparing the effects of disasters to interpersonal violence in the general population, for example, Briere and Elliott (2000) found that interpersonal victimization was associated with far more symptomatology on the Trauma Symptom Inventory (TSI; Briere, 1995) than was disaster exposure. The same study indicated, however, that disasters also were quite capable of producing negative (albeit less common) mental health outcomes that persisted for many years. Because of the typically greater prevalence and psychological impacts of interpersonal violence, this class of traumatic events will receive more attention here than will naturally occurring traumas.

## Disasters

Disasters can be defined as large-scale, potentially injury- or death-producing environmental events that adversely effect a significant number of people. Estimating the prevalence and impacts of disaster in the general population is complicated by whether the term is thought to include technological or human-caused stressors (e.g., toxic spills or nuclear accidents) in addition to natural events such as hurricanes or earthquakes. In either case, however, it appears that disasters are relatively common in the United States. General population surveys suggest that between 13% to 30% of individuals have been exposed to one or more natural disasters in their lifetime (Briere & Elliott, 2000; Green & Solomon, 1995). Ursano, Fullerton, and McCaughey (1994) noted that:

> Between 1965 and 1985, 31 states experienced five or more presidentially declared disasters. Between 1974 and 1980, 37 major catastrophes occurred in the United States. From October 1979 to September 1980, over 688,000 persons and 90,000 different families received emergency care following a disaster. ... In 1990 alone, there were 35 presidentially

declared disasters which involved 585 counties; over $2 billion were obligated by the Federal Emergency Management Agency to assist the victims of these disasters. (p. 4)

A number of studies document the potential psychological effects of exposure to a natural disaster. These include the impacts of earthquakes (e.g., Basoglu, Salcioglu, & Livanou, 2002), fires (e.g., McFarlane, Clayer, & Bookless, 1997), floods (e.g., Green, Lindy, Grace, Gleser, et al., 1990), avalanches (e.g., Finnsdottir & Elklit, 2002), hurricanes (e.g., Sattler et al., 2002), tornados (e.g., North, Smith, McCool, & Lightcap, 1989), and volcanic eruptions (e.g., Goto, Wilson, Kahana, & Slane, 2002). Although disaster can occur in many forms, the experience of physical injury, fear of death, and property loss during a disaster appear to predict most posttraumatic symptomatology (Briere & Elliott, 2000).

Among the psychological symptoms that have been associated with natural disasters are posttraumatic stress (e.g., Johnsen, Eid, Løvstad, & Michelsen, 1997), anxiety (e.g., Cardeña et al., 1998), depression (e.g., Armenian et al., 2002), dissociation (e.g., Cardeña & Speigel, 1993), and somatic complaints (e.g., Norris, Phifer, & Kaniasty, 1994).

## Mass Violence Against Noncombatants

Although sometimes listed under disasters, intentional violence that involves high numbers of injuries or casualties—but does not occur in the context of declared war—requires its own category. The terrorist attacks on the World Trade Center and the Pentagon on September 11, 2001, or the Oklahoma City bombing on April 19, 1995, obviously come to the North American mind in the context of mass trauma. However, there also have been a large number of nonwar atrocities or terrorist attacks against people in various other locales throughout the world (e.g., Alexander, 2001; Boudarene, 2002; Desivilya, Gal, & Ayalon, 1996; Gautam et al., 1998; Gidron, 2002; Kawana, Ishimatsu, & Kanda, 2001; Pfefferbaum et al., 2001).

The effects of the September 2001 terrorist-directed airliner crashes into the World Trade Center have been widely studied.

They suggest that the attacks produced the same general effects found in other mass traumas, especially in terms of elevated anxiety, depression, posttraumatic stress, and substance abuse (Galea et al., 2002; Schlenger et al., 2002; Silver, Holman, McIntosh, Poulin, & Gil-Rivas, 2002; Vlahov et al., 2002). Although the most severe posttraumatic effects tended to be concentrated within a few square miles of the "ground zero" area (Galea et al., 2002; Schlenger et al., 2002), the atrocity obviously affected the entire United States and the world at large, albeit not necessarily symptomatically.

## Large-Scale Transportation Accidents

Transportation accidents involve events such as airline crashes, train derailments, and maritime accidents. These events often involve multiple victims and high fatality rates. Although the incidence of such events is not readily determined, the traumatic stress literature cites a number of transportation-related traumatic events (e.g., Bartone & Wright, 1990; Birmes, Arrieu, Payen, Warner, & Schmitt, 1999; Chung, Farmer, Werrett, Easthope, & Chung, 2001). A review of these studies suggest impacts similar to those of disasters, including PTSD, anxiety, and depression. The rates of PTSD for plane crash survivors may be especially high: Sloan (1988) found, for example, that 54% of those who lived through a chartered plane crash had PTSD soon after the event, and 10% to 15% still had PTSD one year later.

## Motor Vehicle Accidents

It is estimated that between 19% to 23% of individuals in the United States have experienced a serious (e.g., injury-producing) motor vehicle accident (MVA; Blanchard & Hickling, 2004), of which approximately 7% to 45%—depending on the study and the time of measurement—go on to develop PTSD (Blanchard & Hickling, 2004; Mayou, Bryant, & Ehlers, 2001; Kessler et al., 1995; Norris, 1992). Beyond posttraumatic stress responses such as ASD and PTSD, MVAs may lead to depression, panic disorder, generalized anxiety, somatization, and substance abuse (e.g., Malta, Blanchard, Taylor, Hickling, & Freidenberg, 2002; Mayou,

2002; Mayou, Bryant, & Ehlers, 2001). A common post-MVA presentation in trauma treatment centers is phobic avoidance of driving and of the geographic location of the crash, often requiring the use of more *in vivo* desensitization techniques than is sometimes necessary for other traumas. The additional presence of traumatic brain injury in some MVA (and other accident) victims can add to the clinical picture and complicate diagnosis (Harvey & Bryant, 2001).

## Emergency Worker Exposure to Trauma

Because emergency workers often encounter potentially traumatic phenomena, such as grotesque death, dismemberment, disfigurement, and mortal injury, it is not surprising that those who help the traumatized may become traumatized themselves. Among those known to be at risk for such work-related stress are firefighters and rescue workers (e.g., North, McCutcheon, Spitznagel, & Smith, 2002), paramedics and other emergency medical workers (e.g., Galloucis, Silverman, & Francek, 2000), individuals involved in the identification and handling of deceased trauma victims (e.g., McCarroll, Ursano, Fullerton, Liu, & Lundy, 2001), emergency mental health and crisis intervention workers (e.g., Berah, Jones, & Valent, 1984), and law enforcement personnel (e.g., Sewell, 1993). Psychotherapists who treat trauma survivors may also develop a form of vicarious traumatization (e.g., Pearlman & Saakvitne, 1995).

The effects of trauma on emergency workers tend to involve psychological reactions to the actual stressor, such as ASD or PTSD, dissociation, shock, and depression (e.g., Bryant & Harvey, 1996; Rivard, Dietz, Martell, & Wideaski, 2002). Also present may be feelings of helplessness and frustration in the face of seemingly "unfixable" medical or psychological injuries or injustice (e.g., Sewell, 1993) and repeated contact with survivors' extreme distress (e.g., Hodgkinson & Shepard, 1994).

## War

Until recently, much of the study of posttraumatic stress has been the study of war-related psychological disturbance. In fact, the appearance of PTSD as a diagnostic category in *DSM–III* reflected, in large part, the need to categorize the effects of the Vietnam War on those returning from combat (Weathers, Litz, & Keane, 1995). Posttraumatic difficulties have been described in veterans of the American Civil War and World Wars I and II, as well as in those who fought in "conflicts," "police actions," and other combat situations in countries or regions such as Afghanistan, Armenia, Bosnia, Cambodia, the Falklands, Iraq, Israel, Korea, Liberia, the Persian Gulf, Somalia, Turkey, and Vietnam.

War involves a wide range of violent and traumatic experiences, including immediate threat of death or disfigurement, actual physical injury, witnessing injury or the death of others, involvement in injuring or killing others (both combatants and civilians), witnessing or participating in atrocities (including rape), being captured, and prisoner-of-war experiences such as confinement, torture, and extreme deprivation. Further, as noted by Weathers, Litz, and Keane (1995):

> Each war poses its own hardships that color the experience of combatants and produce unique effects on long-term psychological adjustment. Wars differ with respect to climate . . . , terrain . . . , methods of warfare . . . , and types of weapons used. Also, wars may be fought on domestic or foreign soil, and they may be popular or unpopular. Finally, the experience of war may be very different depending on combatants' branch of service . . . and specific duties. . . . (p. 107)

Because of the variability of traumatic exposure and its context, war can produce a wide variety of psychological effects on both combatants and civilians, including dissociative responses, depression, generalized anxiety, chronic guilt, aggression, suicidality, and substance abuse (e.g., Berthold, 2000; Bleich, Gelkopf, & Solomon, 2003; Bremner, Steinberg, Southwick, Johnson, & Charney, 1993; Gray, Reed, Kaiser, Smith, & Gastanaga, 2002; Hicklin, 2003; Kulka et al., 1990; Miller et al., 2002). Most typically, however, PTSD is described as the major sequel of combat. The incidence of PTSD for most wars is nearly impossible to ascertain because the clinical data on them antedate the development of modern PTSD criteria. Kulka et al. (1990), however, estimate the current prevalence of PTSD for Vietnam theater veterans as 15.2% for males and 8.5% for females, whereas the lifetime prevalence for PTSD in this group is 30.6% for males and 26.9% for females, with even higher rates for those with the greatest combat exposure.

## Rape and Sexual Assault

Modern definitions of rape and sexual assault vary considerably across and within legal, clinical, and research contexts, and from state to state. The National Violence Against Women Survey (NVAWS; Tjaden & Thoennes, 2000), developed as a joint project of the National Institute of Justice (NIJ) and the Centers for Disease Control and Prevention (CDC), defines rape as "an event that occurred without the victim's consent, that involved the use or threat of force to penetrate the victim's vagina or anus by penis, tongue, fingers, or object, or the victim's mouth by penis" (p. 4). Not included in this definition, unfortunately, are situations in which the victim is not physically forced or threatened but incapable of giving consent, such as when under the influence of alcohol or drugs, or is sleeping. The definition of sexual assault typically involves any forced or nonconsenting sexual contact short of rape, although some authorities consider sexual assault to involve any forced or nonconsenting sexual contact, including rape.

Using definitions similar to these, the prevalence of rape against women in the United States is generally thought to be somewhere between 14% to 20% (Kilpatrick & Resnick, 1993; Koss, 1993; Tjaden & Thoennes, 2000), although some studies report higher or lower figures. There does not appear to be a widely accepted prevalence rate for sexual assault of women, partially due to definitional and methodological issues. Rape and sexual assault rates for males is somewhat less clear, probably because of the only recent social awareness that men can be rape victims (Stermac, Sheridan, Davidson, & Dunn, 1996). Nevertheless, several studies suggest that between 5% and 10% of all sexual assault victims are men (Forman, 1982; Kaufman, Divasto,

Jackson, Voorhees, & Christy, 1980; Stermac et al., 1996). Congruent with this estimate, two recent studies suggest that between 2% and 4% of men in the general population have been sexually assaulted (Elliott, Mok, & Briere, in press; Tjaden & Thoennes, 2000). Because of the shame and secrecy typically associated with being a victim of rape or sexual assault in many cultures, it is likely that some victims do not identify themselves as such in research studies.

The psychological effects of rape appear to be wide-ranging, including fear, anxiety, anger, depression, low self-esteem, reduced social functioning, sexual difficulties, suicidality, substance abuse, dissociative symptoms, and PTSD (e.g., Dancu, Riggs, Hearst-Ikeda, Shoyer, & Foa, 1996; Elliott et al., in press; Petrak & Campbell, 1999; Resick, 1993; Ullman & Brecklin, 2002). Two longitudinal studies of rape victims presenting to emergency rooms suggest that symptoms of PTSD are very common soon after the assault and often decrease in frequency as time passes. Rothbaum, Foa, Riggs, Murdock, and Walsh (1992) found that 94% of their sample of rape victims met symptomatic criteria for *DSM–III–R* PTSD an average of 13 days after the assault, 65% met full PTSD criteria after an average of 35 days, and 47% still had PTSD at 94 days. Similarly, Kramer and Green (1991) found that 73% of the rape victims they studied met *DSM–III* criteria for PTSD six to eight weeks after the assault. Some rape victims experience posttraumatic difficulties for an indefinite period of time (Gilbert, 1994). Kilpatrick and Resnick (1993), for example, reported that approximately 15 years after being raped, 12.5% of the victims they studied still had PTSD. In another study, sexual assault victims in the general population continued to have elevated scores on the TSI an average of 14 years after the assault (Elliott et al., in press).

## Intimate Partner Violence

Intimate partner violence (also known as spouse, wife, or partner battering; spouse abuse; or domestic violence) has been defined as physical, visual, verbal, or sexual acts against an intimate partner that are experienced as a threat, invasion, or assault and that have the effect of hurting or degrading the person or taking away her or his ability to control contact with another individual (from Koss et al., 1994, p. xvi, adapted to reflect both victim genders). Although males may be assaulted by their wives or partners (e.g., Straus, Gelles, & Steinmetz, 1980), more violent acts are perpetrated by men against women (Straus, 1979), and women are more likely to sustain injury during attacks by their partners than are men (Stets & Straus, 1990). As noted by Jordan, Nietzel, Walker, and Logan (in press), domestic violence by women against men often involves different etiologies, behaviors, and outcomes than man-on-woman intimate violence.

Historically, data on the epidemiology of wife battering (used hereinafter to refer to physical violence against a cohabitating female sexual partner by a man) typically used the Conflict Tactics Scale (CTS; Straus, 1979) as a measurement instrument. The CTS asks individuals to indicate whether they engaged in, or were exposed to, a number of specific violent or abusive behaviors during a dispute in the previous year. Three large general population studies (Straus & Gelles, 1990; Schulman, 1979 [described in Dutton, 1992]; Straus et al., 1980) indicate that severe assaults against wives (e.g., kicking, biting, hitting with a fist, beating up, using a knife, firing a gun) were reported on the CTS for between 9% and 13% of couples. If the definition included any violence against wives (e.g., including slapping, pushing, and shoving), the rates increased to 21% to 28%. In another recent study, using a measure other than the CTS, 28% of 472 women from the general population reported at least one incident of partner physical violence in their lives (Elliott & Briere, in press).

Some of the newest large-sample research in this area is the NVAWS study (Tjaden & Thoennes, 2000). Using a modified version of the CTS, this survey of 8,000 women and 8,000 men from the general population found that 22% of women and 7% of men reported having been raped or physically assaulted by a current or former spouse, cohabiting partner, boyfriend or girlfriend, or date at some point in their lifetime.

Generally included in working definitions of intimate partner violence are four forms of battering: (a) physical, (b) sexual, (c) destruction of property and pets, and (d) psychological (Ganley, 1981; Stordeur & Stille, 1989). Importantly, however, research shows that when one form of abuse exists, it is most often accompanied by other forms. Partner physical violence, for example, often occurs in the context of coexisting psychological abuse (O'Leary, 1999) and sexual assault (Campbell & Soeken, 1999). Among women who are physically assaulted by a partner, concomitant rates of sexual assault as high as 45% have been reported (Campbell & Soeken, 1999), and for women who seek protective shelter from violence, the incidence of marital rape may be as high as 59% (Shields, Resick, & Hanneke, 1990). Rates of sexual assault of women by partners or spouses—irrespective of their history of physical battering—range from 8% to 14% (Finkelhor & Yllo, 1985; Hanneke, Shields, & McCall, 1986; Tjaden & Thoennes, 2000). In general agreement with these findings, the study cited earlier, by Elliott and Briere (in press), found that 15% of a sample of general population women reported at least one sexual assault by a partner.

The psychological effects of spouse or partner abuse frequently have been described in terms of a "battered woman syndrome" (e.g., Walker, 1984, 1991). Clinical descriptions of this syndrome generally refer to symptoms of PTSD, as well as depression, fearfulness, guilt, poor self-image, and learned helplessness (Houskamp, 1994). Empirical studies generally support this symptom list (especially with reference to PTSD), as well as documenting greater somatization, substance abuse, and various anxiety disorders (e.g., Astin, Ogland-Hand, Coleman, & Foy, 1995; Dutton, Hohnecker, Halle, & Burghardt, 1994; Elliott & Briere, in press; Jordan, Nietzel, Walker, & Logan, in press; Mechanic, Uhlmansiek, Weaver, & Resick, 2000; Mertin & Mohr, 2001). The notion of whether there is a specific battered woman syndrome, however, is debatable (see page 66).

## Stalking

Taking a variety of legal definitions into account, stalking can be defined as intentionally and repeatedly following or harassing another person in such a way that would reasonably cause her or him to feel terrorized, frightened, intimidated, threatened, or alarmed. Although verbal threats are common, they are not always required for the definition. Examples of stalking include following an individual to or from work or home; repeatedly leaving unwanted notes, phone messages, or objects; continually surveilling someone from a distance; cyber-stalking via computer; and repeatedly vandalizing a person's property.

Although stalking only recently has been appreciated as a form of victimization, the NVAWS study found that approximately 8% of women and 2% of men in the United States have been stalked by someone known or unknown to them (Tjaden & Thoennes, 1998). Often terrorizing in and of itself, stalking also is associated with the various forms of interpersonal violence described in this chapter. For example, according to the NVAWS study, 81% of women who were stalked by a former intimate partner were also physically assaulted by that person, and 31% were also sexually assaulted.

As might be predicted, exposure to stalking produces effects similar to other forms of interpersonal trauma. These include posttraumatic stress, depression, anxiety, suicidality, guilt, and helplessness (e.g., Kamphuis, Emmelkamp, & Bartak, 2003; Mechanic, Uhlmansiek, Weaver, & Resick, 2000; Pathé & Mullen, 1997).

## Torture

Torture has been defined by the United Nations (reproduced in Vesti & Kastrup, 1995, p. 214) as "Any act by which severe pain or suffering, whether physical or mental, is intentionally inflicted on a person for such purposes as obtaining from him [sic] or a third person information or confession, punishing him for an act he has committed or is suspected of having committed, or intimidating him or a third person." Although this definition is quite broad, it does not include other, less intrinsically political acts such as random torture of citizens by invading military forces, the abduction and subsequent sexual torture of women for sadistic gratification, or the ongoing physical and sexual torture that sometimes occurs in severe domestic violence. A review of the prevalence and characteristics of torture worldwide (Amnesty International, 2002) indicates that most politically based torture occurs at the hands of police officers, especially in totalitarian states, and often begins within a few hours or days of arrest.

Regardless of context, the actual methods of torture involve both physical and psychological techniques. Physical torture activities include beatings, near strangulation, electric shocks, insertion of objects into bodily orifices, various forms of sexual abuse and assault, crushing or breaking of bones and joints, and exposure to extreme heat, cold, or chemical corrosives. Psychological methods include sensory deprivation, threats of death or mutilation, forced nakedness and sexual exposure, mock executions, being made to feel responsible for the death or injury of others, sleep deprivation, and being forced to engage in grotesque or humiliating acts.

The incidence of torture is not known, although Amnesty International (2002) estimates that more than 111 nations currently sanction the use of—or at least tacitly allow—this practice. Torture victims are dramatically overrepresented among refugees (e.g., Baker, 1992)—it is estimated, for example, that 500,000 torture survivors from other countries currently live in the United States (Center for Victims of Torture, 2004). Unfortunately, such individuals are rarely questioned about a potential torture history when they come in contact with North American mental health systems. Additionally, those who have been tortured may be especially reluctant to describe or report injuries at the hands of authorities to seemingly new examples of institutional authority (e.g., agencies, hospitals, or medical or psychological personnel).

The psychological effects of torture are diverse, partially because of the many types of torture and the various contexts in which they occur. Minimally, torture has been associated with posttraumatic stress, depression, anxiety disorders, sleep disturbance, sexual problems, psychosis, somatic symptoms, guilt, self-hatred, and suicidality (e.g., Eisenman, Gelberg, Liu, & Shapiro, 2003; Ekblad, Prochazka, & Roth, 2002; El Sarraj, Punamaki, Salmi, & Summerfield, 1996; Engdahl & Eberly, 1990; Okawa, Gaby, & Griffith, 2003; Silove, Steel, McGorry, Miles, & Drobny, 2002; Turner, Yuksel, & Silove, 2003; Van Ommeren et al., 2002).

Because torture victims seen in North America and Europe are typically refugees from other countries who bring with them a wide variety of cultural perspectives, clinical work with torture-related psychological disorder is often quite complicated. Beyond the difficulties associated with conducting assessment (not to mention therapy) through translators, such work requires geopolitical awareness and cross-cultural sensitivity. The interested reader is referred to the Web site for the International Rehabilitation Council for Torture Victims (www.irct.org).

## Prostitution and Sex-Trafficking

Although not covered in most general discussions of trauma exposure (see, however, Herman, 1992b; and Dutton, Kilpatrick, Friedman, & Patel, 2003), commercial sexual exploitation is a significant world phenomenon with substantial mental health impacts on its victims (Farley, in press). Included in this category are those involved in prostitution, sex shows, massage parlors, escort services, cyber-sex Web sites, and pornography. An increasing number of these individuals are women who have been trafficked into the North America sex industry from other countries. A report from the U.S. Central Intelligence Agency estimates, for example, that "of the 700,000 to two million women and children who are trafficked globally each year, 45,000 to 50,000 of those women and children are trafficked to the United States" (Richard, 2000, p. 3).[2] Most trafficked people in the United States and Canada originate from Southeast Asia, Latin America, and the former Soviet block countries. Upon their arrival into North America, these individuals are typically forced into brothels, street prostitution, or various forms of sexual "entertainment" (Richard, 2000).

Whether trafficked from other countries or born in North America, those involved in prostitution almost inevitably live difficult lives. In fact, research on prostitutes and others in the sex industry indicates that so-called sex work is less a freely chosen occupation than the effects of poverty, social deprivation, and previous victimization (Farley & Kelly, 2000; McClanahan,

---

[2]This report is available on the Web at www.cia.gov/csi/monograph/women/trafficking.pdf

McClelland, Abram, & Teplin, 1999; Nixon, Tutty, Downe, Gorkoff, & Ursel, 2002; Potter, Martin, & Romans, 1999; Simons & Whitbeck, 1991). A number of studies, for example, indicate that the rate of childhood sexual abuse among prostitutes ranges from 50% to 90% (e.g., Bagley & Young, 1987; Farley et al., in press; James & Meyerding, 1977; Silbert & Pines, 1981, 1982).

Those enmeshed in the sex industry are at considerable risk of additional victimization, as well. Studies suggest that prostitutes have at least a 40% to 80% probability of rape (Farley & Barkan, 1998; Miller & Schwartz, 1995; Silbert & Pines, 1982; Valera, Sawyer, & Schiraldi, 2000) and experience considerable physical and emotional abuse (Farley, Baral, Kiremire, & Sezgin, 1998; Miller & Schwartz, 1995; Vanwesenbeek, de Graaf, van Zessen, Straver, & Visser, 1995). In combination with maltreatment by pimps (Nixon et al., 2002; Williamson & Cluse-Tolar, 2002), risk of life-threatening diseases such as acquired immune deficiency syndrome (AIDS) and hepatitis (e.g., Jackson, Highcrest, & Coates, 1992), psychological distress associated with the experience of prostitution (El-Bassel & Schilling, 1997; Kramer, in press) and the childhood abuse that often precedes it, such victimization produces unusually high rates of PTSD, substance abuse, anxiety, depression, and other forms of psychological disturbance among prostitutes (Dutton et al., 2003). For example, using the civilian version of the PTSD Checklist (PCL–C; Weathers, Litz, Herman, Huska, & Keane, 1993), Farley and Barkan (1998) found that 68% of 130 prostitutes interviewed in San Francisco satisfied *DSM–IV* criteria for PTSD. Other studies also have found high PTSD rates for prostitutes, ranging from 42% to 86%, in studies that span a number of countries (Farley et al., 1998; Farley et al., in press; Valera et al., 2000).

## Life-Threatening Illness

Illnesses and medical procedures involving potential life-threat are known to produce posttraumatic stress in some individuals, along with anxiety, depression, and other psychological symptoms (Mohta, Sethi, Tyagi, & Mohta, 2003; Tedstone & Tarrier, 2003). For example, studies indicate that PTSD (and, presumably, ASD) may arise in the context of myocardial infarction (Bennet,

Conway, Clatworthy, Brooke, & Owen, 2001), stroke or brain hemorrhage (Sembi, Tarrier, O'Neill, Burns, & Faragher, 1998), miscarriage (Engelhard, van den Hout, & Arntz, 2001), HIV infection (Kelly et al., 1998), and cancer (Kangas, Henry, & Bryant, 2002). In addition, invasive medical procedures such as heart surgery or intensive care treatment are associated with elevated PTSD rates (Stoddard & Todres, 2001; Stoll et al., 2000), as are related medical complications, such as unexpected awareness under anesthesia (Osterman, Hopper, Heran, Keane, & van der Kolk, 2001).

The actual prevalence of PTSD in individuals exposed to life-threatening illness or medical procedures is widely variable in these studies, ranging from a few individuals to greater than half of those in some acute medical contexts. This variability probably arises from the same sorts of variables found to be moderators of posttraumatic impacts in other areas. For example, Tedstone and Tarrier (2003) noted in their review of medical illness and PTSD that demographics, personality style, previous traumas or adversities, psychiatric history, and reduced social support all appear to predict a greater likelihood of posttraumatic stress in response to life-threatening medical conditions. Interestingly, the severity of the illness itself does not appear to be especially contributory to the development of posttraumatic disturbance.

## Child Abuse

Although child abuse is not an adult trauma, its psychological impacts often continue into the long term and can affect individuals' responses to later stressors (Breslau, Chilcoat, Kessler, & Davis, 1999). For these reasons, child maltreatment and its effects are presented here.

Childhood sexual and physical abuse is unfortunately quite prevalent in North American society, if not the world. U.S. government publications indicate that, in 2000 alone, approximately 879,000 children were determined by child protective agencies to be abused or neglected, and 1,200 were killed as a result of child abuse or neglect (U.S. Department of Health and Human Services, 2002). These statistics are likely to be substantial underestimates, because they rely on (a) incidents reported to agencies, and (b) incidents that were accompanied by sufficient evidence to warrant a determination of abuse. Studies of retrospective child abuse reports by adults in the general population (e.g., Bagley, 1991; Briere & Elliott, 2003; Finkelhor, Hotaling, Lewis, & Smith, 1990; Russell, 1983; Wyatt, 1985) suggest that approximately 25% to 35% of women and 10% to 20% of men, if asked, describe being sexually abused as children, and approximately 10% to 20% of men and women report experiences congruent with definitions of physical abuse. Even the most severe levels of sexual victimization of children are not uncommon in the general population. For example, the NVAWS study (Tjaden & Thoennes, 2000) found that approximately 9% of women in the general population reported having experienced a completed rape before age 18, and 22% these women stated that their rape occurred before age 12. In the case of men, 1.9% reported having been rape before age 18, and 48% of these rapes were said to occur before age 12.

Probably because of the negative effects of such maltreatment, several recent studies suggest that approximately 35% to 70% of female mental health patients (according to type of clinical setting) self-report, if asked, a childhood history of sexual abuse (e.g., Briere, Woo, McRae, Foltz, & Sitzman, 1997; Briere & Zaidi, 1989; Bryer, Nelson, Miller, & Kroll, 1987; Chu & Dill, 1990).[3]

The child maltreatment literature indicates that adults abused as children, as a group, exhibit a wide range of psychological and interpersonal problems (see reviews by Berliner & Elliott, 2002; Briere, 1992a; Finkelhor, 1990; Kolko, 2002; Neumann, Houskamp, Pollock, & Briere, 1996). These include symptoms of chronic PTSD (e.g., Carlson et al. 2001; Ullman & Brecklin, 2002) and dissociative symptomatology (e.g., Briere & Runtz, 1990a; Simeon, Guralnik, Schmeidler, Sirof, & Knutelska, 2001). Also present may be more personality-related problems in personal identity, interpersonal boundaries, and affect regulation

---

[3] Equivalent data on male mental health patients are largely unavailable at this time, although clinical experience suggests that the incidence of sexual and physical abuse is elevated in this group as well.

(Brodsky et al., 2001; Cole & Putnam, 1992; Elliott, 1994b). Together, the various sequelae of childhood maltreatment are described well by the notion of "complex PTSD" outlined in chapter 2, although that label may not always fit the average clinically presenting child abuse survivor (Briere & Spinazzola, in press).

# General Determiners of Posttraumatic Response

Specific stressor types aside, the extant trauma literature suggests that the amount of posttraumatic symptomatology an individual experiences is a function of at least four broad variables: variables specific to the victim, characteristics of the stressor, subjective responses to the stressor, and how those around the victim respond to him or her. As will be noted below, none of these variables exist independently of one another. For example, certain victim characteristics (e.g., sex, socioeconomic status, lower psychological functioning) may increase the likelihood of interpersonal victimization and may limit the amount of social support or clinical intervention available to the victim during and after the event. Similarly, characteristics of the traumatic events may interact with victim variables and posttrauma social response to determine the individual's subjective response to the stressor. As a result, it may be difficult to tease out the relative contributions of specific traumatic events, preexisting psychological or demographic variables, and social system response to the victim when attempting to determine the specific etiology of a given posttraumatic psychological state. As will be noted in later chapters, the complexity of these relationships supports the use of multiple measures and assessment foci when evaluating trauma-related phenomena.

## Victim Variables

Yehuda and McFarlane (1995) noted that research reveals a number of predisposing or antecedent factors that increase the likelihood that a given stressor will produce posttraumatic stress disorder. In fact, they concluded that the multiplicity of victim-level risk factors for PTSD "appears to call into question the most fundamental assumption of PTSD as potentially occurring in any individual as a result of exposure to traumatic stress" (p. 1708). Although it probably would be erroneous to consider PTSD and related posttraumatic states as solely disorders of inadequate stress tolerance, there is little question that certain variables increase the likelihood of a posttraumatic stress response (Brewin, Andrews, & Valentine, 2000; Ozer, Best, Lipsey, & Weis, 2003). These appear to include the following:

- ☐ Female gender (e.g., Breslau et al., 1991; Leskin & Sheikh, 2002);
- ☐ Age (e.g., Norris, Kaniasty, Conrad, Inman, & Murphy, 2002; Rosenman, 2002);
- ☐ Race (e.g., Kulka et al., 1990; Ruch & Chandler, 1983);
- ☐ Lower socioeconomic status (e.g., Kulka et al., 1990; Rosenman, 2002);
- ☐ Previous psychological dysfunction or disorder (e.g., Brady, Killeen, Brewerton, & Lucerini, 2000; Kulka et al., 1990; Ursano et al., 1999);
- ☐ Less functional coping styles (e.g., Fauerbach, Richter, & Lawrence, 2002; Silver, Holman, McIntosh, Poulin, & Gil-Rivas, 2002);
- ☐ Family dysfunction or history of psychopathology (e.g., Bassuk, Dawson, Perloff, & Weinreb, 2001; Breslau et al., 1991; Ursano et al., 1999); and
- ☐ Genetic predisposition (e.g., Stein, Jang, Taylor, Vernon, & Livesley, 2002; Segman et al., 2002).

As noted later in this chapter, however, several of these variables increase the likelihood of exposure to trauma (especially interpersonal violence) in the first place, thereby potentially confounding risk factors for PTSD with those for experiencing traumatic events.

Also relevant to an individual's response to traumatic stressors is his or her previous history of other aversive events. Generally, those who have experienced previous traumas, including childhood maltreatment, are prone to exacerbated reactions to current traumas (e.g., Coker et al., 2002; King, King, Foy, & Gudanowski,

1996; Ozer et al., 2003). This phenomenon may be even more likely if the previous trauma and the current one are similar in important respects. In some instances, the restimulated response to an earlier trauma may summate with the current reaction, producing, in a sense, a "double PTSD." In other cases, the previous response may interact with the current reaction in such a way that the current response is more extreme or especially exacerbated.

As an example of previous trauma effects (as well as their complexity), a number of studies indicate that childhood abuse is a significant risk factor for subsequent victimization as an adult (e.g., Briere & Elliott, 2003; Classen et al., 2002; Cloitre, Tardiff, Marzuk, Leon, & Portera, 1996; Messman-Moore & Long, 2003; Neumann et al., 1996; Stermac, Reist, Addison, & Millar, 2002; Tjaden & Thoennes, 2000). Because both childhood and adult traumas can produce psychological difficulties, current symptomatology in such individuals may represent (a) the effects of the more recent sexual or physical assault, (b) the chronic effects of childhood abuse, (c) the additive effects of childhood abuse and adult assault (e.g., flashbacks to both childhood and adult victimization), or (d) the exacerbating interaction of child abuse and adult assault (e.g., especially severe, regressed, dissociated, or even transiently psychotic responses).

Apropos of the relationship between multiple trauma effects, Zaidi and Foy (1994) reported that individuals with child abuse experiences were considerably more likely to develop PTSD in response to adult combat experiences than were those without an abuse history. In a similar vein, Breslau and colleagues (1999) found that individuals in the general population who had experienced multiple assaults in childhood were considerably more likely to experience PTSD in response to adult traumas. Beyond the interaction between childhood and adult traumatic events, a general finding in the trauma literature is that the more traumatic events that have occurred in a given individual's life, the more posttraumatic symptomatology is likely to be present (e.g., Dougall, Herberman, Delahanty, Inslicht, & Baum, 2000; Follette, Polusney, Bechtel, & Naugle, 1996; Nishith, Mechanic, & Resick, 2000). Thus, the client's recent and remote trauma history must be taken into account before his or her symptoms can be attributed solely to a given event.

The different victim variables outlined, although often found to effect posttraumatic outcome, do not inevitably do so. In fact, the majority of variables described in this section as potential moderators of posttraumatic states have been found in at least one study to have no significant relationship to posttraumatic outcome. Among the potential reasons for this variability may be (a) the characteristics of the sample studied (for example, race might not emerge as an important moderator of outcome in university students, yet might be an important variable among combat veterans), (b) methodological issues such as restriction of range in the mediating variable or insufficient statistical power (both of which can mask mediator effects), (c) the traumatic event under investigation (e.g., rape vs. a natural disaster), and (d) the instrument or procedure used to assess posttraumatic outcome (e.g., a PTSD scale versus a diagnostic impression formed during an emergency room evaluation).

Furthermore, not all victim variables operate in the same manner across their entire range, nor is such pretrauma moderation necessarily independent of the specific trauma considered, or even the culture in which it occurs. For example, although older people may be more susceptible to posttraumatic stress following sexual assault than are younger individuals (e.g., Atkeson, Calhoun, Resick, & Ellis, 1982), other research suggests that early trauma—perhaps by virtue of its potential to disrupt development and elaborate over time—may be especially traumagenic (Briere et al., 1997; Koenen et al., 2002; Neria, Bromet, Sievers, Lavelle, & Fochtmann, 2002). In the disaster area, on the other hand, it appears that middle-aged Americans are at greatest risk of negative outcomes (Norris et al., 2002), whereas, among disaster-affected Mexicans and Poles, age has a negative linear and positive linear relationship, respectively, to PTSD (Norris et al., 2002). In a similar vein, although women often are understood to be more vulnerable to the development of posttraumatic states (e.g., Breslau et al., 1991), recent research suggests that adult men are even more likely than women to develop posttraumatic outcomes in response to sexual assault (Elliott et al., in press). As a result, it may be better to consider the interaction between these various potential trauma moderators and the trauma in question, rather than viewing them in isolation.

Finally, it appears that several of the noted risk factors for PTSD are also risk factors for the *DSM–IV*'s traumatic (Criterion A) events. Breslau, Davis, and Andreski (1995), for example, found that past exposure to traumatic events, neuroticism, extraversion, and being African American or Black were all predictive of exposure to a PTSD-level traumatic event. Similarly, Kessler et al. (1995) found that women in the general population were more likely than men to be exposed to events that, in their study, were most likely to produce PTSD (e.g., rape, childhood sexual abuse, adult physical assault). Thus, at least part of the reason why women and people of color in North American culture have higher rates of PTSD (and other posttraumatic states, such as dissociation) may be because they are more frequently exposed to events that may produce posttraumatic stress.

The relationship between risk factors for trauma and PTSD is exemplified by data from the National Vietnam Veterans Readjustment Study (Kulka et al., 1988) on race differences for PTSD. In that investigation, the rate of PTSD in veterans was considerably lower for Whites (14%) than for Hispanics (28%) or Blacks (19%). However, Hispanics and Blacks were also more likely to be exposed to high combat stress than Whites. When differences in level of combat exposure were controlled statistically, the race difference in PTSD between White and Black people disappeared, and the White-Hispanic difference decreased significantly.

In combination, these race and sex data suggest that "vulnerability factors do not increase their influence merely by increasing the likelihood of [PTSD] in persons exposed to environmental stress. The way in which they influence disorder is in part by increasing the likelihood of exposure to adverse experiences" (Breslau et al., 1995, p. 534).

## Characteristics of the Stressor

A number of stressor characteristics appear to affect posttraumatic outcome. Together, these characteristics are thought to reflect a general construct sometimes referred to as *stressor magnitude* or *stressor intensity*. March (1993) reviewed 19 studies where intensity of the stressor was examined in terms of PTSD status and found that in 16 of them "stressor magnitude (was) directly proportional to the subsequent risk of developing PTSD" (p. 40). Unfortunately, because many studies in the literature examine the presence or absence of PTSD, rather than the intensity of PTSD symptoms, somewhat less can be said about the relationship between stressor magnitude and severity of PTSD. Where intensity is also studied, however, the same relationship tends to occur. Variables that appear to increase stressor magnitude, and thus the likelihood or severity of PTSD, include the following:

- ☐ Intentional acts of violence (as opposed to noninterpersonal events; e.g., Briere & Elliott, 2000; Green, Grace, Lindy, Gleser, & Leonard, 1990);
- ☐ Presence of life threat (e.g., Holbrook, Hoyt, Stein, & Sieber, 2001; Ullman, & Filipas, 2001);
- ☐ Physical injury (e.g., Briere & Elliott, 2000; Foy, Resnick, Sipprelle, & Caroll, 1987);
- ☐ Extent of combat exposure during war (e.g., Goldberg, True, Eisen, & Henderson, 1990; Kulka et al., 1990);
- ☐ Witnessing death (e.g., Selley et al., 1997; Ursano & McCarroll, 1994);
- ☐ Grotesqueness of death (e.g., Epstein, Fullerton, & Ursano, 1998; Zaidi & Foy, 1994);
- ☐ Loss of a friend or loved one (e.g., Briere & Elliott, 2000; Green, Grace, Lindy, & Gleser, 1990);
- ☐ Unpredictability and uncontrollability (e.g., Carlson & Dalenberg, 2000; Foa, Zinbarg, & Rothbaum, 1992); and
- ☐ Sexual (as opposed to nonsexual) victimization (e.g., Breslau et al., 1991; Briere et al., 1997).

Although there appears to be a linear relationship between extent or severity of the stressors and subsequent posttraumatic response, in many cases this association is not especially large in magnitude and applies more to group data than to specific individuals. Thus, for example, it is not uncommon to encounter two people who experienced the same stressor (e.g., an earthquake or fire) differ significantly in terms of their posttraumatic response. One individual may develop ASD, followed by PTSD, whereas another may experience few short- or long-term effects. In addition, two stressors may appear objectively equivalent (e.g., two assaults of seemingly equal severity) yet have remarkably different impacts on those involved.

Beyond any unmonitored differences between apparently equivalent events, this variability in posttraumatic symptomatology generally arises from three sets of phenomena: victim characteristics (e.g., age, sex, and previous history, as noted earlier), subjective appraisal of the stressor, and social response. Although this analysis will focus more on those phenomena associated with a negative outcome, it is also true that the extent to which a stressor produces major effects is partially a function of the internal and external resources on which the victim can draw (Briere, 2002a). Such resources are often the "flip side" of the negative moderators presented below (e.g., psychological health versus preexisting distress or disorder, or biologic resilience versus a genetic predisposition toward posttraumatic stress). These factors not only tend to decrease the impacts of potentially traumatic stressors, they are no doubt related to reports of more positive posttraumatic outcomes, such as increased internal capacities or greater empathy (e.g., Affleck, Tennen, Croog, & Levine, 1987; McMillen, Zuravin, & Rideout, 1995).

## Peritraumatic Emotional Responses

As described earlier, the victim's emotional response at the time of the potential stressor is given substantial credence by *DSM–IV*, to the point that the negative event is not deemed a trauma if there is no report of concurrent horror, fear, or helplessness (Criterion A2). Although the use of such responses as an inclusion criteria is potentially problematic, there is little doubt that posttraumatic stress is more likely (and perhaps more intense) when the individual experiences one or more of these emotions peritraumatically (e.g., Brewin, Andrews, & Rose, 2000; Ozer et al., 2003; Roemer, Orsillo, Borkovec, & Litz, 1998). Other negative emotional responses, such as anger, shame, and guilt are also likely to increase the risk of posttraumatic reactions (e.g., Andrews, Brewin, Rose, & Kirk, 2000; Leskela, Dieperink, & Thuras, 2002; Wong & Cook, 1992).

The implication of these findings is that those who interpret a traumatic experience more negatively are more at risk for posttraumatic difficulties, partially because of cognitive predispositions (e.g., the tendency to view life events as outside of one's control, or to perceive challenges as threats), partially as a function of preexisting stress intolerance, and partially because of the specific nature of the trauma (i.e., stressors vary according to the extent that they would motivate negative appraisal in most people). Unfortunately, the subjective response criterion is implicitly circular with respect to psychological symptomatology. By requiring that the trauma be associated with reports of obvious, immediate distress, the revised Criterion A becomes, in part, a symptom category rather than a stressor criterion. As a result, its association with other psychological symptoms is nearly assured.

As a result of these factors, Criterion A2 probably involves a complex combination of stressor, victim, and outcome characteristics. For example, one individual may respond to an event with horror or helplessness because the event itself is horrific and overwhelming, whereas another might respond in a similar manner to a much lower magnitude stressor because of negative cognitive schema arising from previous child abuse experiences (Briere, 2002a; McCann & Pearlman, 1990). A third person might report terror regarding a trauma partially as a function of his or her generally low threshold for emotional reactivity. To compound the complexity of subjective response, such attributions are almost always reported after the traumatic event and its impacts have occurred (March, 1993). As a result, phenomena that occur after the event, such as the level of perceived support from others, subsequent negative or positive events, the effects of posttraumatic symptomatology, financial or interpersonal influences, or the results of professional intervention, may further affect Criterion A2.

## Peritraumatic Dissociative Responses

In addition to emotional distress experienced during a traumatic event, research suggests that peritraumatic dissociative reactions (e.g., depersonalization or derealization around the time of the trauma) predict more extreme psychological outcomes, especially a greater likelihood of PTSD (e.g., Bremner et al. 1992; Marmar et al. 1994; Shalev, Peri, Canetti, & Schreiber, 1996). It has been hypothesized that such responses interfere with the encoding and immediate processing of traumatic memories, thereby increasing the risk of more severe posttraumatic outcomes (Koopman, Classen, Cardeña, & Spiegel, 1995). Although the correlation between peritraumatic dissociation and subsequent PTSD is substantial in some studies (see a review by Ozer et al., 2003), other researchers have failed to replicate this relationship (e.g., Birmes et al. 2001; Marshall & Schell, 2002; Mellman, David, Bustamante, Fins, & Esposito, 2001) or report that the peritraumatic dissociation–PTSD connection disappears once other variables are taken into account (e.g., Briere, Scott, & Weathers, 2003; Holeva & Tarrier, 2001). In one study (Briere et al., 2003), for example, a scale that measures persistent and ongoing dissociation following a specific traumatic event (the Trauma-Specific Dissociation scale of the Detailed Assessment of Posttraumatic Stress [DAPS; Briere, 2001]; see p. 179) was considerably more powerful in the prediction of PTSD than was another scale measuring peritraumatic dissociative symptoms (the Peritraumatic Dissociation scale of the DAPS); in fact, peritraumatic dissociation ceased to be predictive of PTSD once sustained posttraumatic dissociation was taken into account through multiple regression analysis. These data suggest that it may be less whether one dissociates during a traumatic event that is a risk factor for PTSD than whether dissociation associated with the event (perhaps regardless of when it began) persists into the long term.

## Social Response, Support, and Resources

As is especially reported in the interpersonal violence literature, posttraumatic states may vary in intensity as a function of the level of acceptance and support that follow the stressor. However, social response to the victim is not independent of trauma characteristics, victim variables, or environmental effects. Some traumatic events appear to be more socially acceptable than others. For example, a victim of a hurricane or earthquake may be seen as more innocent and worthy of compassion than a rape or "gay bashing" victim. In addition, certain trauma survivors are more likely to receive prejudicial treatment than others, especially those living in poverty; racial minorities; homosexuals;

undocumented immigrants; women; prostitutes and others exploited by the sex industry; and the homeless (Bassuk, Melnick, & Browne, 1998; Berg, 2001; Briere, 1992a; De Zulueta, 1998; Farley et al., 1998; Goodman, Saxe, & Harvey, 1991; Loo et al., 2001; West, 2002). This correlation between certain traumas, victims, and social variables may especially produce stigmatization and, as a result, reports of shame, guilt, or self-hatred (e.g., Chan, 1987; Hardesty & Greif, 1994; Herek, Gillis, & Cogan, 1999; Lisak, 1994).

Holding social prejudice constant, however, it appears that posttrauma support by family members, friends, helping professionals, and others can moderate the intensity of posttraumatic stress. Such support includes accepting (versus rejecting) responses after the trauma disclosure, nurturance from loved ones, an absence of stigmatization or blame by others, and availability of helpers and agencies after a traumatic experience. In this regard, posttrauma social support appears to reduce the effects of disaster (e.g., Armenian et al., 2002), terrorism (e.g., Lee, Isaac, & Janca, 2002), rape (e.g., Fontana & Rosenheck, 1998), being battered in a domestic relationship (e.g., Coker et al., 2002), and war and combat (e.g., Fairbank, Hansen, & Fitterling, 1991).

Significantly, however, Meichenbaum (1994) cited the work of Green (1994) and Solomon and Smith (1994) in noting that—especially for women—very high levels of social support may interfere with recovery from trauma. Solomon and Smith (1994), for example, conclude that "for females, in particular, too much involvement has its costs" (p. 188). Although the basis for this relationship is unclear, one possibility is that women who are actively embedded in social environments are especially required by prevailing sex-roles to be supportive of others—a phenomenon that might produce significant role strain when the woman, herself, needs extensive support from the interpersonal environment. Women also, by virtue of their embeddedness and socialization, may be more sensitive to negative social network responses to their victimization. In other words, the converse of social support is social devaluation—recent research indicates that negative responses from one's social network (e.g., criticism, blaming responses, or stigmatization) are especially powerful predictors of postvictimization outcome, especially for women (Andrews, Brewin, & Rose, 2003).

More generally, writers such as Hobfoll (e.g., Hobfoll, Dunahoo, & Monnier, 1995) have suggested that the trauma victim's overall level of social (as well as physical and psychological) resources, before and after the trauma, is an important moderator of his or her response to a given stressor. Hobfoll (1988) noted that traumatic events not only produce stress, they may also precipitate *loss spirals*, wherein the victim becomes more dependent on (and consuming of) social resources, eventually resulting in depletion of these resources, leading to additional stressors, greater vulnerability, and more stress responses. When the stressor affects an entire community (e.g., during a disaster), it may reduce social and physical resources at the same time that it traumatizes individuals, thereby producing more severe reactions (Norris & Thompson, 1995). When the stressor is more confined to the individual level (e.g., a rape or miscarriage), initial social support may decrease as the victim fails to recover in a time span expected by the social milieu, leading to victim perceptions of abandonment and rejection and, ultimately, potentially more severe stress responses.

# Conclusion

As suggested in this chapter, the notion of what constitutes a traumatic event is less straightforward than might be envisioned. The initial intent of *DSM–III* was to define stressor characteristics, relatively independent of the victim, that were of sufficient intensity to produce a posttraumatic response in almost anyone. However, recent research suggests that the extent to which an event is traumatic is governed by the interaction between trauma magnitude and a range of victim variables that serve as relative risk factors for the development of posttraumatic stress. This interaction is further moderated by concurrent and postevent variables such as peritraumatic responses, level of social support and resources, cultural beliefs and expectations, and postevent attributions regarding the stressor.

It is clear that the interactionist view of traumatic events has lent greater precision to a clinical understanding of posttraumatic states. Among other things, this perspective increases the likelihood that the clinician will consider the stressor, the person, and his or her social network when evaluating the etiology of posttraumatic states. As has been found in other areas of mental health, the interactionist model suggests that posttraumatic stress rarely exists in a vacuum, and that the individual's responses to upsetting events must be considered within the context of his or her environment, resources, and life history.

On the other hand, the growing awareness of predisposing and moderating victim variables in PTSD response should not be used to discount the inherently traumatic nature of many events. Regardless of moderating victim and environmental phenomena, some events are intrinsically traumatic—acts of tremendous intrusion that negatively affect almost all of those who experience them. If these stressors are only considered traumatic when they produce a formal *DSM–IV* posttraumatic stress disorder, there is a danger that the pain and lasting distress of many trauma survivors (e.g., those whose symptoms do not fit precisely into existing PTSD criteria) will be discounted. In contrast, the broader view of posttraumatic disturbance offered in the following chapters takes into account various types of disturbance, including subthreshold posttraumatic stress, ASD, dissociation, and interpersonal sequelae, and thus implicates a wider range of potentially traumatic events.

Chapter

# 2

# Symptoms, Syndromes, and Disorders

This chapter outlines a variety of posttraumatic outcomes, many of which are listed as disorders in *DSM–IV*. It should be reiterated, however, that not all trauma-related difficulties fit into specific *DSM–IV* categories, in part because of the complex relationship between specific traumatic events and those individual and social variables outlined in the previous chapter. As a result, it is not especially helpful to define the clinical significance of a given person's posttraumatic disturbance according to whether he or she meets the criteria for a specific *DSM–IV* stress category.

Described below are two general types of posttraumatic responses (stress and dissociative disorders), as well as a sometimes-relevant differential diagnosis (adjustment disorder). Also discussed are culturally bound stress responses, grief reactions, and several more generic diagnoses that may arise from traumatic events in some people.

## The Stress Disorders

*DSM–IV* recognizes three stress disorders: two as anxiety disorders (acute stress disorder [ASD] and posttraumatic stress disorder [PTSD]), and one as a psychotic disorder (brief psychotic disorder with marked stressor[s] [BPDMS]). In addition, some writers have suggested the existence of a "complex PTSD" (Herman, 1992a, 1992b) or "DESNOS" (Disorders of Stress Not Otherwise Specified; van der Kolk, Roth, Pelcovitz, Mandel, & Spinazolla, in press), although neither is a *DSM–IV* diagnosis.

## Posttraumatic Stress Disorder

PTSD has been available as a diagnosis since *DSM–III*, although some version of its essential premise existed in *DSM–I* (Gross Stress Reaction) and, to a considerably lesser extent, *DSM–II* (Adjustment Reaction of Adult Life). Interestingly, as noted by Wilson (1994), in many ways *DSM–I*'s understanding of traumatic stress responses was more similar to current thinking than the intervening *DSM–II*. *DSM–IV* requires an initiating stressor involving direct personal experience or direct witnessing "of an event that involves actual or threatened death or serious injury or other threat to . . . physical integrity" or learning of similar events that happened to a family member or close associate (p. 424). The most substantial changes from *DSM–III* to *DSM–IV* are (a) the elimination of the former's description of trauma as "outside the range of normal human experience," and (b) the new requirement that the victim's response to an aversive event must involve intense fear, helplessness, or horror before the event can be considered traumatizing.

As presented in Table 2.1, the symptoms of PTSD are divided into three clusters: reexperiencing of the traumatic event, avoidance of trauma-relevant stimuli and numbing of general responsiveness, and persistent hyperarousal. Typically, reexperiencing presents as flashbacks and intrusive thoughts or memories of the trauma, as well as distress and physiologic reactivity on exposure to internal or external stimuli reminiscent of the event. Avoidance may be cognitive (e.g., avoiding or suppressing upsetting thoughts, feelings, or memories), behavioral (e.g., avoiding activities, people, places, or conversations that might trigger memories of the stressor), dissociative (e.g., amnesia for all or parts of the stressor, detachment) and, perhaps, partially physiologic (e.g., emotional numbing). These avoidance responses often align into two different symptom clusters when examined by factor analysis: *effortful avoidance* and *numbing* (Asmundson et al., 2000; King, Leskin, King, & Weathers, 1998; Taylor, Kuch, Koch, Crockett, & Passey, 1998). The third PTSD symptom cluster, hyperarousal, may present as "jumpiness" (a lowered startle threshold), irritability, sleep disturbance, or attention and concentration difficulties. Intrusive and reliving PTSD symptoms are often the first to fade over time, whereas avoidant and hyperarousal symptoms typically are more enduring (e.g., McFarlane, 1988).

As compared to ASD (described in the next section), PTSD can only be diagnosed a month or longer after the stressor and does not include as much dissociative symptomatology. The disorder does not have to appear within a certain time period after the trauma; in some instances "there may be a delay of months, or even years, before symptoms appear" (American Psychiatric Association, 2000, p. 466). Such delayed PTSD appears to be quite rare, however (e.g., Koren, Arnon, & Klein, 2001; North et al., 2002). In fact, some research suggests that most cases of "delayed" PTSD may, instead, involve the activation or exacerbation of already existing posttraumatic stress that was previously unrecognized (Bryant & Harvey, 2002).

In many—but not all—instances, the 30 days of symptoms that antedate the PTSD diagnosis satisfy criteria for ASD (e.g., Koopman et al., 1995), hence the need to change diagnoses at the one month point. When ASD "becomes" PTSD, the dissociative symptoms of ASD that persist are either recategorized as part of the avoidance cluster for PTSD (e.g., numbing, amnesia) or are no longer considered relevant to the diagnosis (e.g., detachment, depersonalization).

As is noted more extensively below under "Complex PTSD," *DSM–IV* acknowledges that the associated features of PTSD—especially following interpersonal victimization—often include not only dissociation but also cognitive distortions and more Axis II-like difficulties in areas such as identity and affect regulation. As a result, a detailed assessment for PTSD also will consider these common sequelae.

As might be expected from the frequency of North Americans' exposure to traumatic events (see chapter 1), the lifetime prevalence of PTSD in the general population is significant. Several

## TABLE 2.1

*DSM–IV* Diagnostic Criteria for Posttraumatic
Stress Disorder

A. The person has been exposed to a traumatic event in which both of the following were present:
  (1) the person, experienced, witnessed, or was confronted with an event or events that involved actual or threatened death or serious injury, or a threat to the physical integrity of self or others
  (2) the person's response involved intense fear, helplessness, or horror.
B. The traumatic event is persistently reexperienced in at least one of the following ways:
  (1) recurrent and intrusive distressing recollections of the event, including images, thoughts, or perceptions
  (2) recurrent distressing dreams of the event
  (3) acting or feeling as if the traumatic event were recurring (includes a sense of reliving the experience, illusions, hallucinations, and dissociative flashback episodes, including those which occur on awakening or when intoxicated
  (4) intense psychological distress at exposure to internal or external cues that symbolize or resemble the traumatic event
  (5) physiological reactivity on exposure to internal or external cues that symbolize or resemble the traumatic event.
C. Persistent avoidance of stimuli associated with the trauma and numbing of general responsiveness (not present before the trauma), as indicated by at least three of the following:
  (1) efforts to avoid thoughts, feelings, or conversations associated with the trauma
  (2) efforts to avoid activities, places, or people that arouse recollections of the trauma
  (3) inability to recall an important aspect of the trauma
  (4) markedly diminished interest or participation in significant activities
  (5) feelings of detachment or estrangement from others
  (6) restricted range of affect (e.g., unable to have loving feelings)
  (7) sense of foreshortened future (e.g., does not expect to have a career, marriage, children, or a normal life span.
D. Persistent symptoms of increased arousal (not present before the trauma), as indicated by at least two of the following:
  (1) difficulty falling or staying asleep
  (2) irritability or outbursts of anger
  (3) difficulty concentrating
  (4) hypervigilance
  (5) exaggerated startle response.
E. Duration of the disturbance is more than one month.
F. The disturbance causes clinically significant distress or impairment in social, occupational, or other important areas of functioning.
*Specify*: Acute (if duration is less than three months) or Chronic (if duration is three months or longer), and With Delayed Onset (if onset of symptoms is at least six months after the stressor).

studies indicate that approximately 7% to 12% of Americans have had (or will have) PTSD at some point in their lifetimes (e.g., Breslau et al., 1991; Kessler et al., 1995; Norris, 1992), although lower rates (as low as 1%) have been reported in earlier studies with less sensitive assessment instruments (e.g., Heltzer, Robins, & McEnvoy, 1987). Most research suggests that women are approximately twice as likely as men to have PTSD at some point in their lives. For example, Kessler et al. (1995) estimate the lifetime prevalence of PTSD to be 10.4% for women and 5.0% for men, similar to Breslau et al.'s (1991) estimates of 11.3% and 6.0%, respectively.

Not surprisingly, individuals from countries that have undergone especially high levels of internal strife, violence, and war appear to have elevated rates of PTSD. In one major study, for example, the estimated prevalence of PTSD is reported to be 37% in Algeria, 28% in Cambodia, 16% in Ethiopia, and 18% in Gaza (De Jong et al. 2001).

## Acute Stress Disorder

According to the *DSM–IV*, "the essential feature of Acute Stress Disorder is the development of characteristic anxiety, dissociative, and other symptoms that occurs within 1 month after exposure to an extreme traumatic stressor" (American Psychiatric Association, 2000, p. 469). In order to be categorized as ASD, the relevant symptoms must last for at least two days but not exceed four weeks in duration. The specific symptoms of ASD are presented in Table 2.2. This disorder is noteworthy for its similarity to PTSD, except that it is diagnosed more acutely, has fewer avoidance and hyperarousal requirements, and includes more dissociative symptomatology than PTSD. In fact, one recommended name for this *DSM–IV* diagnostic category was "brief reactive dissociative disorder" (Cardeña, Lewis-Fernandez, Bear et al., 1996). Especially prominent dissociative features listed in the *DSM–IV* are psychic numbing and detachment, as well as depersonalization or derealization. These dissociative reactions may be peritraumatic; in other words, occurring at the time of the traumatic event or soon thereafter, or may emerge later in time. In some cases, the poor concentration and reduced attention span found in some ASD presentations may be interpreted as

**TABLE 2.2**

*DSM–IV* Diagnostic Criteria for Acute Stress Disorder

A. The person has been exposed to a traumatic event in which both of the following were present:
   (1) the person experienced, witnessed, or was confronted with event(s) that involved actual or threatened death or serious injury, or a threat to the physical integrity of self or others
   (2) the person's response involved intense fear, helplessness, or horror.
B. Either during or after the distressing event, the individual has at least three of the following dissociative symptoms:
   (1) numbing, detachment, or absence of emotional responsiveness
   (2) reduced awareness of his or her surroundings
   (3) derealization
   (4) depersonalization
   (5) dissociative amnesia (i.e., inability to recall an important aspect of the trauma).
C. The traumatic event is persistently reexperienced in at least one of the following ways: recurring images, thoughts, dreams, illusions, flashback episodes, or a sense of reliving the experience; or distress upon exposure to reminders of the traumatic event.
D. Marked avoidance of stimuli that arouse recollections of the trauma (e.g., thoughts, feelings, conversations, activities, places, people).
E. Marked symptoms of anxiety or increased arousal (e.g., difficulty sleeping, irritability, poor concentration, hypervigilance, exaggerated startle response, motor restlessness).
F. The disturbance causes clinically significant distress or impairment in social, occupational, or other important areas of functioning or impairs the individual's ability to pursue some necessary task.
G. The disturbance lasts for a minimum of two days and a maximum of four weeks and occurs within four weeks of the traumatic event.
H. The disturbance is not due to the direct physiological effects of a substance or a general medical condition, is not better accounted for by Brief Psychotic Disorder, and is not merely an exacerbation of a preexisting Axis I or Axis II disorder.

*Note.* From *Diagnostic and Statistical Manual of Mental Disorders* (4th ed., Text Revision, pp. 471–472), by the American Psychiatric Association, 2000, Washington, DC: Author. Copyright 2000 by the American Psychiatric Association. Reprinted with permission.

dissociative symptomatology when, in fact, they represent difficulties in cognitive processing associated with hyperarousal.

The ASD diagnosis is new to *DSM–IV*, although symptoms similar to this disorder have been recognized for some time by trauma-specialized clinicians and researchers (Koopman, Classen, Cardeña, & Spiegel, 1995). For example, many of the symptoms of ASD have been described as the "impact" or "response" phase of a mental health emergency or crisis state (see Forster, 1992, for a review). As well, the diagnosis of "acute stress reaction" has existed for a number of years in the *International Classification of Diseases and Related Health Problems*, 10th ed. (ICD–10; World Health Organization, 1992), although the ICD–10 version is constrained to a shorter time period (48 hours), involves a broader range of anxious and depressive symptoms than the *DSM* version, and does not require dissociative symptoms.

Individuals who experience acute stress reactions such as those listed for ASD sometimes present with labile affect and evidence of psychomotor agitation or retardation, although these symptoms are not included in the *DSM–IV* ASD criteria. Also occasionally present, especially when the stressor is severe or the victim is especially vulnerable psychologically, may be some near-psychotic or psychotic symptoms. These symptoms may include transient cognitive loosening, briefly overvalued ideas or delusions involving persecution or outside control, and auditory hallucinations with trauma-related content. When psychotic features are prominent, however, the appropriate diagnosis is usually brief psychotic disorder, as noted later in this chapter.

The prevalence of ASD in the general population is not known. The incidence of ASD among traumatized individuals varies widely by study and trauma type; motor vehicle accident (MVA) victims usually have about a 13% chance of ASD (Harvey & Bryant, 1998a, 1998b, 1999a), whereas published rates for victims of interpersonal violence and war range from 3% to 33% (Brewin, Andrews, Rose, & Kirk, 1999; Classen, Koopman, Hales, & Spiegel, 1998; Green, Krupnicket al., 2001).

Although interest in ASD has grown, especially given the mass traumas that have occurred since *DSM–IV* was published, there are a number of potential problems associated with this diagnosis. These include the following:

1. Because the symptoms of ASD are generally a frequent—and thus potentially "normal"—response to overwhelming trauma, it has been argued that codifying them as a psychiatric disorder is inappropriate (e.g., Marshal, Spitzer, & Liebowitz, 1999), perhaps especially if the symptoms are less severe or pervasive.
2. The dissociative symptoms emphasized by the ASD diagnostic criterion set do not appear to be an inevitable part of acute posttraumatic stress (Bryant & Harvey, 2000; Harvey & Bryant, 2002; Marshall et al., 1999). As a result, some individuals who are acutely traumatized may not receive the diagnosis because they have no, or insufficient, peritraumatic dissociative symptoms.
3. Although ASD was initially introduced as a marker for the likelihood of later PTSD, a review of the literature suggests that between 27% and 63% of people who develop PTSD did not meet criteria for ASD beforehand (Harvey & Bryant, 2002).
4. ASD requires fewer and slightly different avoidance and hyperarousal symptoms than does PTSD: some PTSD avoidance symptoms are reclassified as dissociative in ASD, and extreme anxiety is a criterion for ASD whereas PTSD conspicuously does not include anxiety in its hyperarousal criterion set. It is not clear why more acute trauma impacts would necessarily involve a lower number (or different classification) of these symptoms than is the case for PTSD.

Together, these issues make it difficult to determine whether ASD is an actual, heretofore less-recognized psychiatric disorder or, instead, a very acute form of PTSD with problematic additional criteria. To resolve this issue, it would be necessary to determine the exact structure of acute posttraumatic response across a large number of individuals and traumas, and to assess whether that symptom structure changed as a function of time (e.g., at one month). Based on current data, it seems likely that ASD and PTSD are essentially the same disorder, albeit measured at different points in time with different criteria. If this turns out to be true, future *DSMs* might fold ASD into PTSD, perhaps with an additional 1- to 30-day acuity specification, and might list peritraumatic dissociation as an associated feature or known risk factor. Regardless of its ultimate classification, however, the distress and symptomatology of a significant minority of acute trauma survivors is of sufficient severity to require a clinical diagnosis and should not be overlooked or underassessed merely because of its time frame.

## Brief Psychotic Disorder With Marked Stressors

This disorder appeared in *DSM–III–R* as brief reactive psychosis. In *DSM–IV*, however, the focus is on the chronology of the disorder, not its etiology; as a result, the clinician can apply the diagnosis when there is no stressor (i.e., brief psychotic disorder without marked stressors; BPDMS) or where stressors exist (brief psychotic disorder with marked stressors). There also is an option to diagnose brief psychotic disorder with postpartum onset. In the case of marked stressors, the precipitating event is generally equivalent to that of ASD or PTSD, although *DSM–IV* is less specific here and more reminiscent of *DSM–III*—noting that "psychotic symptoms develop shortly after and apparently in response to one or more events that, singly or together, would be markedly stressful to almost anyone in similar circumstances in that person's culture" (p. 330).

BPDMS is noteworthy for the fact that the psychotic episode often begins abruptly and may be quite florid in nature. The diagnosis requires at least one of four psychotic symptoms (delusions, hallucinations, disorganized speech, or grossly disorganized or catatonic behavior), although several are usually present simultaneously. Like other acute psychotic phenomena, BPDMS is sometimes accompanied by extreme agitation, emotional distress, and confusion. *DSM–IV* lists suicide attempts as an associated feature, and notes that those with this disorder may require close supervision. Duration of BPDMS ranges from one day to less than one month.

It is not always clear whether a psychotic episode that follows a traumatic stressor is, in fact, BPDMS. In some cases, the psychosis may appear to be trauma-related, but may persist for several months or longer (American Psychiatric Association, 2000, pp. 330–331). Unfortunately, because such symptoms exceed the (somewhat arbitrary) one month limit, they cannot be diagnosed as BPDMS but instead must be diagnosed as some other (non-stressor-related) psychotic disorder. In other instances, psychotic responses to a marked stressor may represent the activation of a latent predisposition toward psychosis, or the acute exacerbation of an already existing—but previously undetected—psychotic illness, such as schizophrenia, schizophreniform disorder, or a delusional disorder. It also is not uncommon for a severe trauma to produce or trigger a psychotic depression, as noted later in this chapter—a diagnosis that takes precedence over BPDMS (American Psychiatric Association, 2000, p. 332). Finally, some instances of severe posttraumatic stress may include psychotic symptoms (e.g., paranoid ideation, looseness of thought, or hallucinations) in the context of a more prominent ASD or PTSD presentation (Davidson, 1994; Okawa, Gaby, & Griffith, 2003; Petty et al., 2001; Pinto & Gregory, 1995). For example, it has been estimated that 30% to 40% of treatment-seeking Vietnam combat veterans with PTSD experience at least some hallucinations or delusions (David, Kutcher, Jackson, & Mellman, 1999). In a similar vein, research on the more severe and complex impacts of child abuse suggests that some psychotic symptomatology can arise from early child trauma and maltreatment (Read, Perry, Moskowitz, & Connolly, 2001).

Taken together, these issues highlight three problems associated with the current diagnostic criteria for trauma-related psychosis: (a) as the *DSM–IV* acknowledges, the symptoms of BPDMS often extend well beyond 30 days, at which point another, often less relevant diagnosis must be made, (b) according to the *DSM–IV*, psychotic symptoms are an associated feature of PTSD (American Psychiatric Association, 2000, p. 465) and are often seen in large samples of chronic posttraumatic stress—suggesting a clinical phenomenon that might be labeled "PTSD with psychotic features," and (c) there may be chronic psychotic presentations that develop following extended child abuse and neglect, with symptoms that do not obviously resemble those of classic schizophrenia or psychotic depression. Although resolution of these inconsistencies awaits further investigation and analysis, available evidence suggests the existence of one or more "posttraumatic psychotic disorders," whose expression may vary as a function of predisposition (genetic and otherwise), type of trauma exposure, and the passage of time. At minimum, the "brief" descriptor in BPDMS may need to be revised.

# The Dissociative Disorders

Dissociation has been characterized in various ways since its introduction into the psychological nomenclature in the late 1800s (Janet, 1887). Nemiah (1993), for example, describes this phenomenon as "the exclusion from consciousness and the inaccessibility of voluntary recall of mental events, singly or in clusters, of varying degrees of complexity, such as memory, sensations, feelings, fantasies, and attitudes" (p. 107). The *DSM–IV*, on the other hand, refers to "a disruption in the usually integrated functions of consciousness, memory, identity, or perception of the environment" (p. 519). Central to most definitions of dissociation is a variation in normal consciousness that arises from reduced or altered access to one's thoughts, feelings, perceptions, or memories, typically in response to a traumatic event.

The *DSM–IV* lists five dissociative disorders: *depersonalization disorder*, involving perceptual alienation and separation from one's body; *dissociative amnesia*, consisting of psychogenic, clinically significant inability to access memory; *dissociative fugue*, characterized by extended travel with associated identity disturbance; *dissociative identity disorder* (formerly multiple personality disorder), involving the experience of having two or more personalities within oneself; and *dissociative disorder not otherwise specified* (DDNOS), used when significant dissociative symptoms are present but cannot be classified into one of the preceding diagnostic categories. As indicated by the phenomenological range of these disorders, the symptoms attributed to dissociation are numerous and vary considerably in form.

Despite this variability, however, dissociative phenomena are often considered to be manifestations of a single underlying state or trait, variously referred to as "dissociation," "dissociativity," or "dissociative capacity." This perspective holds that dissociative symptoms exist on a continuum, whereby phenomena such as dissociative identity disorder or fugue states are thought to represent more severe dissociation than, say, depersonalization. The continuum approach, while noting differences among various dissociative presentations, implies that these differences are because of the extremity of the dissociation, as opposed to representing qualitatively different phenomena. Other researchers, however, note that dissociative symptoms tend to form a number of only moderately correlated clusters when examined by factor analysis (e.g., Amdur & Liberzon, 1996; Briere, Weathers, & Runtz, in press). These analyses support a growing consensus in the field that "dissociation" refers to a group of phenomenologically distinct experiences that differ in form but ultimately produce similar outcomes, that is, reduced experience of emotional distress (Briere et al., in press).

This relatively wide definitional net is accompanied by controversy regarding the psychophysiologic and functional basis of dissociation. As noted by Steinberg (1993), "Contemporary reviews relate dissociation to a variety of phenomena, including habitual and automatic activities, parallel processing, neuropsychophysiologic state-dependent learning, and divisions between executive and monitoring functions or between mental representations of the self and representations of experience, thought, and action" (pp. 59–60).

Although the phenomenology of dissociative response has yet to be resolved, less in doubt is its frequent posttraumatic etiology. Each of the dissociative disorders (other than the residual category DDNOS) are linked to traumatic events in *DSM–IV*, albeit not always exclusively. Among the stressors related to dissociative symptoms in the trauma literature are child abuse (e.g., Chu, Frey, Ganzel, & Matthews, 1999), combat (e.g., Bremner et al., 1992), sexual and physical assaults (e.g., Cooper, Kennedy, & Yuille, 2001), and natural disasters (e.g., Koopman, Classen, & Speigel, 1996). This trauma–dissociation relationship probably explains the prominence of dissociative symptoms in ASD and their presence as "associated features" in PTSD.

Interestingly, although dissociation is correlated with trauma exposure, this relationship is not as large as might be expected. For example, van IJzendoorn and Schuengel (1996) reported that, across 26 studies, the average variance in Dissociative Experience Scale (DES; Bernstein & Putnam, 1986) scores accounted for by participants' sexual or physical abuse history was 6%. Similarly, Briere, Weathers, and Runtz (in press) found that respondents' lifetime history of trauma exposure accounted for an average of 4.4% of the variance in Multiscale Dissociation Inventory (MDI; Briere, 2002b) subscale scores. These studies suggest that trauma exposure may be an important but—in and of itself— insufficient factor in the genesis of dissociative responses, much as has been found for posttraumatic stress disorder (Yehuda & McFarlane, 1995). Studies indicate, for example, that dissociative reactions are also related to insecure (especially disorganized) parent–child attachment early in life (e.g., Coe, Dalenberg, Aransky, & Reto, 1995; Ogawa, Sroufe, Weinfield, Carlson, & Egeland, 1997), which, in turn, is associated with early trauma exposure and with more negative psychological responses to later traumas (e.g., Allen, 2001; Ogawa et al., 1997). Dissociative symptoms are also likely to vary as a function of sensitivity to stress, socioeconomic status, culture, and other variables that intervene between trauma and posttraumatic outcome, as has been found for PTSD.

Because dissociation is a frequent response to extreme stress, the clinician should consider dissociative symptoms and disorders as well as posttraumatic ones when assessing or treating trauma survivors (Dalenberg, 1999). Each of the dissociative disorders are described briefly below, along with their diagnostic criteria.

## Dissociative Amnesia

*DSM–IV* refers to dissociative amnesia as "an inability to recall important personal information, usually of a traumatic or stressful nature, that is too extensive to be explained by normal forgetfulness" (American Psychiatric Association, 2000, p. 519). In *DSM–III* and *DSM–III–R* this disorder was named *psychogenic amnesia. DSM–IV* identifies five forms of memory disturbance that may occur in this disorder:

- □ *Localized amnesia,* in which "the individual fails to recall events that occurred during a circumscribed period of time" (p. 520);
- □ *Selective amnesia,* in which "the person can recall some, but not all, of the events during a circumscribed period of time" (p. 520);
- □ *Generalized amnesia,* involving rare circumstances wherein there is no memory for the person's entire life;
- □ *Continuous amnesia,* in which there is "the inability to recall events subsequent to a specific time up to and including the present" (p. 520); and
- □ *Systematized amnesia,* involving a "loss of memory for certain categories of information, such as all memories relating to one's family or to a particular person" (p. 520).

A review of medical journals published around the time of World Wars I and II suggests that psychogenic amnesia (then considered a symptom of hysteria) was a broadly accepted concept among combat physicians and was frequently documented in reports of war effects. Henderson and Moore (1944), for example, reported that of the first 200 war-related cases admitted to a military hospital for psychiatric reasons, 5% had amnesia for combat-related events. Similarly, Torrie (1944) found that 9% of 1,000 cases of war-related "anxiety neurosis and hysteria" presented with symptoms of amnesia. Finally, in a study of war stress in 1,000 admissions to a neurological hospital unit, Sargant and Slater (1941) reported that "severe" war stress ("prolonged marching and fighting under heavy enemy action") produced amnesia for war events in 35% of patients, whereas "moderate" stress (e.g. "experiences like periodical dive-bombing at home bases and aerodromes") resulted in amnesia for 13% of patients (p. 758).

Other traumatic events, such as torture, concentration camps, physical assaults, motor vehicle accidents, and rape have been linked to reduced memory access (see Loewenstein, 1993, for a review). In a study of trauma and memory in a large sample of the general population, Elliott (1997) found a significant number of individuals who reported periods of incomplete or absent memories for a wide variety of traumatic experiences, ranging from war to motor vehicle accidents to instances of sexual or physical assault. In a smaller, but more detailed study of acute trauma survivors presenting to an emergency room, Yovell, Bannett, and Shalev (2003) found evidence of both reversible and irreversible amnesia for traumatic events.

Most recent research in this area, however, has been concerned with amnesia for severe childhood abuse experiences. A number of studies of clinical and nonclinical research participants have found either (a) that a substantial proportion of those who report childhood trauma experiences (especially sexual abuse) also describe periods of partial or complete amnesia for said traumas (e.g., Chu et al., 1999; Elliott & Briere, 1995; Epstein & Bottoms, 2002; Feldman-Summers & Pope, 1994; Goodman et al., 2003; Herman & Schatzow, 1987), or (b) that some research participants with independently established histories of childhood sexual abuse will, on follow-up as adults, fail to report any memory of these experiences (Williams, 1994).

Although there are problems with each of these studies, including retrospective reporting, lack of independent confirmation of self-reported trauma history, and the potential confounding of amnesia with reluctance to disclose (Berliner & Briere, 1998; Loftus & Ketcham, 1993; McNally, 2003), it seems unlikely that all of them misidentify lack of trauma-related memories as something else. In support of the likelihood that at least some trauma is inaccessible to some survivors, recent functional magnetic resonance imaging (fMRI) research indicates specific neural systems associated with blocking unwanted memories from consciousness (Anderson et al., in press). More generally, the last three diagnostic and statistical manuals (*DSM–III, DSM–III–R,* and *DSM–IV*) have each referred to the existence of dissociative amnesia, with *DSM–IV* noting that amnesia for traumatic events can also occur in ASD, PTSD, and somatization disorder (pp. 471, 468, 490).

It should be noted that the mere absence of a specific trauma memory does not necessarily mean that the individual is experiencing dissociative amnesia in any form. The material may be encoded in implicit (as opposed to narrative) memory, may be unretrievable or distorted as a result of brain injury, may be state-specific (i.e., may be encoded in the context of high emotional arousal and only be accessible in similar arousal states at a later point), or it may be sufficiently fragmented by stress or peritraumatic dissociative processes that it is not readily retrievable as a coherent recollection (Berliner & Briere, 1998; Goodman et al., 2003; van der Kolk, 1996).

In addition to the multiple potential etiologies of incomplete memory, the probable existence of trauma-specific amnesia does not rule out the possibility of confabulated memory (Courtois, 1999; Lindsay & Briere, 1997). Furthermore, as *DSM–IV* notes, "there is currently no method for establishing with certainty the accuracy of [recovered memories] in the absence of corroborative evidence" (p. 523). As a result, the clinician must approach any given report of memory recovery (or any other uncorroborated historical statement) with some level of care, neither ruling in nor ruling out such reports without due consideration of all relevant information.

Finally, the potential presence of amnesia for a traumatic event does not necessarily mean that the memory of that event will ever be "recovered." If memory of the event was never encoded, was encoded in a fragmentary way, or was encoded in implicit memory alone, there may be no explicit memory (or coherent version of memory) to retrieve. For example, if an individual was overwhelmed by extreme autonomic arousal associated with the trauma, or the event occurred before the offset of infantile amnesia, or extreme peritraumatic dissociation interfered with perception and thus encoding, one would not expect explicit verbal memories of the trauma to exist.

Implications of these additional issues include the likelihood that (a) not all amnesia is dissociative; (b) when dissociation is relevant to amnesia, it may occur at the encoding level as well as (or instead of) during retrieval; and (c) not all amnesia is potentially resolvable, either during the assessment process or at any other time.[1]

---

[1]It is not clear, in fact, that examiners should attempt to reduce amnesia during assessment. Not only may aggressive memory recovery techniques fail to accurately reinstate traumatic memory (McNally, 2003), such techniques are potentially problematic, if not harmful, in the treatment of posttraumatic disturbance (Courtois, 1999; Lindsay & Briere, 1997).

## Dissociative Fugue

As described by *DSM–IV*, dissociative fugue involves "sudden, unexpected travel away from home or one's customary place of daily activities, with (an) inability to recall some or all of one's past . . . This is accompanied by confusion about personal identity or even the assumption of a new identity." (p. 523). Also present must be significant symptom-related distress or impairment.

Contrary to earlier clinical belief, the taking on of an entirely new identity, without knowledge of the old one, is relatively uncommon in fugue states (Riether & Stoudemire, 1988). In this regard, *DSM–III–R* probably incorrectly required the assumption of a new identity for a fugue diagnosis, thereby causing fugue suffers who were amnestic for (or confused about) their past identity but who did not take a new one to be diagnosed as DDNOS (Loewenstein, 1993). Fortunately, as noted in this definition, *DSM–IV* no longer requires the development of a new identity for the fugue diagnosis, thereby improving the coverage of this diagnosis as well as increasing its usage.

As noted by *DSM–IV* and others (e.g., Lowenstein, 1993), fugue states often begin after a significant trauma or stressful life event. Putnam (1985) suggests that this disorder may be more common during wartime or major natural disasters, perhaps especially those requiring forced relocation. Loewenstein (1993) added that "factors related to avoidance of responsibility may be quite prominent in many of these cases, with sexual indiscretions, legal difficulties, financial problems, or fear of anticipated combat being part of the clinical matrix" (p. 61). Clinical experience suggests that although not all fugue states involve secondary gain, in those instances where avoidance of punishment or responsibility appears to be present, some clinicians may suspect malingering when, in fact, a dissociative disorder is at least part of the clinical picture.

## Dissociative Identity Disorder

The most dramatic of the dissociative disorders is dissociative identity disorder (DID), previously referred to as multiple personality disorder (MPD) in *DSM–III* and *DSM–III–R*. *DSM–IV* diagnostic criteria for DID include (a) "the presence of two or more distinct identities or personality states (each with its own relatively enduring patterns of perceiving, relating to, and thinking about the environment and self"), (b) "at least two of these identities or personality states recurrently take control of the person's behavior," and (c) an "inability to recall important personal information that is too extensive to be explained by normal forgetfulness" (p. 529).

Although *DSM–IV* specifies "two or more" identities, it is not uncommon for individuals with diagnoses of DID to report many more discrete identities, as well as less coherent personality "fragments" (Kluft, 1988; Putnam, Guroff, Silberman, Barban, & Post, 1986). Some DID patients report considerable conflict between personality states, with some identities seeking to take control from others, although this is not inevitably the case (Kluft, 1993). DID patients typically report an amnestic barrier between at least some identities, such that one personality state may have little or no knowledge of the existence of one or more other personality states (Putnam, 1989). Although *DSM–III–R* did not require the presence of amnesia, *DSM–IV* reintroduced it as a diagnostic criterion. Because different identities are thought to take control at different times, this amnestic barrier often results in any given personality state (especially the primary or "host" identity) reporting blanks in memory, possession of items that they do not recall collecting or owning, and other indicators of discontinuous awareness.

Of the various disorders, DID has been most frequently linked to extreme abuse during childhood, often severe sexual abuse (e.g., Ellason, Ross, & Fuchs, 1996; Putnam et al., 1986). For example, Ross and his colleagues (1990) examined structured interview data from 102 patients diagnosed with multiple personality disorder, across four different sites in North America, and found that 95% of cases reported instances of childhood sexual or physical abuse. Other childhood traumas also have been implicated in DID, including death or loss of a significant other and witnessing the intentional killing of another or others (Kluft, 1993).

The diagnosis of DID is relatively controversial in mental health circles. A number of writers either question the validity of DID as a naturally occurring phenomenon, dispute the connection between DID and child abuse (especially reports of ritualistic abuse), or suggest that at least some cases are iatrogenically associated with suggestibility during treatment, involvement in self-help groups, or exposure to mass media coverage of the issue (e.g., Aldridge, 1993; Merskey, 1993). Although this issue is unlikely to be resolved to all parties' satisfaction, it seems likely that DID (a) can occur as a natural psychological phenomenon, albeit a rare one; (b) usually arises from extended and extreme childhood trauma; and (c) is sometimes misdiagnosed in the context of poorly conducted psychological assessment or treatment. In fact, as a result of the heightened suggestibility found among some extreme dissociators, iatrogenically induced pseudo-DID is a valid assessment concern. As is noted in chapter 5, the use of validated structured interviews for dissociative disorders may improve, to some extent, diagnostic accuracy in this area.

## Depersonalization Disorder

*DSM–IV* defines the central feature of depersonalization disorder as

> persistent or recurring episodes of depersonalization characterized by a feeling of detachment or estrangement from oneself . . . The individual may feel like an automaton or as if he or she is living in a movie. There may be a sensation of being an outside observer of one's mental processes, one's body, or parts of one's body. Various types of sensory anesthesia, lack of affective response, and a sensation of lacking control of one's actions, including speech, are often present. The individual with Depersonalization Disorder maintains adequate reality testing. (p. 530)

Also present may be feelings of derealization, as well as déjà vu experiences and perceptual distortions, wherein objects or body parts appear to change shape or size. Sensory anesthesia often presents as feeling "dead" or "wooden." Because depersonalization is an ego-dystonic, often frightening symptom, panic attacks and extreme anxiety may accompany such episodes. In other instances, panic attacks may trigger depersonalization, rather than arising from it.

Feelings of depersonalization are common in North American society, especially among psychiatric patients (Brauer, Harrow, & Tucker, 1970; Cattell & Cattell, 1974) and only reach disorder level when such symptoms are persistent and cause clinically significant distress or impairment. Actual depersonalization disorder is therefore less frequent, although various writers have suggested that it is often underdiagnosed (Edwards & Angus, 1972; Moran, 1986). Steinberg (1993) has suggested a number of reasons why this may occur, including (a) the relative absence of valid assessment tools that are sensitive to depersonalization phenomena, (b) the wide variety of depersonalization symptoms, (c) the overlap between depersonalization disorder symptoms and those of other disorders (e.g., schizophrenia, depression, and seizure disorders), and (d) the fact that most psychiatric patients do not refer to depersonalization symptoms in their presenting complaints (p. 82).

Depersonalization and depersonalization disorder often arise from traumatic or highly stressful experiences (e.g., Shilony & Grossman, 1993; Simeon et al., 2001), although other etiologies, such as epilepsy, drug intoxication, or panic attacks, are also possible (e.g., Alper et al., 1997; Marshall et al., 2000). Traumas reported to produce depersonalization symptoms or the disorder include vehicular accidents and other immediately life-threatening experiences (e.g., Bryant & Harvey, 1999), child abuse (e.g., Simeon et al., 2001), natural disasters (e.g., Cardeña & Spiegel, 1993), burn injuries (Van Loey, Maas, Faber, & Taal, 2003), and the death of one's child (e.g., Hazzard, Weston, & Gutterres, 1992).

## Dissociative Disorder Not Otherwise Specified

The DDNOS category is intended to be used when an individual presents with demonstrable dissociative symptoms but does not satisfy criteria for any specific disorder. The use of residual categories is common in *DSM–III–R* and *DSM–IV*; in the dissociative area, however, it is especially invoked. The frequent use of DDNOS appears to represent at least three phenomena: (a) the wide variety of dissociative responses experienced by trauma-tized individuals, only some of which are codified in current diagnostic systems; (b) potential problems with some diagnostic criteria, such that numerous individuals with major dissociative difficulties do not quite meet the requirements of the disorder; and (c) the fact that, in the absence of specific diagnostic criteria, this label can be applied whenever a given clinician believes a dissociative disorder is present.

Although the first scenario may be unavoidable, given the need for reasonable limits on the number of diagnoses contained in *DSM–IV*, the other two suggest the need for further adjustment in diagnostic criteria or clinical practice. The second scenario, for example, was a factor in *DSM–III–R* vis-à-vis the dissociative fugue disorder. As noted, *DSM–III–R* required that the person assume a new identity after his or her dissociated travel to a new location. In reality, however, many individuals with fugue symptoms do not take on new identities, instead reporting amnesia (or substantial confusion) regarding their current identity. As a result, some of those who would have been diagnosed as having a fugue disorder in *DSM–IV* received a diagnosis of DDNOS in *DSM–III–R*.

Other phenomena that increase the DDNOS diagnosis are (a) the absence of a derealization disorder in *DSM–IV*, such that those with derealization but not depersonalization must be diagnosed as DDNOS (American Psychiatric Association, 2000, p. 532); and (b) the *DSM–IV* requirement that DID suffers have two or more distinct identities "each with its own relatively enduring pattern of perceiving, relating to, and thinking about the environment and self" (p. 529). As noted by Ross (1989), seemingly DID-like clients who present with multiple, indistinct or fragmentary identities (none of which have sufficiently enduring patterns of perception, relationship, and thought) "are not at all atypical, and are probably common" (p. 80). Currently, this group of individuals receive the diagnosis DDNOS.[2]

---

[2]This is not always a negative outcome, however; the use of DDNOS circumvents the premature or inappropriate use of the DID diagnosis, and thus is less likely to convince the suggestible client that he or she has "multiple personalities" when, in fact, they are not multiple, distinct ego states (J. Armstrong, personal communication, February 1996).

Also potentially problematic is a third issue, that of the subjectivity of the DDNOS diagnosis. Because there are no formal *DSM–IV* criteria for this category (only that the person have a "disorder" [undefined] "in which the predominant feature is a dissociative symptom" [p. 532]), clinical impressions become the basis for diagnosis. Although such subjectivity need not result in incorrect diagnoses, the risk of arbitrary diagnostic decision-making is obviously higher for this category.

# Adjustment Disorder

Adjustment disorder is sometimes confused with more classic posttraumatic presentations, such as ASD or PTSD. This is often because the *DSM–IV* criterion set for adjustment disorder is sufficiently broad and nonspecific (Strain, Wolf, Newcorn, & Fulop, 1996) that the diagnosis is occassionally applied inappropriately. In almost all cases, however, careful differential assessment of the relevant diagnostic criteria will resolve the issue.

According to *DSM–IV*, there are six types of adjustment disorder:

- □ With anxiety;
- □ With depressed mood;
- □ With disturbance of conduct;
- □ With mixed anxiety and depressed mood;
- □ With mixed disturbance of emotions and conduct; and
- □ Unspecified (American Psychiatric Association, 2000, p. 683).

Associated features include suicidal behavior, substance abuse, and somatic complaints. The prevalence of adjustment disorders in outpatient mental health samples is estimated to be between 10% and 30% (American Psychiatric Association, 2000). As opposed to PTSD or ASD, the event associated with an adjustment disorder can be any identifiable stressor (i.e., not necessarily an extreme trauma) that occurred within three months before the onset of symptoms (American Psychiatric Association, 2000, p. 683). The symptoms of adjustment disorder are only "marked distress" or impairment in social or occupational functioning that is beyond what would normally be expected in response to that particular stressor. Furthermore, in order to be considered an adjustment disorder, symptoms must last for less than six months after the termination of the stressor. Because this broad symptom description would appear to include many instances of ASD, PTSD, BPDMS, and other posttraumatic diagnoses, *DSM–IV* specifies that adjustment disorder can only be applied when no other Axis I disorder is relevant and when the symptoms do not reflect normal bereavement.[3]

Because of the range of adverse events potentially associated with an adjustment disorder, this diagnosis usually is used when the stressor falls short of ASD/PTSD Criterion A (e.g., divorce, a serious—but not life-threatening—medical condition, financial difficulties, or being fired from one's job). In addition, the hallmark symptoms of an adjustment disorder typically are sustained dysphoria or maladaptive behavior, as opposed to the specific reliving, avoidant, and hyperarousal symptoms most characteristic of a posttraumatic stress disorder. It should be noted, however, that the diagnosis can be applied in cases where there was an extreme (e.g., PTSD-level) trauma, but where the symptoms arising from it do not meet criteria for any other, more specific, disorder. When the differential diagnosis involves high-level (i.e., Criterion A) stressors, three questions should be asked, in the following order:

1. Are the symptoms best described as a classic stress disorder or other Axis I condition?
   If yes, consider *ASD, PTSD, BPDMS,* and so on.
2. If not #1, do the symptoms involve subthreshold posttraumatic stress?
   If yes, consider *Anxiety disorder, not otherwise specified.*
3. If not #2, have the symptoms been present within six months of the offset of the stressor, and do they appear to be something other than a normal grief reaction?
   If yes, consider *Adjustment disorder.*

---

[3]When bereavement is "in excess of, or more prolonged than, what would be expected" (American Psychiatric Association, 2000, p. 862), but does not meet criteria for a depressive disorder, an adjustment disorder diagnosis may be the appropriate *DSM–IV* stand-in for what is described as "complicated grief" on p. 68).

# Other Trauma-Related Presentations

Beyond the posttraumatic stress, dissociative, and adjustment disorders, several other trauma-related syndromes have been suggested by trauma clinicians and researchers. Complicating the issue is a much-debated concern: Given the significant psychiatric comorbidity associated with PTSD (e.g., Brown, Campbell, Lehman, Grisham, & Mancill, 2001; Kessler et al., 1995; Kulka et al., 1990), how does one determine whether a given symptom presentation is related to a separate but concurrent disorder (e.g., PTSD with a coexisting psychosis or depression) or, instead, reflects a broader syndrome of which PTSD or ASD symptoms are only a subset?

Apropos of this issue, Heltzer et al. (1987) found that nearly 80% of the cases of PTSD in their general population study either had some other psychiatric disorder as well or had a lifetime history of some other disorder. Similarly, Kessler et al. (1995) found in a large general population sample that "a lifetime history of at least one other disorder was present in 88.3% of the men with lifetime PTSD and 79% of the women with lifetime PTSD" (p. 1055). On the other hand, various writers have made a good case for mixed or complex posttraumatic disorders that includes a range of other cognitive, affective, or interpersonal symptoms (e.g., Herman, 1992a; Kroll, 1993; van der Kolk, Roth, Pelcovitz, Mandel, & Spinazzola, in press).

## Posttraumatic Depression

A number of clinicians and researchers have noted a tendency for posttraumatic and depressive symptoms to arise from the same stressor (e.g., Pickens, 1995; Winfield et al., 1990; Yehuda, Kahana, Southwick, & Giller, 1994). As well, a number of studies indicate significant comorbidity between PTSD and depression (see Davidson & Foa, 1993, for a review, and Kessler, Sonnega, Bromet, Hughes, & Nelson, 1995). Although neither literature proves the existence of posttraumatic depression, both suggest that events severe enough to produce posttraumatic stress can also produce or exacerbate depressive symptoms.

In commenting on the relationship between posttraumatic and depressive symptoms, Herman (1992b) noted that

> Protracted depression is reported as the most common find-
> ing in virtually all clinical studies of chronically traumatized
> people. ... Every aspect of the experience of prolonged
> trauma combines to aggravate depressive symptoms. The
> chronic hyperarousal and intrusive symptoms of PTSD fuse
> with the vegetative symptoms of depression. ... The dis-
> sociative symptoms of PTSD merge with the concentra-
> tion difficulties of depression. The paralysis of initiative of
> chronic trauma combines with the apathy and helplessness
> of depression. The disruptions in attachments of chronic
> trauma reinforces the isolation and withdrawal of depres-
> sion. The debased self image of chronic trauma fuels the
> guilty ruminations of depression. And the loss of faith
> suffered in chronic trauma merges with the hopelessness
> of depression. (p. 382)

When posttraumatic and depressive symptoms arise in tan-
dem from the same traumatic events, victims often report themes
of loss, abandonment, isolation, and irrevocable life change.
Some victims appear to present with a dissociative depression,
wherein apathy and numbness appear to combine with dysthymia to produce a singular level of avoidance and nonresponsivity
(Briere, 1995). Also evident may be preoccupation with loss,
alternately presenting as cognitive distortions and ruminations,
and intrusive thoughts and images. As noted later in this chapter,
when these responses arise from the traumatic death of a loved
one, the resultant syndrome is sometimes referred to as "complicated" or "traumatic" grief.

## Complex Posttraumatic Stress Disorder and Disorder of Extreme Stress, Not Otherwise Specified

Perhaps the best known of the non–*DSM–IV* posttraumatic presentations is that of "complex PTSD" (Herman, 1992a, 1992b) or,
when certain criteria are met, "disorder of extreme stress, not
otherwise specified" (DESNOS; Pelcovitz et al., 1997; van der
Kolk et al., in press). This syndrome is thought to arise from
severe, prolonged, and repeated trauma, almost always of an
interpersonal nature. Examples of such stressors are torture,
captivity as a prisoner of war or concentration camp internee,
extended child abuse, sex-trafficking, and chronic spouse abuse.

Such traumatic processes (as opposed to single catastrophic events) have been linked to a wide variety of subsequent psychological difficulties, many of which are associated with Axis II disorders (see reviews by Briere & Spinazzola, in press; Herman, 1992a; Kroll, 1993; van der Kolk et al., in press). These include cognitive, somatic, and dissociative disturbance, as well as what has been described as *impaired self-capacities* (e.g., Briere & Runtz, 2002; McCann & Pearlman, 1990), involving chronic difficulties in identity and boundary awareness, interpersonal relatedness, and affect regulation. Self-capacity problems, in turn, may result in self-destructive—or other-destructive— activities, such as substance abuse, self-injurious behaviors (e.g., suicidality, self-mutilation), aggression or abusive behavior, chronic involvement in chaotic or abusive relationships, and dysfunctional sexual behavior (Brennan & Shaver, 1995; Briere & Gil, 1998; Grilo et al. 1997; Zlotnick, Donaldson, Spirito, & Pearlstein, 1997).

By including such sequelae, complex PTSD approximates Horowitz, Weis, and Marmar's (1987) notion of a posttraumatic personality disorder and other models of complex disturbance (e.g., Briere, 2002a; Kroll, 1993; Shea, 1996), as well as calling on the probable relationship between childhood trauma and borderline personality disorder (e.g., Herman, Perry, & van der Kolk, 1989; Yen et al., 2002). This inclusion of personality features is in relative opposition to the traditional *DSM* distinction between Axis I and Axis II disorders.

Because the notion of complex PTSD includes so many divergent symptoms, the diagnostic criteria for such a disorder seemingly would be equally complex. The Disorders of Extreme Stress criteria used in the *DSM–IV* field trials, for example, included the following major categories (Pelcovitz et al., 1995):

- □ Alteration in regulation of affect and impulses;
- □ Alterations in attention or consciousness;
- □ Somatization;
- □ Alterations in self-perception;
- □ Alterations in perception of perpetrator (this symptom group was eventually eliminated from the final DESNOS criterion set);

☐   Alterations in relations with others; and
☐   Alterations in systems of meaning.

The reader will note that these proposed criteria do not include the reliving, avoidance, and hyperarousal found in PTSD. This is, at first glance, confusing; the use of "PTSD" in the term "complex PTSD"—as well as the frequent presence of posttraumatic symptoms in such presentations—seemingly argue for both posttraumatic stress and the additional symptoms outlined. However, a reading of Herman (1992a, 1992b), Pelcovitz et al., (1997), and others clearly indicates that this syndrome does not, in fact, include classical symptoms of posttraumatic stress. This confusion is remediated when the term "DESNOS" is used, because it does not refer to PTSD except as a common comorbid disorder.

As suggested earlier, it is not clear that all the symptoms included in complex PTSD or DESNOS necessarily represent posttraumatic outcomes, as opposed to antecedent or comorbid clinical phenomena, or preexisting risk factors for posttraumatic stress (Yehuda & McFarlane, 1995). Furthermore, research on the Structured Interview for Disorders of Extreme Stress (SIDES; Pelcovitz et al., 1997) suggests that the various domains of DESNOS vary significantly among individuals with a trauma history. For example, when the prevalence of DESNOS was assessed in a PTSD research sample, 13% of individuals were found to meet full diagnostic classification for DESNOS, more than 30% of this sample met criteria for at least five of the six domains, more than 50% met criteria for four or more domains, and the remainder met three criteria or less (Spinazzola, Blaustein, & Van der Kolk, 2002). Such findings suggest that the various symptoms listed within Complex PTSD (or DESNOS) do not necessarily operate in concert with one another, but rather reflect the range of symptoms potentially present in any one traumatized individual (Briere & Spinazzola, in press). These concerns aside, the central message implicit in DESNOS is important: Chronic interpersonal violence or maltreatment effects do not reside exclusively in PTSD or ASD, or even solely on Axis I. In fact, a compelling case can be made for locating most of the symptoms of complex PTSD on Axis II, as was unsuccessfully proposed for *DSM–IV* (Shea, 1996).

## Assault Syndromes

In contrast to DESNOS/Complex PTSD, which is a relatively new clinical construct, two syndromes have been part of the trauma lexicon for several decades: *rape trauma syndrome* (RTS; Burgess & Holmstrom, 1974, 1979) and *battered woman syndrome* (BWS; Walker, 1984, 1991). Symptoms of RTS are typically described as including anxiety, depression, anger, emotional and social withdrawal, sleep and eating disturbance, posttraumatic stress, guilt and self-blame, shame, somatization, and sexual dysfunction (Burgess & Holmstrom, 1979). Similar symptoms have been attributed to BWS, although the latter typically also includes helplessness and passivity in the face of violence (Walker, 1991).

A historic contribution of RTS and BWS has been their focus on response complexity, suggesting that the effects of rape and domestic violence may involve a variety of symptoms beyond, for example, depression or PTSD. In addition, because the idea of an assault syndrome directly implies posttraumatic (not pretraumatic) symptoms, RTS and BWS potentially reduce stigmatization by suggesting that the event, itself, was instrumental in producing the disorder, not the other way around (Koss et al., 1994). Although rarely appearing in modern diagnostic nomenclature, these labels continue to be used (and disputed) in legal settings and other advocacy situations. Problems may arise, however, when it is assumed that RTS and BWS are discrete and unidimensional syndromes that one "has" or "doesn't have," or when the presence or absence of the syndrome is used as evidence that one has or has not been victimized (Briere & Jordan, in press).

With regard to dimensionality, the presence or intensity of postrape symptoms appears to vary as a function of, among other variables, gender (Elliott et al., in press), age (Acierno et al., 2002), culture (Lefley, 1999), previous victimization history (Classen et al., 2002), relational status of the perpetrator (Culbertson & Dehle, 2001), severity of the assault (Ullman & Filipas, 2001), and extent of social support (Yoshihama & Horrocks, 2002) after the assault. Such variability virtually ensures that most rape victims will have different symptomatic outcomes, as opposed to a single "rape trauma" syndrome. Similar issues arise in the case of partner battering, where, in addition to victim and trauma variables, relationship factors may vary dramatically from couple to couple and influence postbattering outcomes.

The second problem for assault syndromes, whether the presence of said syndrome necessarily means that the assault took place, has significant forensic implications. To the extent that a syndrome is assumed to be specific to an assault type, it is understandable that clinicians or the legal system might use RTS or BWS as a litmus test for the likelihood that rape or partner battering did or did not occur. However, there is very little reason to believe that the presence or absence of RTS or BWS is diagnostic of assault exposure. Symptoms that might be attributed to spouse abuse, for example, could be in response to an earlier assault or a history of child abuse or may not even be victimization-related at all. Similarly, denying the possibility that a woman was raped based on the absence of RTS symptoms is clearly untenable, because vulnerability to the effects of an assault varies as a function of a wide variety of victimization, victim, and social variables, and—as described elsewhere in this volume—some victims may experience numbing or dissociative states that reduce their visible distress or symptom expression (Briere & Jordan, in press).

Although the issue of complex posttraumatic or postassault syndromes (including complex PTSD) will not be resolved in the near future, it is likely that different types of stressors, varying on dimensions such as chronicity, intrusion, life-endangerment, locus (e.g., intrafamilial versus environmental), and intentionality (e.g., torture vs. natural disaster), as well as different victim and cultural variables, can produce different manifestations of posttraumatic disturbance. Whether these different responses can comprise separate disorders, require separate diagnoses, or should just be described as associated features of ASD or PTSD is unclear. However, it is important that the clinician be cognizant of the complexity of posttraumatic response, such that he or she does not evaluate formal ASD/PTSD symptoms alone in the traumatized individual.

## Posttraumatic Grief

Grief is a normal human response to major loss that tends to resolve naturally over time. Recent events, such as the attacks on the World Trade Center in New York, have caused clinicians and researchers to focus more on grief than ever before, especially bereavement arising from the sudden, unexpected death of loved ones. This scrutiny reveals that especially traumatic death of a valued other or major losses in one's life may lead to grief responses that are more complicated, enduring, and associated with lasting mental health problems. For example, traumatic loss may be accompanied by clinical depression, anxiety, PTSD, decreased social functioning, substance abuse, and, in some cases, serious physical illness (e.g., Prigerson, Frank, et al., 1995; Shear & Smith-Caroff, 2002; Zisook, Chentsova-Dutton, & Shuchter, 1998). The grief component of such responses appears to be phenomenologically (and statistically) separable from the depression and anxiety that also may be present (Boelen, van den Bout, & de Keijser, 2003; Prigerson, Frank, et al., 1995; Prigerson et al., 1996). This core symptom cluster has been referred to by various authors (e.g., Horowitz et al., 1997; Prigerson et al., 1999; Raphael & Minkov, 1999; Shear & Smith-Caroff, 2002) as a *complicated grief* or *traumatic grief*, and appears to involve some combination of the following (summarized across sources):

- ☐ Feeling shocked, stunned, or numbed by the loss;
- ☐ Intrusive thoughts and fantasies about the death of a loved one;
- ☐ Intense spells or pangs of extremely negative emotion;
- ☐ Distressing yearnings;
- ☐ Disbelief and lack of acceptance;
- ☐ Searching for the lost person, especially if his or her death is uncertain or denial is a predominant symptom;
- ☐ Chronic feelings of aloneness and emptiness;
- ☐ Purposelessness and feelings of futility;
- ☐ Excessive avoidance of stimuli reminiscent of the loss;
- ☐ Unusual levels of sleep disturbance;
- ☐ Excessive anger or irritability;
- ☐ Excessive somatic concerns;
- ☐ Detachment; and
- ☐ Major loss of interest in personal activities.

Other researchers, however, appear to view these symptoms less as a unique syndrome than as the co-occurrence of PTSD and persistent depression (e.g., Kaltman & Bonanno, 2003). Although no *DSM–IV* diagnosis fully encompasses these various outcomes of traumatic loss (see, however, p. 61 for the possible use of adjustment disorder), several criterion sets have been proposed for *DSM–V* (Horowitz et al., 1997; Prigerson et al., 1999).

## "Culture-Bound" Stress Responses

As indicated in chapter 1, posttraumatic presentations are influenced by a variety of individual and environmental variables. As a result, people from different cultures or subcultures may experience trauma and express posttraumatic symptoms in ways that diverge from mainstream Western culture. Thus, it may not always be helpful to insist on classical North American notions of posttraumatic stress and dissociation when evaluating traumatized members from other cultures (Chakraborty, 1991; Friedman & Jaranson, 1994). For example, it appears that individuals from non–North American or European societies "often fail to meet PTSD diagnostic criteria because they lack avoidant/numbing symptoms despite the presence of reexperiencing and arousal symptoms" (Marsella, Friedman, Gerrity, & Scurfield, 1996, p. 533). Furthermore, in many cultures, classic PTSD symptoms are often accompanied (or supplanted) by somatic and dissociative symptoms whose frequency and characteristics are less common in Anglo/European cultures (Marsella et al., 1996).

Growing clinical awareness that not all posttraumatic stress responses are captured by the PTSD diagnosis, especially in non-Western contexts, has led to the concept of *culture-bound* stress syndromes, as described below. It should be noted, however, that PTSD, itself should be considered culture-bound, because it probably best applies to those born in English-speaking countries. This does not mean that PTSD does not ever occur in people from other societies (see, e.g., Kroll et al., 1989; Sack, Seeley, & Clarke, 1997), only that some symptoms of posttraumatic stress may vary according to culture.

Appendix I of the *DSM–IV* lists several culture-bound syndromes that appear to involve dissociation, somatization, and anxiety-related stress responses. Among these are *ataques de nervios, dhat, latah, nervios, pibloktoq, shin-byung, susto,* and *zar,* although Kirmayer (1996) questions whether *latah* and *pibloktoq* should be in this list. In most of these instances, an acute stressor is not inevitably associated with the syndrome in question, and thus these presentations may or may not be posttraumatic stress responses. Three of these syndromes are often posttraumatic, however, and are briefly described. Although each of these is found among Hispanic populations, culture-bound stress syndromes occur in a variety of world locales. For example, clinical experience suggests that people of the Indochinese region experience stress responses partially specific to their cultures, although these responses are not well codified or understood by North American clinicians (Marsella et al., 1996). Culture-bound symptom clusters occur not only in their nations-of-origin, of course, but also are reported by refugees and immigrants from these countries. As a result, clinicians in North America are likely to encounter these specific stress responses, although they may not recognize them as such.

## Ataques de nervios

This disorder is most commonly described as occurring in Puerto Rico (e.g., Guarnaccia, Rivera, Franco, & Neighbors, 1996; Hough, Canino, Abueg, & Gusman, 1996), although it is prevalent in other Latin American, Latin Caribbean, and Latin Mediterranean countries as well (American Psychiatric Association, 2000; Norris et al., 2001). Triggering stressors for *ataques* include automobile accidents, funerals, violent victimization, family arguments, natural disasters, or hearing of or observing the death of a family member. In Guarnaccia et al.'s (1993) study of a Puerto Rico flood and mudslide disaster, for example, 16% of their sample reported symptoms characteristic of *ataques de nervios*. Interestingly, there is disagreement among researchers as to whether *ataques* are related to childhood trauma (Lewis-Fernandez et al., 2002; Schechter et al., 2000). Typical symptoms of this disorder are crying, trembling, heart palpitations, intense heat rising from the chest to the head (often referred to as *calor*), followed by (in some cases) shouting or physical aggression, convulsions, and loss of consciousness. Amnesia for the *ataque* is often reported.

## Nervios

Although sometimes confused with *ataques de nervios, nervios* is a syndrome common in Mexico and other Latin American countries that incorporates a much wider (and potentially less extreme) group of symptoms and sometimes refers to an individual's general tendency to respond to stressors with anxiety and somatization. As well, the stressors thought to produce *nervios* are often less acute (e.g., chronic family dysfunction) than those leading to *ataques*, and some etiologies may not be related to a stressful event at all. In other instances, however, *nervios* appears to reflect chronic anxiety, dissociation, and somatization that arise from an acute stressor (e.g., interpersonal victimization, earthquakes). As noted by *DSM–IV, nervios*

> includes a wide range of symptoms of emotional distress, somatic disturbance, and inability to function. Common symptoms include headaches and "brain aches," irritability, stomach disturbances, sleep difficulties, nervousness, easy tearfulness, inability to concentrate, trembling, tingling sensations, and *mareos* (dizziness with occasional vertigo-like exacerbations). . . . Nervios is a very broad syndrome that spans the range from cases free of a mental disorder to presentations resembling Adjustment, Anxiety, Depressive, Dissociative, Somatoform, or Psychotic disorders. (American Psychiatric Association, 2000, p. 901)

## Susto

Also referred to (with slight symptomatic variation) as *espanto, espasmo, pasmo, pérdida del alma, miedo,* or *saladera,* this disorder is most typically found in Mexico, Central America, and South America. The precipitant is often a frightening or life-threatening event thought to cause the soul to leave the body (hence its frequent English translation as "soul loss"). Typical symptoms are anxiety and hyperarousal, leading to appetite loss, sleep disturbance, frequent startle responses, and constant worrying, as well as depressive symptoms such as chronic sadness, decreased motivation, and decreased self-worth. Also present may be multiple somatic complaints, including headaches, muscle aches, stomachaches, and diarrhea (American Psychiatric Association, 2000; Hough et al., 1996).

# Disorders Sometimes Associated With Traumatic Experience

In addition to the disorders and stress responses outlined above, there are several *DSM–IV* diagnoses that, although not inevitably associated with traumatic experience, often are. Five of these disorders—conversion disorder, somatization disorder, panic disorder, major depression with psychotic features, and borderline personality disorder—are outlined in this section. It should be noted, however, that other disorders (e.g., some anxiety, depressive, and psychotic disorders) may be triggered or exacerbated by traumatic or stressful experiences as well.

## Conversion Disorder

This diagnosis is applied when an individual experiences "one or more symptoms or deficits affecting voluntary motor or sensory function that suggest a neurological or other general medical condition" but, in fact, "psychological factors are judged to be associated with the symptom or deficit because the initiation or exacerbation of symptoms or deficit is preceded by conflicts or stressors" and the symptom(s) cannot be fully explained medically (American Psychiatric Association, 2000, p. 498).

Examples of conversion symptoms are any of the following, if psychogenic in origin:

- Seizures;
- Paralysis;
- Aphonia;
- Difficulty swallowing;
- Blindness;
- Deafness;

- ☐  "Stocking-glove" anesthesia; and
- ☐  Hallucinations.

Until *DSM–III,* conversion symptoms were considered part of hysteria and thus more closely aligned with dissociation. *DSM–III, DSM–III–R,* and *DSM–IV,* however, consider conversion disorder to be a somatoform disorder, undoubtedly because its primary symptoms are somatic in nature. Nevertheless, dissociative disorders are listed as associated mental disorders of conversion in *DSM–IV,* and controversy continues among some as to the logic of moving conversion symptoms into the somatoform arena (e.g., Nemiah, 1993; Ross, 1989).

*DSM–IV* notes that conversion disorder may occur after a major stressor (e.g., combat or the recent death of a significant other), although it is also thought to arise from extreme psychological conflict (usually with associated guilt) and the availability of secondary gain. When trauma appears to be contributory, the stressors most frequently implicated in the clinical literature are child abuse (e.g., Roelofs, Keijsers, Hoogduin, Naring, & Moene, 2002), combat (e.g., Neill, 1993), and torture (e.g., Van Ommeren et al., 2001.

As noted by Kirmayer (1996), conversion symptoms vary by culture and may reflect ethnocultural models or explanations for psychological disorder. As well, in cultures where psychological symptoms have less legitimacy, physical distress or disability may serve as a more acceptable way of expressing posttraumatic stress. Whatever their cultural functions, conversion responses appear to be considerably more frequent in some societies than in North America (Marsella et al., 1996) and appear to be more common among immigrants or refugees seeking medical or psychological services.

### Somatization Disorder

This disorder consists of a wide variety of symptoms whose only commonality is their somatic focus and the fact that they either cannot be explained medically or that their intensity is beyond that expected from their medical etiology. According to the *DSM–IV,* in order to diagnose somatization disorder, the individual must endorse

- ☐ Four pain symptoms (e.g., headaches, backaches);
- ☐ Two gastrointestinal symptoms (e.g., nausea, vomiting);
- ☐ One non-pain-related sexual symptom (e.g., sexual dysfunction, sexual indifference); and
- ☐ One pseudoneurological symptom (e.g., paralysis, amnesia).

A related disorder, undifferentiated somatoform disorder, requires only one physical complaint for which no medical explanation can be found or for which the symptom(s) exceeds its expected intensity. This second diagnosis, however, also requires that the symptom(s) lasts for at least six months. The symptoms of both somatization disorder and undifferentiated somatization disorder symptoms must be neither factitious nor feigned.

Somatization, although potentially arising from a variety of factors, has been linked on multiple occasions to a history of childhood maltreatment, especially sexual abuse (e.g., Drossman et al., 1990; Springs & Friedrich, 1992; Walker et al., 1993; Walker et al. 1988), as well as other traumatic events, such as war, disaster, or adult assault (Beckham et al., 1998; Kimerling & Calhoun, 1994). The reason for an association between trauma and somatization is unclear, although possibilities include the effects of sustained autonomic arousal on organ systems especially responsive to sympathetic activation, and posttraumatic perceptions of vulnerability (with subsequent hypervigilance) based on where in the body the trauma was most salient (e.g., chronic pelvic pain in sexual abuse survivors; Briere, 1992b).

Somatic symptoms also may represent "idioms of distress" (Nichter, 1981) in some cultures, such that physical symptoms function as ways to express nonphysical concerns. As a result, "culture bound" somatic syndromes have been described in several studies (e.g., Moore et al., 2001). Kirmayer (1996) noted that

> This idiomatic use of symptoms allows people to draw attention to and metaphorically comment on the nature of their quandaries. When reduced to symptoms of a disorder [by clinicians], this meaningful personal and social dimension of distress may be lost. (p. 133)

In this regard, as with conversion responses, somatic symptoms may allow communication of posttraumatic distress and symptomatology within cultures where psychological symptoms are either unacceptable or not easily expressed. In such instances, traditional Western interpretations of somatization as neurotic or conflict-based may be somewhat misleading.

## Psychotic Depression

Given the relationship between PTSD and both depression and psychosis, described earlier, it may not be surprising that major depression with psychotic features also has been linked to posttraumatic stress. More unexpected is the fact that PTSD is more common among depressed individuals with psychotic symptoms than among depressed individuals without psychosis. For example, in a sample of 500 psychiatric outpatients, Zimmerman and Mattia (1999) found that those with psychotic depression were nearly four times more likely to have PTSD than those with a nonpsychotic depression (58% vs. 16%). Such data align with findings that, among combat veterans with PTSD, psychotic symptoms are often comorbid with major depression (e.g., David et al., 1999; Hamner, Frueh, Ulmer, & Arana, 1999).

The elevated risk of PTSD in those with psychotic depression may be explained in several ways. First, it may be that extreme trauma produces both psychosis and depression, such that some individuals present with both sets of symptoms simultaneously. Second, it is possible that some of the "psychotic" symptoms in those PTSD sufferers with comorbid depression actually represent severe intrusive and dissociative symptomatology relayed to posttraumatic stress. Finally, given the fact that more than half of all those psychotically depressed outpatients in Zimmerman and Mattia's (1999) study had PTSD, it is possible that some cases of major depression with psychotic features represent a syndromal variant of severe PTSD or BPDMS (the latter minus the "brief" designation). Whatever the ultimate reason for the association, the assessing clinician should be alert to the possibility of a severe trauma in those who complain both of psychotic symptoms and clinical depression.

## Panic Disorder

Although panic disorder is not traditionally understood as trauma-related, *DSM–IV* notes that panic attacks can arise from loss or disruption of important interpersonal relationships and suggests a possible link between panic disorder and posttraumatic stress (American Psychiatric Association, 2000, p. 435). Leskin and Sheikh (2002), for example, reported a substantial comorbidity between panic disorder and PTSD in the general population, concluding that "trauma may act as a risk factor for panic disorder, as well as comorbid panic disorder and PTSD" (p. 599). In a direct investigation of panic and trauma exposure, Falsetti and Resnick (1997) found that 69% of clients seeking treatment for trauma-related symptomatology reported trauma-specific panic attacks. In addition, various investigators (e.g., Kellner & Yehuda, 1999; Southwick et al., 1997) suggested that panic disorder and PTSD may involve hyperactivation of similar neurobiological (e.g., noradrenergic or serotonergic) circuits in the brain.

These data and clinical experience suggest that panic can be a posttraumatic stress response, although, clearly, not all panic attacks arise from traumatic events. When panic is trauma-related, several etiologic pathways are possible. First, panic attacks may arise from the inescapable fear associated with some traumas and thus may represent a classically conditioned response that can be activated by stimuli reminiscent of the original traumatic event. Second, panic episodes may arise from the experience of PTSD, wherein repeated frightening and intrusive flashbacks, along with autonomic hyperarousal, activate anticipatory fear responses. Finally, it is possible that, in some susceptible individuals, traumatic events enhance or kindle reactivity of the sympathetic nervous system, making panic symptoms (and panic disorder) more likely.

Despite the link between panic and PTSD however, *DSM–IV* notes that panic attacks cannot be considered evidence of panic disorder if they are specifically triggered by recollections or reminders of a traumatic event. Thus, for example, a rape victim's panic attack on seeing someone similar to her assailant might be classified as an associated feature of PTSD, if she had that disorder, but would not be categorized as a symptom of panic disorder. If, however, after the rape, she began having unexpected panic attacks in a situation that did not trigger rape memories, panic disorder would be a relevant diagnosis (American Psychiatric Association, 2000, p. 438).

## Borderline Personality Disorder

*DSM–IV* describes borderline personality disorder as a chronic disturbance in which there is "a pervasive pattern of instability of interpersonal relationship, self-image, and affects, and marked impulsivity beginning by early adulthood and present in a variety of contexts" (American Psychiatric Association, 2000, p. 706). The primary symptoms of this disorder, according to *DSM–IV* (p. 710), are

- ☐ "Frantic efforts to avoid real or imagined abandonment";
- ☐ "A pattern of unstable and intense interpersonal relationships" (e.g., idealization, manipulation, and marked shifts in attitude);
- ☐ "Identity disturbance: markedly and persistently unstable self image or sense of self";
- ☐ "Impulsivity in at least two areas that are potentially self damaging" (e.g., spending, sex, substance use, reckless driving, binge eating)";
- ☐ "Recurrent suicidal behavior, gestures, or threats, or self-mutilating behavior";
- ☐ "Affective instability due to a marked reactivity of mood";
- ☐ "Chronic feelings of emptiness";
- ☐ "Inappropriate, intense anger or difficulty in controlling anger"; and
- ☐ Transient, stress-related paranoid ideation or severe dissociative symptoms."

Most traditional theories of borderline personality development (e.g., Kernberg, 1976; Masterson, 1976) trace the genesis of this disorder to dysfunctional parental (primarily maternal) behavior in the first several years of the child's life. In classic psychoanalytic theory, the soon-to-be-borderline child is rewarded for enmeshed dependency and punished (often through abandonment) for independence. Such children (and later adults) are thought to be arrested at a "pre-Oedipal" level, such that they are unable to form the capacity for healthy object relations.

Although childrearing of this nature might be expected to produce significant disturbance in children, there is little empirical support for this model vis-à-vis borderline symptom development. In contrast, a number of studies indicate that severe childhood trauma, neglect, and loss are, in fact, associated with later borderline personality disorder (e.g., Briere & Zaidi, 1989; Heffernan & Cloitre, 2000; Herman et al., 1989; Ogata et al., 1990; Yen et al., 2002). As suggested by Herman's (1992a) formulation of "complex PTSD," it is likely that the early developmental disruption associated with pervasive childhood trauma (i.e., chronic sexual and/or physical abuse) and parental acts of omission (e.g., neglect-related emotional deprivation) may later produce borderline personality in some people.

# Conclusion

This chapter has outlined a number of disorders that are either intrinsically associated with traumatic events or that may arise from traumatic events or processes. As well, several newer trauma-related diagnoses have been presented, although these latter entities have yet to be fully accepted or codified by the general mental health community. This chapter also described several stress-related syndromes that, although not often seen in mainstream North American/European society, are prevalent in other cultures.

As the role of trauma in psychological disorder becomes more widely understood by practitioners and researchers, other diagnoses probably will be found to relate, in some instances, to traumatic stress as well. Trauma can be etiologically associated with mental disorders in at least two different ways, for example: first, by directly producing posttraumatic responses (e.g., as in PTSD, ASD, or the dissociative disorders), or second, by triggering an already latent or prepotent process into a visible disorder (e.g., acute exacerbations of chronic schizophrenia or depression, secondary to a major stressor).

It is likely that as psychological diagnosis becomes more sophisticated, clinicians will find that the very notion of dichotomously present-or-absent disorders often is an oversimplification. Especially with regard to PTSD-related phenomena, it is probably more accurate to refer to posttraumatic spectrum responses of various types that—if determined to be of sufficient severity or frequency—may meet diagnostic criteria and become a "disorder."

Fortunately, although the exact etiologic pathway to various diagnoses may not be fully known, and the longstanding controversy between symptom continua and discrete disorders has yet to be settled, the clinician need not resolve these issues in order to assess potentially posttraumatic states. As noted in later chapters, the evaluator's responsibility is to evaluate the current level and configuration of symptomatology presented by the client, determine whether his or her self-reported (or otherwise determined) history appears to contain traumatic events sufficient to produce such symptoms, consider the relative contribution of mediating risk factors, and make, if necessary, hypotheses about potential links between these two phenomena. Although a clearly appropriate *DSM–IV* diagnosis may arise from this process, in some cases it will not; the symptomatology—although potentially of clinical import—may be too diverse or of insufficient intensity or frequency to justify a specific *DSM* label. As discussed in the next chapter, in many cases the examiner will also not be able to state with absolute certainty that a given disorder or symptom pattern arose directly and exclusively from a specific traumatic event.

Nevertheless, posttraumatic states are relatively common, often arise from events that trigger clinical, judicial, or compensatory interventions from society (and thus require detailed evaluation), and yet may be overlooked by the clinical evaluator who has insufficient information on posttraumatic responses. The remainder of this book addresses the various issues that must be considered if an accurate and meaningful psychological assessment is to be made.

# II

# General Issues in the Assessment of Posttraumatic Stress

# 3

# Critical Issues in Trauma-Relevant Assessment

$P$ sychological assessment of posttraumatic states, whether by diagnostic interview or formal psychometric testing, must take into account certain issues if it is to be successful. Among these are the quality of the evaluation environment, the need to assess both trauma-related and more generic symptoms, the potential for the client to under- or overreport traumatic events and symptoms, and potential constraints on the interpretation of trauma-relevant psychological assessment data. Along with these concerns, this chapter also considers the effects of assessor interactional style on the client (and, thereby, the test data), the occasional need to stabilize the client who is overwhelmed by the assessment stimuli or environment, cross-cultural issues, the interface between medical illness or injury and posttraumatic stress, and the limits of evaluator testimony in the courtroom.

## Approach to Assessment

Because trauma victims, by definition, have been exposed to danger and intrusion, it is not uncommon for them to approach the assessment process with trepidation, if not distrust. When the trauma has just recently occurred or is especially overwhelming in some way, the victim may experience psychological evaluation as yet another component of the traumatic event itself and view the interviewer as an additional stressor. For example, crisis workers occasionally find that their attempts to engage in initial mental status evaluations and triage with victims of mass trauma are perceived by some victims as intrusive, bureaucratic, or even malignant.

In fact, the assessment process is inherently stressful for some victims (e.g., Litz, Penk, Gerardi, & Keane, 1992). The request that a victim describe (and thereby recall) traumatic events can reactivate upsetting memories and painful affects, producing more posttraumatic stress than may have been present before the interview. For example, victims of political torture may sharply fear what they view as interrogation by an authority figure; adult survivors of childhood abuse may expect betrayal or violation rather than assistance; and rape victims may experience renewed distress if evaluated by someone in some way similar (e.g., by gender, ethnicity, or personal characteristics) to the rapist.

In some sense, the assessor is constrained by a psychological version of the uncertainty principle; just as, in physics, observation of an event inevitably changes that event, so it is true that aspects of the assessment process may temporarily alter the client's current state and influence the results of assessment. A classic example of how this dynamic can go awry is in some forensic or clinical evaluations where the examiner appears unnecessarily distant and skeptical, is excessively abrupt or intrusive with questions, or is, ironically, too invasively sympathetic regarding assumed traumatic experience. In response, the interviewee may become avoidant (e.g., nondisclosing or dissociative) or restimulated (e.g., angry or cognitively disorganized), ultimately leading to an inaccurate psychological report regarding his or her history or current psychological symptoms.

The evaluator should take this reactive dimension of trauma assessment into account, so that the client is not unduly stressed by the interview, nor are the resulting assessment data contaminated by the client's negative reactions to assessment or the assessor. In some instances, this approach may mean that certain psychological tests (e.g., projective instruments) are not administered until the client is more stable and less distressed, whereas in others even a trauma-based mental status exam or detailed description of the traumatic event may have to be delayed. Despite the sometimes pressing need to acquire assessment data from the client, the ultimate issue is the client's continuing well-being and the importance of avoiding any further harm.

For these reasons, the assessing clinician should work to provide a manifestly safe evaluation environment and to develop as much rapport with the client as possible (Armstrong, 1995). Among other things, this approach requires that the evaluator (a) be sensitive to the client's current situation, stressors, and level of functioning; (b) pace the interview so that the client is not overwhelmed by questions or demands for information; (c) explain testing procedures in advance; and (d) obtain the client's implicit, if not explicit, permission for each step in the assessment process. More generally, the clinician must attempt to find a psychological "place" in relation to the trauma victim that is neither so distant as to be nonempathic or uncaring nor so close as to be intrusive or threatening.

It is also generally a good idea to inform the client beforehand that assessment may be stressful—without, of course, suggesting that it is intrinsically injurious. In this way, the client is more able to give informed consent and is, to some extent, prepared for possible assessment-related distress. In some cases, the examiner may even debrief the client after the evaluation, inviting him or her to discuss, process, and place into context the impacts of talking about the trauma.

Interestingly, however, even a brief or superficial discussion of traumatic events has been shown to significantly decrease psychological symptoms and increase indices of physical health (e.g., Brown & Heimberg, 2001; Petrie, Booth, Pennebaker, Davison, & Thomas, 1995). As well, Brabin and Berah (1995) reported that the minority of research participants in their study who found trauma questions stressful also described positive impacts of such inquiry. Thus, the potentially stressful effects of trauma-focused assessment should not be seen as necessarily enduring and may be psychologically helpful in the longer term.

Nevertheless, on rare occasion, the severely traumatized client may react adversely to the assessment process. This may occur either because assessment stimuli (for example, test materials or the examiner's physical or psychological characteristics) reactivate significant posttraumatic stress in an otherwise seem-ingly stable individual, or because, especially in acute trauma settings, the client is already sufficiently destabilized that any additional psychic demands exacerbate his or her posttraumatic state. In either instance, the evaluatee may present with evidence of increased stress, such as panic, anger, flashbacks, dissociative responses, or even tangentiality or confusion.

Obviously, in such unusual cases, further assessment is almost always contraindicated, and the primary task becomes emotional stabilization. Clinical experience suggests that this process may be aided by reduced stimulation, reassurance, and grounding. First, the evaluator will typically terminate the assessment pro-cess as soon as is reasonably possible, generally refrain from further activating inquiries or statements, and reduce environ-mental stimuli that could cue or trigger posttraumatic stress. If evaluation took place near the traumatic event (for example, near a disaster site or in an emergency setting where other victims are visible), the clinician may consider moving the noninjured client to a less stimulating environment.[1] If the upsetting stimulus is a Rorschach card or psychological inventory, the examiner may choose to visibly put away such materials, so that direct restimulation will be reduced and symbolic termination of the upsetting event may occur. If the examiner's characteristics (e.g., his or her gender or physical appearance) are significantly restim-ulating by virtue of their similarity to those of a trauma perpetra-tor, it is often a good idea to seek a new evaluator (if possible) for the client. When this is done, the change and the reason for the change usually should be explained to the client in a nonthreatening and nondemeaning manner.

Reassurance and grounding are also important parts of de-escalating evaluation-related distress or disturbance. The client is typically reminded of the safety of the assessment environ-ment, and his or her emotional reactions may be framed as

---

[1]This should not be done automatically, however. For some survivors of multivictim trauma, some degree of proximity to other affected individuals may be more helpful than being isolated from them. In most cases, a simple inquiry will resolve this issue.

reasonable given his or her situation. During this normalization process, the evaluator's voice and demeanor should be calming and reassuring. When necessary, the clinician may draw the client's attention to the concrete aspects of the immediate environment in such a way as to distract from escalating internal states. When the client has returned to a more stable emotional state, assessment either may be carefully reinitiated or delayed to a later point in time.

## Goals of Trauma-Relevant Assessment

Assuming that assessment can occur without overstressing the victim, a central issue concerns the actual goal of such evaluation. For example, in the assessment of a rape victim, is the ultimate intent to determine (a) whether the victim's current symptoms are directly attributable to the rape, (b) whether the victim is experiencing posttraumatic distress or disorder, or (c) the extent to which the victim is suffering from any sort of psychological disturbance, including posttraumatic stress?

Although the first option might seem important, it is often the case that a given psychological presentation cannot be absolutely linked to an earlier traumatic event. Even if the client reports definitive symptoms of acute stress disorder (ASD) or acute posttraumatic stress disorder (PTSD), it is possible that some other traumatic experience produced some or all of the symptoms in question. Even more problematic are chronic PTSD, dissociative, and personality-level symptoms, because the etiology of these responses may reside far in the past. In those instances when a cause–effect relationship must be specifically evaluated (e.g., in some forensic situations), important issues include the temporal sequence (i.e., did the posttraumatic disturbance appear after the traumatic event, in the absence of other intervening traumas) and the nature of the intrusive symptoms (e.g., does the client report flashbacks or intrusive images and memories of the specific rape experience in question). If these two conditions are met, and the validity of the test data can be assured, the clinician may be able to hypothesize (but not promise) that the rape, in fact, produced the posttraumatic symptoms found in the client.

More typically, however, the traumatic event may be long past (e.g., in childhood or at some point earlier in life), the symptoms may be less clear-cut (e.g., dissociative symptoms or depression), and other negative life events may have intervened between the hypothesized stressor and the observed clinical state (e.g., more recent traumas or victimization experiences). In such cases, and in the absence of other relevant data, the evaluating clinician may be left with the conclusion that (a) the client's report of an earlier trauma(s) appears to be valid, and (b) his or her current state is consistent with the possibility that the trauma produced the current symptom pattern, but that (c) a definitive connection between these two events cannot be asserted absolutely. In other words, there are rarely psychological "litmus tests" for the existence or effects of a given trauma, especially one long past. Fortunately, other than in some forensic contexts (i.e., civil litigation for psychological damages), this trauma–response connection need not be definitive. Instead, the clinician may determine that the best-fitting hypothesis is that the trauma and the post-traumatic stress are related, without ruling out other potential etiologies.

The second issue, that of determining whether a posttraumatic condition exists, is typically possible in a sensitive and competent psychological evaluation. In certain instances, however, even this goal may be elusive. As noted elsewhere in this volume, many generic psychological tests are relatively insensitive to posttraumatic states and instead misclassify such symptoms as evidence of other disorders, such as personality disorder or psychosis. As well, the clinician unfamiliar with (or negatively predisposed toward) posttraumatic disturbance may misinterpret or overlook existing trauma-related symptoms in a clinical interview. Finally, as discussed later in this chapter, the client's need for avoidance may cause him or her to deny or mask posttraumatic symptomatology, thereby reducing the visibility of such symptoms during evaluation. Given these issues, the most effective evaluator will be familiar with the complexities of posttraumatic clinical presentation, will administer trauma-sensitive psychological tests along with a sensitive clinical interview (see chapter 7), and will work to provide an evaluation environment that minimizes the presence of client avoidance or distortion.

Even though the assessment focus may be on posttraumatic stress and stressors, the ultimate goal of a competent evaluation is not solely to define the relationship between aversive experiences and outcomes, or to identify specific posttraumatic difficulties. Instead, the client's entire symptom experience should be assessed. For example, although a 33-year-old earthquake victim's ASD is an obvious target for evaluation, his preexisting obsessive–compulsive symptoms and current panic disorder are also important components of his clinical picture. Similarly, individuals with psychotic disorders or certain Axis II difficulties (especially those residing in Cluster B) are thought to be especially prone to PTSD when exposed to moderate stressors, and thus a complete psychological assessment will include data on these clinical antecedents as well. Finally, some nontrauma-related symptoms (e.g., certain obsessional, psychotic, or anxiety symptoms) may mimic posttraumatic symptomatology. In such instances, failure to consider all relevant diagnostic possibilities may lead to a misidentification of posttraumatic disturbance.

Generally, as noted in chapter 2, diagnostic notions such as "complex PTSD" or "posttraumatic depression" reflect the fact that posttraumatic stress is often present in the context of other symptoms and disorders. Studies suggest, for example, that those with PTSD may also suffer from other, coexisting disorders such as depression, anxiety disorders (especially panic disorder, phobias, and obsessive–compulsive disorder), alcohol and drug abuse, and borderline or antisocial personality disorder (Breslau & Davis, 1992; Green, Lindy, Grace, & Gleser, 1989). This overlap appears to represent not only the comorbidity of various disorders with PTSD, but also the fact that some PTSD diagnostic criteria are similar to those for depressive and anxiety disorders (Davidson & Foa, 1991; Kessler et al., 1995). Such symptom and disorder overlap emphasizes the need to evaluate for the full range of psychological disorders when assessing the traumatized client.

In summary, clinical evaluation of trauma victims must take into account the client's entire psychological experience, including the complexity of potentially etiologic, predisposing, and moderating events, and the possibility of significant comorbidity with other, less trauma-related conditions. Failure to consider these broader issues may result in erroneous conclusions or unnecessarily constrained clinical data.

# Avoidance and Underreporting

Because most living organisms tend to withdraw from noxious stimuli, it is not surprising that traumatic events can motivate the development and use of avoidance strategies. Avoidance may present as emotional or cognitive suppression, denial, dissociation, memory distortion, or involvement in activities that numb or distract. For example, a combat veteran may attempt to suppress thoughts about his or her war experiences, may avoid situations where he or she has to talk about the war, may enter a dissociative state when exposed to combat-relevant stimuli, or may use alcohol or drugs to numb posttraumatic distress.

Although such avoidance strategies can be superficially adaptive, they often impede the treatment process (Briere & Scott, in press; Resick & Schnicke, 1993) and can easily interfere with accurate psychological evaluation. Regarding the latter, the client's tendency to avoid or attenuate distress may decrease his or her response to psychological assessment, in some instances leading to a significant underreporting of trauma history or posttraumatic effects. This underreporting may especially occur if a given assessment technique requires the victim to recall or reexperience trauma-related events. More generally, Epstein (1993) noted that "The avoidant symptoms of PTSD can serve as a 'self-cloaking' device that may hinder or prevent timely diagnosis" (p. 457).

Avoidance also may present in the form of psychogenic amnesia, in which case the victim may have insufficient recall of traumatic experiences and thus will not report them during the evaluation interview. As noted, several studies suggest that some instances of childhood or adult trauma may be relatively unavailable to conscious memory for extended periods of time, during which, presumably, the subjects of these studies would deny or underestimate historical events that did, in fact, occur. Newer research suggests a neurological basis for such cognitive avoid-

ance. Anderson et al. (in press) used functional magnetic resonance imaging (fMRI) to demonstrate that increased prefrontal
activation and reduced hippocampus activation were associated
with the unconscious suppression of unwanted memories in the
laboratory. By definition, such memory suppression might easily
alter the trauma disclosure process.

Defensive avoidance of painful material also may suppress
clients' scores on symptom measures. Shedler, Mayman, and
Manis (1993) demonstrated in a more general context, for example, that "standard mental health scales appear unable to distin-
guish between genuine mental health and the facade or illusion
of mental health created by psychological defenses" (p. 1117). In
support of this notion, Elliott and Briere (1994) reported on a
subsample of children for whom there was compelling evidence
of sexual abuse (e.g., unambiguous medical findings, photo-
graphs taken by the abuser, or abuser confession) but who, none-
theless, both (a) denied that they had been abused, and (b) scored
significantly lower than control group (children without known
sexual abuse histories) on the Trauma Symptom Checklist for
Children (TSCC; Briere, 1996b). As noted in that paper, it is
likely that these children were using denial and other cognitive
avoidance strategies to keep from confronting both their abuse
and its psychological impacts. In the absence of outside corroboration, these children probably would have been judged as nonabused and nondistressed on interview or by psychological
evaluation.

Symptom underreporting, while potentially an important issue in the assessment of abuse survivors and other traumatized
individuals, is difficult to identify through psychological tests.
At present, the practitioner is limited to reliance on validity scales
that, for example, index defensiveness or "fake good" responses
(e.g., the L and K scales of the Minnesota Multiphasic Personality
Inventory [MMPI], Positive Impression Management scale of the
Personality Assessment Inventory [PAI; Morey, 1991], Disclosure
and Desirability indices of the Millon Clinical Multiaxial Inventory [MCMI], or Response Level scale of the Trauma Symptom
Inventory [TSI; Briere, 1995]). Unfortunately, although these validity indicators identify more extreme cases of underreporting, it is likely that many other instances will go unidentified

unless the clinician can somehow detect it during the evaluation interview.

As a result of these various processes, the clinician should not rule out the possibility of an unreported traumatic event or trauma-related disturbance in a given individual's life history, whether the missing information occurs as the result of conscious suppression of upsetting material or more unconscious defensive processes. The possibility of significant avoidance-based underreporting does not mean, however, that an individual who is symptomatic but denies a victimization history is necessarily "in denial" about or "repressing" a specific traumatic event. For example, some clinicians have attributed a variety of mental health complaints to completely repressed sexual abuse trauma in clients who denied abuse histories, a practice not supported by current knowledge (Berliner & Briere, 1998). As noted at various points in this volume, there are a variety of traumatic and nontraumatic events and processes that may produce any given symptom or state, such that an automatic assumption of a specific undisclosed trauma as etiologic is not tenable (Meyers, 1996). Furthermore, although complete dissociation of a trauma-related memory appears to be possible, such extreme avoidance responses are not the norm and should not be assumed unless there are specific data in support of that hypothesis.

# Overreporting

In contrast to underreporting, some individuals may overreport or misrepresent trauma histories or trauma-related symptomatology (Fairbank, McCaffrey, & Keane, 1985; Frueh, Hamner, Cahill, Gold, & Hamlin, 2000). Occasionally, overreporting of trauma histories may occur in the context of psychosis or extreme personality disorders. On the other hand, as noted, borderline personality disorder may also arise from, among other things, severe child abuse; and recent research implicates trauma in some psychotic presentations, including, obviously, brief psychotic disorder with marked stressor[s] (BPDMS). In addition, there are no data to suggest that more disturbed individuals have a lower probability of being traumatized than other people, and considerable cause to expect that psychologically impaired or incapacitated people are more easy prey for predatory individuals. As a result, the trauma reports of psychotic or borderline individuals should not be discounted automatically but, instead, should be evaluated for their credibility and meaning in the same manner as any other historical statements might be considered.

Because of concerns over the likelihood of some "false memories" of childhood maltreatment (e.g., Lindsay, 1994), the specific validity of adults' reports of childhood trauma (especially abuse) has been the subject of considerable debate. Some have contended, for example, that a given abuse allegation may be the result of psychopathology, greed, or vindictiveness, or that an evaluator/therapist has implanted "false memories" of abuse in a client who, in fact, has no abuse history (e.g., Loftus & Ketcham, 1994). Others suggest, however, that adult reports of childhood abuse are often reality-based, especially in terms of their central features (e.g., Courtois, 1999).

Clinical experience, as well as the data on amnesia presented in chapter 2, tends to support the latter position regarding trauma and memory, while not discounting the former. Prospective data from a study by Williams (1995) suggested that the content of self-identified recovered memories of sexual abuse is no less accurate than the recollections of those who report that they have always remembered their abuse, and research by Elliott (1997) and others (e.g., Epstein & Bottoms, 2002) suggested that it is not unusual for trauma survivors to report having at least temporary amnesia for part or all of very stressful events. In a similar vein, *DSM–III–R*, *DSM–IV*, and *DSM–IV–TR* each refer to dissociative amnesia and include as a criterion for PTSD the possibility that the individual may experience, for example, an "inability to recall an important aspect of the trauma" (American Psychiatric Association, 2000, p. 468).

Unfortunately, some undetermined fraction of trauma disclosures, whether "always remembered" or not, are likely to be significantly distorted or confabulated (McNally, 2003). Such overreporting can have major negative impacts on innocent parties, as well as, obviously, distracting the treatment focus during psychotherapy. As such, the possibility of distortion or confabulation must be taken into account during the assessment process.

The charge that therapists can encourage the production of pseudomemories of abuse may lead some clinicians to avoid inquiring at all about trauma histories during evaluation or treatment (Enns et al., 1995). Such clinicians may fear that they will be sued for implanting false memories of abuse, or that the mere asking about trauma will lead to a confabulated history. However, a leading proponent of the false memory perspective noted,

> Criticism of memory work in psychotherapy are not directed at survivors of CSA [child sexual abuse] who have always remembered their abuse or at those who spontaneously remember previously forgotten abuse. Furthermore, most critics of memory work in psychotherapy do not claim that all memories of CSA recovered in therapy are false. Finally, most critics do not suggest that practitioners should never broach the subject of CSA, nor do they claim that a few probing questions about CSA are likely to lead clients to create illusory memories. (Lindsay, 1995, p. 281)

Although Lindsay's position may not be supported by all of his colleagues, his statement should be reassuring to those who fear that any assessment procedure that addresses abuse-related memories is likely to produce intrinsically false memories. As Enns et al. (1995) noted, "when inquiries are embedded within a thorough assessment about various aspects of a person's psychological status, it is highly unlikely that these questions will pressure the client to falsely believe they were abused" (p. 230). On the other hand, the exact conditions that govern when a given respondent will or will not misreport or confabulate a trauma history are largely unknown. As a result, clinicians must do as much as they can to ensure that their queries and interventions do not encourage false reports.

Given the reliable correlation between child abuse and later psychological difficulties, it is recommended that clinicians inquire about childhood abuse experiences (as well as adult traumas) as a routine part of all those clinical evaluations where such questions can be tolerated and are likely to be valid. These questions should be posed as a regular part of history-taking, as opposed to being given special attention or emphasis in such a way as to suggest that a specific answer is desired (see chapter 4 for more on taking a trauma history). It is also strongly recommended that such questions not occur during hypnosis, drug-assisted interviews, or within any other context that might capitalize on suggestibility or lead the client to report more than he or she actually recalls (Lindsay & Briere, 1997). As Courtois (1995) outlined in the specific instance of sexual abuse:

> Paraphrasing Judith Herman [1992b] on this matter, the therapist must be technically neutral while being morally cognizant of the prevalence and possibility of an abuse history. But technical neutrality does not mean not asking and cognizance does not mean that the therapist assumes sexual abuse to the exclusion of other issues. The therapist should be open to the possibility of other childhood events and trauma that might account for the symptom picture and should not prematurely foreclose these other possibilities. (p. 21)

Beyond trauma and memory concerns, the client may suffer from a factitious disorder, wherein he or she is driven to report nonexistent traumatic events as a result of psychological disorder. Although factition is typically associated with attempts to appear as if one has a physical disorder, trauma specialists occasionally come across individuals whose presenting description of traumatic events and posttraumatic stress appears to serve a neurotic need for psychological or medical attention and intervention (Baggaley, 1998; Fear, 1996; Neal & Rose, 1995). For example, an individual without military experience may present to a crisis center or outpatient clinic with credible reports of traumatic combat experiences and resultant posttraumatic stress. Although factitious trauma presentations are probably uncommon, they are not unheard of and should be considered in instances where the presenting problem seems overstated or in some other way suspect.

Because our legal system entitles victims to file suits against their alleged perpetrators and some institutions appropriately provide financial support or compensation to those who have been traumatized (e.g., the Veterans Administration and state victim compensation boards), there also may be a financial motivation for some trauma reports and trauma symptom endorsements (Gold & Frueh, 1999; Litz et al., 1992; McNally, 2003). Thus, a competent forensic assessment during, for example, a psychological damages suit, should consider the possibility of malingering (Simon, 1995). Similarly, a more treatment-focused evaluation should not overlook the possibility of intentional misrepresentation, because such phenomena obviously require different sorts of intervention strategies. This possibility should be a normal "rule out" issue, however, as opposed to a way to act out undue skepticism or countertransference regarding actual traumatic events and posttraumatic states. Clinical experience suggests that false reports of trauma or trauma-related symptomatology are more rare than common in non-forensic clinical settings and should not be automatically assumed, just as other reports should not be automatically accepted in their entirety.

Beyond factitious disorder and financially driven malingering, it is not especially uncommon for some individuals who have suffered stigmatization and rejection to amplify their subsequent complaints in an effort to draw attention to injuries that they fear otherwise would be overlooked. When this occurs on psychological tests, it is sometimes referred to as a "cry for help," typically involving a generic overendorsement of symptom items. Unfortunately, in the process of such amplification, the trauma survivor's "real" symptoms may be overlooked or misinterpreted. This phenomenon may be lessened to the extent that the clinician conveys a nondismissive attitude toward the client's complaints, and does not assume that the presence of one overstated complaint necessarily negates the validity of the next one.

As with underreporting, it is somewhat difficult to reliably identify cases of overreporting through the use of psychological tests. Some overreporting of symptomatology, for example, may be detected through validity scale scores, such as elevations on the F, Fp (Infrequency Psychopathology), and Ds (Dissimulation) scales (along with F–K) of the MMPI and MMPI-2, the Debasement scale of the MCMI, or the Atypical Response scale of the TSI (Briere & Elliott, 1997; Bury & Bagby, 2002; Freuh et al., 2000; Rogers, 1997). However, those who have experienced interpersonal victimization, combat, or other severe traumas tend to score more deviantly on such validity scales, thereby lessening to some degree the usefulness of such scales with trauma victims (Elhai et al., 2002; Elliott, 1993; Frueh et al., 2000). For example, the elevated invalidity scores of some Vietnam combat veterans and child abuse survivors appear to reflect the chronic posttraumatic stress, dissociation, cognitive distortions, affective symptoms, or substance abuse often found in these groups, as opposed to motivated symptom overendorsement (e.g., Hyer, Woods, Harrison, et al., 1989; Jordan, Nunley, & Cook, 1992; Klotz Flitter, Elhai, & Gold, 2003; Smith & Frueh, 1996). Given this confounding of validity responses with posttraumatic symptomatology, the clinician or forensic evaluator is faced with a difficult trade-off: Does one strictly apply validity cutoffs, thereby catching some cases of overreporting but also potentially eliminating valid protocols of especially traumatized individuals? Or does one use more liberal cutoffs to retain valid trauma protocols, yet run the risk of incorrectly interpreting overreported or false test responses?

## Overreporting and the Minnesota Multiphasic Personality Inventory–2

Fortunately, it appears that several MMPI–2 validity indicators, although elevated for trauma survivors, are even more elevated for those who intentionally overreport. Wetter, Baer, Berry, Robinson, and Sumpter (1993) found that, consistent with the general trauma literature, 20 patients with PTSD had an average F (T-score) of 79.8 ($SD = 23.7$). As high as this score was, 22 nonclinical research participants instructed to fake PTSD (after being given information on the disorder and being promised a monetary reward for success) had a substantially higher mean F score (111.3, $SD = 17.1$). Wetter et al. found that the Ds and F–K indices were even better at detecting "motivated faking": Raw Ds scores for the PTSD group averaged 24.4 ($SD = 9.7$) whereas the mean score for the faking group was 42.3 ($SD = 11.1$), and raw F–K for the PTSD group was 4.4 ($SD = 12.0$) as compared with 27.4 ($SD = 15.8$) for the motivated fakers. The Variable Response Inconsistency Scale (VRIN) did not differ between PTSD and motivated faking groups—a finding that replicated previous data (Wetter Baer, Berry, Smith, & Larson, 1992). Similarly, a later study by Wetter, Baer, Berry, and Reynolds (1994) found that an F–K value of 14 or higher discriminated motivated fakers of borderline personality disorder from nonfakers. Finally, Smith and Frueh (1996) reported that an F–K of 14 or higher was a reasonable index of "apparent exaggerators" of PTSD. By way of caution, however, it should be noted that the sample sizes in these studies were relatively small and the standard deviations for the relevant validity indicators were relatively large. As a result, it may not be appropriate to use the means of these studies as definitive cutoffs for malingering or overreporting in any given client. Nevertheless, they reinforce the notion that F–K and Ds, along with F, are reasonably good at detecting malingerers and other overreporters, but that even optimal cutting-scores run the risk of labeling some true PTSD cases as misrepresenting themselves. A more recent study of malingering and PTSD on the MMPI–2 (Elhai, Gold, Frueh, & Gold, 2000) drew similar conclusions.

In addition to the F, F–K, and Ds scales, recent research suggests that an additional validity indicator, the Fp (Arbisi & Ben-Porath, 1997) may be helpful in the assessment of traumatized individuals. The Fp was developed to address the fact that those with high levels of psychopathology tend to score highly on F and thus may be inappropriately seen as malingering. Because those with PTSD often endorse a fair amount of general (i.e., not PTSD-specific) symptomatology as well on the MMPI, it would be reasonable to assume that Fp might be better than F in detecting valid versus invalid PTSD profiles. This assumption was born out in two studies, wherein Fp demonstrated greater sensitivity than the F scale in discriminating valid from invalid PTSD protocols (Elhai, Gold, Sellers, & Dorfman, 2001; Elhai et al., 2002). A third study, however, failed to demonstrate a clear advantage of Fp over F (Elhai, Gold, Frueh, & Gold, 2000).

Based on the partial success of Fp in controlling for psychopathology while still detecting valid versus invalid MMPI responses, a promising new validity scale, the Infrequency-Posttraumatic Stress Disorder Scale (Fptsd; Elhai et al., 2002) has been developed. This scale attempts to measure overreporting while, at the same time, avoiding the usual elevation of validity scales in the presence of posttraumatic stress. Created from

MMPI–2 items that were rarely endorsed by male combat veterans in a large Veterans Administration sample, this scale was significantly less related to psychopathology and distress and better at discriminating simulated from actual PTSD than other MMPI validity scales. Although these findings are quite encouraging, further research is indicated before this measure can be generally applied with confidence in clinical practice.

## Non–Minnesota Multiphasic Personality Inventory Overreporting Indicators

Unfortunately, almost all the research available on validity indicators and PTSD concerns the MMPI–2. The few studies available on the PAI and MCMI–III, however, suggested that validity scales are helpful in detecting malingering or overreporting, but that they may also eliminate a significant proportion of valid cases of PTSD (Calhoun, Earnst, Tucker, Kirby, & Beckham, 2000; Lees-Haley, 1992; Liljequist, Kinder, & Schinka, 1998).

The use of independent malingering scales or interviews (e.g., the Structured Interview of Reported Symptoms [SIRS; Rogers, Bagby, & Dickens, 1992] and the Malingering Probability Scale [MPS; Silverton & Gruber, 1998]) also may be indicated when there is a significant possibility of intentional misrepresentation (e.g., in some forensic domains). However, clinicians usually administer the SIRS to detect malingering of schizophrenia or psychosis (Rogers et al., 1992), and, with the exception of one small study (Rogers, Kropp, Bagby, & Dickens, 1992), the SIRS's ability to detect falsified trauma presentations is unknown. Similarly, although the MPS includes items that might allow the clinician to discriminate true from factitious PTSD, there is no "malingered PTSD" scale (only a total malingering score across depressive, schizophrenic, dissociative, and PTSD symptoms), and there are as yet no data available regarding the actual ability of the MPS to detect malingering of PTSD symptoms (Smith, 1997).

In addition to validity scale data, elevated psychosis scores on standardized instruments—if found to represent true psychotic symptoms—may suggest that the client is too cognitively disorganized or delusional to respond in valid ways to psychological tests of traumatic stress. Interestingly, however, some individuals with less acute psychotic symptoms are still able to respond in a valid way to trauma measures. Finally, the client whose historical reports or symptom presentation appear especially unlikely (e.g., descriptions of technically impossible scenarios or especially florid or nonsensical symptomatology) obviously may be overreporting, although even such individuals may have experienced other, actual victimization events and may nevertheless report at least some events or symptomatology accurately.

## Misidentification and Distortion Effects

Because most standard psychological tests (e.g., the MMPI or Rorschach) were not developed at a time when psychological trauma was well recognized, these instruments may underidentify or distort trauma effects (Briere & Elliott, 1997; Jacobs & Dalenberg, 1998). As described in chapter 6, older instruments may confuse intrusive posttraumatic symptomatology with hallucinations, obsessions, primary process, or "fake bad" responses; misinterpret dissociative avoidance as fragmented thinking, chaotic internal states, or the negative signs of schizophrenia; and misidentify trauma-based cognitive phenomena (e.g., hypervigilance or generalized distrust) as evidence of paranoia or other delusional processes. Furthermore, these tests may misinterpret the effects of childhood trauma as personality disorders to the extent that they involve interpersonal difficulties, chaotic internal states, and tension-reduction or other affect-avoidance activities.

This tendency for traditional measures to misinterpret posttraumatic symptoms as psychosis or personality disorder might seemingly preclude their use in trauma assessment. However, the issue may be less that of intrinsically bad data (i.e., the test items themselves) as erroneous interpretation (i.e., how the items and scales are understood). For example, as described in chapter 6, although many sexual abuse survivors have elevations on scales 4 and 8 of the MMPI or MMPI–2, it is often inappropriate to view these individuals as potentially schizophrenic (scale 8), psychopathic (scale 4), or "borderline" (e.g., a 4–8 profile). Instead, examination of specific items and available subscale scores may indicate the presence of nonpsychotic reexperiencing symptoms, interpersonal distrust or social alienation, and dissociative responses, as well as accurate reporting of familial discord during childhood. Thus, to the extent that more trauma-relevant interpretations can be made, standard psychological tests can be a helpful part of the trauma assessment process. This is important, because there are tremendous databases available on clients' responses to the MMPI, MCMI, Rorschach, and other tests, data that can be well used when applied with care.

Important issues to consider when using traditional psychological test data are at least fourfold:

1. The test, itself, must be generally understood, in terms of how it was developed and normed, its relevant psychometric qualities, including its reliability, sensitivity (the percentage of instances that it detects actual cases of the disorder in question), and specificity (the percentage of instances that it correctly detects noncases of the disorder), and the underlying theory on which interpretation of scores is based. For example, a test normed on a relatively homogeneous sample of Midwestern adults may have diminished applicability to an African American combat veteran with severe and chronic PTSD. Similarly, a projective test interpretation system that regularly relies on traditional psychoanalytic theory may be of limited validity in the assessment of an individual who was repeatedly incestuously assaulted as a child.

2. The item domain of the instrument should be evaluated: Do the items tap the labeled construct well, or can they misinterpret other phenomena as evidence of the construct? To the extent that the items within a given scale reflect multiple phenomena, some of which are more trauma-relevant than others, are there interpretable subscales available? For example, scale 8 (Sc) of the MMPI contains the following Harris and Lingoes (1968) content subscales: Social

Alienation; Emotional Alienation; Lack of Ego Mastery, Cognitive; Lack of Ego Mastery, Conative; Lack of Ego Mastery, Defective Inhibition; and Bizarre Sensory Experiences. Because such subscales are typically more unidimensional than summary scale scores, their meaning with regard to the client's current state may be more transparent and therefore more helpful.

3. The presence of more specific trauma scales within the instrument should be taken into account. The MMPI–2, PAI, and MCMI–III, for example, each have PTSD scales. Although, as described in chapter 6, each PTSD scale has less than perfect content coverage (all underestimate certain posttraumatic symptoms and two contain less trauma-relevant symptoms such as depression), they may alert the examiner to the possibility of significant posttraumatic stress, and thus to alternate explanations for other scale elevations. Further, ad-hoc, trauma-specific scoring rules for a given instrument often are available (e.g., Armstrong and Loewenstein's [1991] Traumatic Content Index for the Rorschach), thereby adding more information for interpretation.

4. Standard psychological tests should be augmented with additional, more trauma-specific instruments. Because the notion of posttraumatic stress is a relatively new one, however, there are a limited (albeit growing) number of standardized instruments available in this area thus far. Trauma-focused tests should be normed on large, sociodemographically diverse samples, have demonstrated reliability and validity, and measure a number of areas of posttraumatic disturbance. Regarding the latter, a scale that yields a single summary PTSD score is often less helpful because PTSD minimally involves three separate, only moderately correlated components: reexperiencing, avoidance, and hyperarousal—each of which may vary in magnitude in any specific instance. The most useful measures provide scores on each component,

so that a more detailed assessment of posttraumatic stress can be made. For example, whereas a summary measure of PTSD (e.g., as found in the MMPI–2) might indicate that an assault victim is experiencing moderately high posttraumatic stress, a more detailed instrument might suggest that his or her levels of intrusion and arousal are high but his or her avoidance is within normal limits.

## Cross-Cultural Issues

As noted in chapter 1 and elsewhere in this volume, the notion of posttraumatic stress and—to some extent—the idea of trauma, itself, is culturally determined. Negative events may be seen as more traumatic in one society or group than in another, by virtue of attitudes and beliefs each holds regarding the meaning of such events and their social implications for the individual exposed to them. As well, cultures vary significantly in what idioms of distress and underlying models they use to understand and communicate psychological injury. One culture, for example, may locate the effects of trauma in the psyche, whereas a second may assume the impact is on the body, and a third may interpret the injury as spiritual. For this reason, diagnoses such as "PTSD," or even "depression" presuppose certain etiologies, mechanisms, and phenomenologies; assumptions that may not be shared by all cultures. As a result, it is important that the clinical assessor be aware of the cultural relativity of the terms he or she uses, and the limits to their generalizability. To put it bluntly, "PTSD" may have no more value as a diagnosis than do *ataques de nervios*, *shin-byung*, or another non-*DSM*/ICD label, except as it relates to professional mental health communications about "Western" symptoms in English-speaking cultures. The implications of this are several, ranging from the realization that PTSD, itself, is partially a culture-bound disorder, to recognizing the need for clinicians to consider other possible forms of mental disturbance when evaluating immigrants or refugees or when engaging in outreach to traumatized people elsewhere in the world. The need for cultural awareness is obvious when one is working in a center for immigrant torture victims; it is just as significant, however, in the multicultural contexts found in most urban mental health clinics.

## Trauma-Related Testimony in Court

Although this is not a text on forensic psychology, a few points should be made with regard to expert testimony in trauma cases. There are at least two ways in which a trauma evaluator or clinician may become involved in the courts. First, the clinician who treats or evaluates trauma survivors may easily find him- or herself testifying with regard to one of his or her clients, either in a criminal case or in a civil suit. Second, a forensic evaluator may be called on to render an expert opinion regarding the presence of posttraumatic distress or disorder in someone who is involved in a criminal or civil proceeding. In the author's opinion, only the second clinician should offer expert testimony as to the effects of trauma and the potential validity of a specific allegation. The first clinician, to the extent that he or she has formed a therapeutic relationship with the client, is less likely to be objective regarding the facts of the case. Of course, this does not preclude the clinician's testimony regarding the process or content of therapy.

During testimony, the examiner would do well to adhere to four principles of expert testimony, sometimes expressed as the acronym HELP: honesty, evenhandedness, limits of expertise, and preparation (Meyers, 1996). Honesty with regard to trauma testimony typically means acknowledging an unavoidable set of realities: (a) in the absence of external corroboration, it may be impossible to determine with complete certainty whether a traumatic event has occurred; (b) it is not always possible to rule out the existence of symptom underreporting, overreporting, or malingering; and (c) when a pattern of symptoms has been established, it is rarely possible to assert with complete confidence that the symptoms in question arose entirely from a specific past traumatic event.

That these limitations exist does not, however, mean that the evaluator has no role in the courtroom. First of all, the judge and jury may need to be appraised as to the limits of "medical certainty" with regard to potential posttraumatic states. Second, although the expert witness may not be able to provide definitive testimony regarding trauma or effect, he or she can assist the court in considering the various possibilities and the general likelihood of each.

In this regard, evenhandedness and an acknowledgment of the limits of expertise means that the evaluator should consider all reasonable explanations for the client's reports of trauma and posttraumatic difficulty, and, to the extent that data are available, offer a carefully constrained opinion as to the likelihood of each. For example, although the interviewer may believe that, on balance, the alleged victim's reports have merit, he or she should also be prepared to discuss the possibility of misrepresentation or malingering. Similarly, even though an expert may have been hired by the plaintiff's attorney regarding the possibility that a given traumatic event caused short- or long-term damages, the evaluator must also consider the possibility that other antecedent or intervening negative experiences produced at least some of the symptoms in question, or that the plaintiff's reports are distorted by financial considerations. Finally, an interviewer who believes that a given allegation of posttraumatic stress is false must also consider the possibility that his or her expectations, demeanor, or even choice of assessment procedures precluded access to information that would have contradicted that belief. He or she must also accept the fact that an absence of evidence does not mean that an event did not take place. In this regard, psychological testimony that a traumatic event did not occur may be as inappropriate as unsupported testimony that it did.

Forensic experience suggests that those expert witnesses who come to significant grief in the courtroom are often those who are not well prepared regarding the actual needs of the court. Such individuals may argue one "side" without considering the other, failing to evaluate competing hypotheses for the complainant's allegations, symptoms, and presentation. For example, the examiner who categorically states that event A occurred and produced posttraumatic response B is less likely to be viewed as an objective expert by judge or jury—and is much more easily discredited upon cross-examination—than the examiner who offers several potential hypotheses regarding what may have occurred. By applying relevant test and interview data to these hypotheses, along with an understanding of the relevant literature, the expert may then offer a considered, but explicitly probabilistic conclusion regarding A and B. Such testimony not only honors the ethical responsibilities incumbent on psychologists and other mental health professionals, it carries with it greater professionalism and probity and, ultimately, greater credibility. For additional information on the forensic aspects of trauma practice, see Simon (1995), Armstrong, and High (1999) and, in the specific instance of childhood abuse, Myers (1998).

# Conclusion

Posttraumatic states are in some sense unique in the clinical field because of their tendency to become reactivated during the assessment of their presence. This reactivation, in turn, may distort psychological test or interview data. This concern is compounded by the fact that many evaluation approaches used in this area were developed without specific reference to posttraumatic phenomena and thus may misinterpret trauma responses as evidence of other clinical states. Because psychologists and others have only recently considered these issues in psychological assessment, no definitive information is available regarding the exact meaning of posttraumatic stress tapped by traditional assessment methodologies. As a result, some trauma victims are likely to be seen as suffering from non-trauma-related psychopathology, and some nontraumatized individuals who seek to present themselves as posttraumatic are likely to go undetected. Thus, the examiner is on shaky ground to the extent that he or she absolutely concludes, based on test or interview data, that a given incident of trauma and subsequent stress have occurred and are related.

Fortunately, research on the assessment and diagnosis of posttraumatic states is proceeding at a rapid pace, and new, more trauma-specific tests are being developed on an ongoing basis. The remainder of this book outlines what we have learned thus far, and highlights new approaches to posttrauma assessment that substantially increase the sensitivity and specificity of trauma-relevant clinical evaluation.

# Assessment of Traumatic Events

As outlined in chapters 1 and 2, traumatic events are not un-common in people's lives and may lead to psychological distress and impairment, if not a posttraumatic stress disorder (PTSD). For this reason, when conditions allow—that is, if the client is not acutely psychotic, overwhelmed, or suffering from substantial cognitive impairment—the interviewer should in-quire about childhood and adulthood trauma history in those seeking psychological assistance. To some extent, how this in-quiry is done is up to the interviewer, but it should minimally include general questions about major negative experiences throughout the lifespan. As described later in this chapter, such questions should be behaviorally anchored, as opposed to solely asking about "child abuse," "rape," or exposure to "disasters."

Taking a routine trauma history may result in considerable information about important traumatic events (e.g., Lanktree, Briere, & Zaidi, 1991; Read & Fraser, 1998)—material that often is not volunteered without specific inquiry. For example, Briere and Zaidi (1989) surveyed the psychiatric emergency room (ER) charts of 50 randomly selected women for references to a child-hood history of sexual abuse and found that only 6% documented such events. In a second phase of the study, ER clinicians were requested to routinely ask patients about any history of child-hood sexual victimization. When 50 charts from this phase were examined, reference to a positive sexual abuse history increased more than tenfold. Furthermore, abuse history from this second phase was associated with a wide variety of presenting problems, ranging from suicidality and substance abuse to multiple Axis I diagnoses and an increased rate of borderline personality disorder diagnoses. As we noted:

> Diagnostic work-ups and evaluations are of necessity constrained in the emergency room and appropriately focus most on acute concerns. In such a context, issues relating to childhood history are easily seen as irrelevant to the patient's immediate or presenting problem. . . . The current data clearly suggest, however, that sexual abuse histories are both frequent and predictive in emergency room populations and that questions regarding childhood maltreatment are a useful component of psychiatric emergency protocols. (p. 1605)

Although simply asking about interpersonal violence is associated with substantially higher self-reports of trauma, the clinician's overall awareness of trauma issues and knowledge of trauma-oriented interview techniques further facilitates this process. For example, Currier and Briere (2000) compared the amount of trauma identified by two groups of psychiatry trainees and staff: one group who received a one-hour lecture on the prevalence, impacts, and assessment of interpersonal violence, and one group who received no specific information on trauma. Each of 167 male and female psychiatric ER patients were then evaluated by a member of one group or the other, using a standardized trauma interview. Clinicians exposed to the orientation identified more sexual violence (45% vs. 24%), physical violence (74% vs. 54%), and total interpersonal violence (79% vs. 63%) than did those without the one-hour lecture.

The trauma interview used in the Currier and Briere study was an early version of the Initial Trauma Review–Revised (ITR–R) presented in the appendix. There are other detailed and validated interviews and measures available for the evaluation of trauma history, however. When time and logistics allow, the clinician may choose to use one of the structured clinical interviews or inventories for traumatic events presented in the following sections.

# Trauma (Criterion A) Interviews and Measures

Although there are a number of structured clinical interviews that survey clients' adult trauma histories, only some of the best known are presented below. Each of these interviews evaluates a range of traumatic experiences. Most may be used either to prompt interviewer questions or may be given to the client to fill out. Other *DSM–IV* Criterion A instruments address specific traumatic events and are not described here. These include measures evaluating combat experiences (e.g., Keane et al., 1989; Wolfe, Brown, Furey, & Levin, 1993), adult sexual assault (e.g., Koss & Gidycz, 1985), and adult spouse abuse (e.g., Shepard & Campbell, 1992; Straus, 1979; Tolman, 1989). For a detailed review of Criterion A measures, the reader should consult the chapter by Norris and Hamblen in Wilson and Keane's (in press) volume on PTSD assessment.

It should be noted that although these instruments are designated "Criterion A measures," few do, in fact, evaluate all of *DSM–IV* Criterion A. As discussed previously, *DSM–IV* includes a second component to Criterion A for adults: the requirement that the stressor induce intense fear, horror, or helplessness in the client (A2). Because the structured interviews outlined below tend to focus on events rather than on subjective reactions to them, they typically provide insufficient information regarding whether the event in question satisfies *DSM–IV*'s requirements for an ASD- or PTSD-level stressor. Future versions of some of these Criterion A measures will undoubtedly include an assessment of (A2). In the meantime, clinicians using the majority of the measures listed below should ask, independently, about intense fear, horror, or helplessness regarding any stressor identified as present.

The clinician also is reminded of the need to attend to the client's reaction to the structured interview as it unfolds, so that it can be modified or even terminated if necessary. These interviews tend to move rapidly from one traumatic event to the next, typically without any formalized acknowledgment of the emotional impact of such questions, or of the rapport and sensitivity required in such contexts. As a result, the interviewee may become overwhelmed or even retraumatized by the process, thereby defeating the purpose of the interview (ultimately, to help the client) as well as decreasing the quality of the interview data (i.e., by motivating avoidance or producing confusion). Although structured interviews allow for the acquisition of information in a reliable and focused manner, the clinician should see the interview items as a series of helpful prompts, rather than as a script that must be followed regardless of the respondent's distress or psychological state.

Another issue to be discussed before reviewing specific Criterion A measures is that of trauma description. Although most of the measures reviewed below provide a seemingly exhaustive list of potential stressors, not all offer behavioral descriptions of these events. Instead, they merely ask respondents to report whether, for example, they have ever been "raped," "physically assaulted," or "sexually abused as a child." Although some stressors may not require much elaboration (e.g., earthquakes or motor vehicle accidents), others—especially acts of interpersonal victimization—often must be described behaviorally before accurate assessment can occur. Hanson, Kilpatrick, Falsetti, and Resnick (1995), for example, discussed the specific problems inherent in screening for a sexual assault history:

> Studies have documented that the use of behaviorally specific questions to detect trauma history produce significantly higher prevalence rates (and presumably more accurate) [sic] than single item screening questions. For sexual assault, studies find that asking respondents if they have been "raped" elicits much lower prevalence rates than if behaviorally specific structured questions are used to define sexual assault (Koss, 1983; 1993). One reason for this is that people do not always perceive a sexual assault incident to be a rape. If the assailant was a family member, a friend, or a dating partner, some individuals may not label the incident as a rape. If the assault did not involve vaginal penetration, but did involve some other type of sexual penetration (i.e., oral or anal), individuals may not categorize the event as a rape. (p. 135)

Similar to concerns of Hanson et al. (1995) regarding rape, it is not at all uncommon for a respondent to deny a history of childhood "sexual abuse" or "physical abuse" because of differing interpretations of these words. For example, some clients may not consider their sexual intercourse at age 15 with a 28-year-old "boyfriend" to be sexual abuse, and some respondents are known to interpret relatively extreme examples of physical maltreatment as, instead, appropriate parental discipline (Briere, 1992a). Similarly, some battered women may reframe their experiences as "fighting" or "not getting along" with their partner, or they may not consider it abuse if they believe they deserved to be beaten. In some instances this confusion appears to represent a lack of definitional understanding, whereas in others it is more likely to arise from psychological defenses against acknowledging traumatic events.

Given this variability in response to screening items, the clinician is advised to avoid merely presenting a list of potentially traumatic events during trauma assessment. Instead, acts of interpersonal violence should be described in such a way that their definitions are unambiguous. Furthermore, brief preassessment comments regarding victimization may be helpful to the extent that they normalize or destigmatize the reporting of interpersonal violence experiences (Falsetti & Resnick, 1995; Resnick, Kilpatrick, & Lipovsky, 1991). These comments should not, however, take the form of pressuring or prescribing trauma disclosures, such that the respondent believes he or she *should* have something traumatic to report.

## Potential Stressful Events Interview

The Potential Stressful Events Interview (PSEI; Falsetti, Resnick, Kilpatrick, & Freedy, 1994; Kilpatrick, Resnick, & Freedy, 1991) is best known for its use in the *DSM–IV* PTSD field trials. This interview serves as an important example of how a research measure can be useful as a clinical tool.

Components of the PSEI relevant to this section are modules tapping stressor type (divided into low- and high-magnitude stressors), objective/behavioral characteristics of the stressor, and subjective reactions to the stressor. High-magnitude stressors evaluated include events such as war zone or combat experiences, natural disasters, childhood sexual abuse, and aggravated physical assaults. The low-magnitude stressors module evaluates events that may contribute to stress, although few would qualify as *DSM–IV* stressors themselves.

Following the stressor modules, the PSEI inquires about various qualities of the stressor and subjective reactions to it. These items are used to characterize responses to the first, most recent, and worst event. The module examining characteristics of the high-magnitude stressor evaluates injury to self and others; perceived cause of the event; perception of the perpetrator's intent to harm (if relevant); the suddenness of the event; its expectedness; and whether there was a warning regarding the event. Finally, the subjective reaction module consists of 15 items tapping feelings of surprise, detachment, panic, embarrassment, shame, and disgust. Not all subjective (A2) reactions required for *DSM–IV* traumas are included, however.

There is a shorter version of the PSEI, named the Trauma Assessment for Adults (TAA; Resnick, Best, Kilpatrick, Freedy, & Falsetti, 1996). This measure goes into less detail, but its greater brevity probably makes it more clinically useful in some cases.

## Stressful Life Events Screening Questionnaire

Developed by Goodman, Corcoran, Turner, Yuan, and Green (1998), the Stressful Life Events Screening Questionnaire (SLESQ) is a newer measure that evaluates 13 traumatic events. In contrast to some measures, the SLESQ has been shown to have good test–retest reliability, adequate convergent validity, and good discrimination between Criterion A and non-Criterion A events. The authors have shown in several studies that this measure is a good predictor of posttraumatic distress and disturbance (Green et al., 2000; Green et al., 2001). The SLESQ tends to focus on interpersonal traumas, about which it queries significant detail. It does not evaluate Criterion A2 responses, however. Subject to replication of its reported psychometric properties, this measure appears to be a clinically useful review of interpersonal trauma exposure.

## Traumatic Events Questionnaire

The Traumatic Events Questionnaire (TEQ; Vrana & Lauterbach, 1994) taps 11 stressors relevant to Criterion A. Little additional information is assessed in the TEQ, such as detailed behavioral characteristics of the trauma or the client's subjective response to it. The major advantage of an interview such as the TEQ is its relative brevity and the fact that it systematically examines a wide variety of traumatic events. However, the relative lack of codable detail on the TEQ may discourage its use when detailed trauma information is needed. As well, some traumas listed in this questionnaire require further elaboration before responses to them can be considered fully valid. Representative studies using the TEQ include Lauterbach and Vrana (2001) and Scarpa et al. (2002).

## Traumatic Events Scale

The Traumatic Events Scale (TES; Elliott, 1992) is a comprehensive measure that assesses a wide range of childhood and adult traumas. Both childhood and adult stressors are operationalized in detail, so that subjective interpretations of what constitutes a traumatic event are less likely. Of the 30 interpersonal and environmental traumas examined by the TES, 20 evaluate adult events and 10 are devoted to childhood events. Adult traumas include natural disasters, sexual and physical assault, torture, war, auto accidents, and witnessing a murder. Among the characteristics evaluated for each trauma are frequency of occurrence over the life span; age at the time of the first, last, and worst incident; and level of distress at the time of the event and currently, including the helplessness, terror, and horror criteria of A2. A version of the TES was used in part of the Trauma Symptom Inventory standardization project, where it predicted a wide variety of symptoms on multiple measures (e.g., Briere, Elliott, Harris, & Cotman, 1995; Elliott & Briere, 1995).

## Traumatic Stress Schedule

Norris first published the Traumatic Stress Schedule (TSS) in 1990 and revised it soon thereafter (Norris, 1992). The revised version inquires about 10 potentially traumatic events. The TSS also allows each identified trauma to be further probed according to the extent of loss it produced (i.e., people, property), its scope (number of people involved), threat to life and physical integrity, whether the individual was blamed, and familiarity of the trauma. As with most other measures in this area, the TSS uses single questions to tap each content area. The TSS is widely used in clinical research and has been correlated with a variety of posttraumatic outcomes (e.g., Dougall et al. 2000; Flett, Kazantzis, Long, MacDonald, & Millar, 2002).

## Traumatic Life Events Questionnaire

The Traumatic Life Events Questionnaire (TLEQ; Kubany et al., 2000) is a relatively new measure that, nevertheless, has been used in several studies (e.g., Kubany & Watson, 2002). It evaluates 17 potentially life-threatening events. A major (and relatively unusual) benefit of this questionnaire is its inclusion of *DSM–IV's* Criterion A2, allowing researchers and clinicians to determine if a given instance of trauma exposure meets all of Criterion A.

## Initial Trauma Review–Revised

When use of one of the measures listed is not possible, either because of time pressures or because a more face-to-face trauma evaluation is indicated, the clinician may find the Initial Trauma Review–Revised useful. This semi-structured interview, presented in the appendix, consists of a series of questions, each of which can be asked (or paraphrased) at the onset of an evaluation interview. Items are behaviorally anchored, and tap each of the three A2) criteria. (See also www.JohnBriere.com for a copy of this measure.)

## Trauma Exposure Sections Within Larger Traumatic Stress Measures

Three readily-available trauma impact measures have specific sections for assessing trauma exposure.

**Harvard Trauma Questionnaire.** The Harvard Trauma Questionnaire (HTQ; Mollica et al., 1992; Mollica et al., 1995) was developed specifically for the assessment of refugees, primarily those from Indochina. However, there are now six officially translated versions of the HTQ: Vietnamese, Cambodian, Laotian, and, more recently, Japanese, Croatian, and Bosnian. In addition to the stressor section reviewed here, the HTQ has a symptom section that evaluates *DSM–IV* PTSD and other stress symptoms relevant to the Indochinese culture (see chapter 7). The stressor section has 17 items, tapping common refugee-related traumas, including torture, rape, starvation, and exposure to the murder of others. Unfortunately, like most other trauma questionnaires, the HTQ does not describe or define these stressors in detail, and thus confusion and underreporting is possible. There is also an open-ended question that inquires about the most terrifying events that have happened.

Research on 91 refugees (Mollica et al., 1992) indicates that the stressor section is reliable, both in terms of internal consistency ($\alpha$ = .90) and stability over one week (test–retest $r$ = .89). The HTQ is a frequently cited measure of refugee traumatic experiences, both because of its structural quality and because there are few other established measures of refugee experiences (especially torture) available.

**Posttraumatic Stress Diagnostic Scale.** Part 1 of the Posttraumatic Stress Diagnostic Scale (PDS; Foa, 1995) surveys 12 types of trauma exposure, one of which (the one "that bothers you the most") the respondent uses to rate subsequent PTSD symptoms. For the index trauma, the client also rates how long ago it occurred, whether physical injury or life threat was involved, and whether, during the traumatic event, the respondent felt helpless or terrified. Like the HTQ and the Detailed Assessment of Posttraumatic Stress (described below), the effect of this approach is to determine A2 responses to the chosen trauma, but not to all possible traumas. The third A2 criterion, feeling horrified, is not included in the PDS, however, because both intense fear and horror were thought to be subsumed under the term "terrified" (E. Foa, personal communication, September 28, 2003).

The range of traumas presented in the PDS appears to cover all relevant stressful events. However, Part 1 overlooks the fact that child sexual abuse does not require threatened or actual violence or injury to be considered traumatic in *DSM–IV* (p. 464). Instead, like other stressors on the list, the PDS requires that sexual abuse be accompanied by either life threat or physical injury to be considered to be a Criterion A trauma (p. 43).

**Detailed Assessment of Posttraumatic Stress.** The Detailed Assessment of Posttraumatic Stress (DAPS; Briere, 2001) includes a trauma specification module, which lists 13 potentially traumatic events, all of which (except childhood physical abuse and childhood sexual abuse) include the requirement that the respondent was "seriously hurt or afraid you would be hurt or killed." The physical abuse item refers to physical injury, and sexual abuse, as noted, does not require threat or injury to be categorized by *DSM–IV* as a trauma. An unfortunate side effect of asking only about traumas that meet Criterion A1, however, is that the examiner does not learn about events such as motor vehicle accidents or potential disasters that were not associated with threat or injury.

The DAPS requires the client to choose the one experience "that bothers you the most now," or to respond to the event prechosen by his or her therapist or evaluator, and then to rate its time of onset and whether there were (A2) subjective responses to it. In the case of the DAPS, these include not only the horror, intense fear, and helplessness listed in *DSM–IV* (A2), but also guilt, shame, disgust, and so on. Together, these ratings are summed to form an overall *Peritraumatic Distress* scale. Also queried is whether the respondent experienced a range of dissociative symptoms at the time of the chosen trauma that sum to form a *Peritraumatic Dissociation* scale.

# Childhood History Interviews and Measures

Most instruments that evaluate traumatic events in adulthood either overlook childhood abuse or merely include it—typically without operational definition—as one of many traumas that the respondent can endorse. There are, however, five scales known to the author that examine adults' childhood maltreatment history in detail. These scales vary considerably in terms of the number of forms of abuse or neglect they assess and the amount of abuse-specific detail they offer.

## Assessing Environments III, Form SD

The Assessing Environments III, Form SD (AEIII–Form SD; Rausch & Knutson, 1991) is a revision of the AEIII, first introduced by Berger, Knutson, Mehm, and Perkins in 1988. This scale consists of 170 items, forming the following scales: Physical Punishment scale, Sibling Physical Punishment scale, Perception of Discipline scale, Sibling Perception of Punishment scale, Deserving Punishment scale, and Sibling Deserving Punishment scale. The reliability of scales making up the SD version of the AEIII was evaluated in a sample of 421 university students, yielding KR–20 coefficients ranging from .68 to .74 (Rausch & Knutson, 1991). No test–retest data were presented. In a study using the AEIII, DiTomatasso and Routh (1993) found that the Physical Abuse Scale (presumably equivalent to the Physical Punishment Scale of the AEIII–Form SD) correlated with several measures of dissociation.

## Child Maltreatment Interview Schedule

The Child Maltreatment Interview Schedule (CMIS; Briere, 1992a) is a 46-item measure, with some items containing a number of subquestions that yield greater detail on a given abuse or neglect experience. The CMIS evaluates level of parental or caretaker physical availability, parental disorder (i.e., history of inpatient or outpatient psychological treatment, alcoholism or drug abuse, and domestic violence), parental psychological availability, psychological abuse, physical abuse, emotional abuse, sexual abuse, and perception of physical and sexual abuse status. For each area, specific questions probe the age of onset, the relationship to the abuser, and the severity of the maltreatment. The Psychological Abuse component of the CMIS is a seven-item scale taken from Briere and Runtz (1988; 1990b), where it has demonstrated moderate internal consistency ($\alpha$'s ranging from .75 to .87). The CMIS is also available in a short form

(CMIS–SF; Briere, 1992a) that contains most of the material of the original measure, but without quite as much detail. The CMIS–SF is more often used for research purposes than is the CMIS (e.g., Cloitre, Cohen, Edelman, & Han, 2001; Walker et al., 1997).

## Childhood Maltreatment Questionnaire

The Childhood Maltreatment Questionnaire (CMQ; Demaré, 1993) focuses extensively on psychological abuse and neglect, although it includes scales for sexual and physical maltreatment. This questionnaire contains three components: the Psychological Maltreatment Questionnaire (PMQ), the Physical Abuse Questionnaire (PAQ), and the Sexual Abuse Questionnaire (SAQ). The PMQ has 12 scales, each tapping a form of child maltreatment identified as significant in the psychological abuse literature. The PAQ has a single scale, whereas the SAQ consists of Parental and Nonparental versions. Demaré and Briere (1994) examined the psychometric characteristics of these scales in a sample of 1,179 university students and found them relatively reliable ($\alpha$'s ranged from .67 to .95) and predictive of symptomatology for both males and females.

## Childhood Trauma Questionnaire

The Childhood Trauma Questionnaire (CTQ; Bernstein et al., 1994) is a 70-item measure that assesses childhood trauma in six areas: physical, sexual, and emotional abuse, physical and emotional neglect, "and related areas of family dysfunction (e.g., substance abuse)" (p. 1133). Probably the most widely used abuse-exposure instrument in the child abuse literature, this measure reportedly requires 10 to 15 minutes to administer. Items in the CTQ begin with the phrase "When I was growing up," and are rated on 5-point Likert-type scales ranging from "never true" to "very often true." Principal components analysis of the CTQ in a sample of 286 substance dependent patients yielded four factors that subsequently made up the scales of this measure: physical and emotional abuse, emotional neglect, sexual abuse, and physical neglect. Internal consistency of these factor sub-scales was moderately high ($\alpha$'s range from .79 to .94) and, in a subsample of 40 patients, test–retest correlations ranged from .80 to .83 for an average intertest interval of 3.6 months (Bernstein et al., 1994). Later analyses suggest a five-factor solution, wherein physical and emotional abuse form separate factors (Bernstein, Ahluvalia, Pogge, & Handelsman, 1997; Scher et al., 2001). Because the Scher et al. (2001) study examined 1,007 community participants, the authors suggested that the means and standard deviations they report can be considered normative data for the CTQ.

## Traumatic Events Scale

As noted for adult traumas, the Traumatic Events Scale (TES) evaluates a number of childhood traumas. Among these are exposure to disasters, peer sexual and physical assault, witnessing school and neighborhood violence, physical abuse, psychological abuse, sexual abuse, and witnessing spouse abuse. Considerable detail is obtained vis-à-vis characteristics of the various reported traumas. For example, in the case of child abuse, the client is asked about age at first and last incident, relationship to perpetrator, and level of distress about the abuse—both at the time it occurred and currently. Additional details are ascertained for sexual abuse in particular, such as whether the abuser used threats or force to gain sexual access and whether oral, anal, or vaginal penetration occurred.

# Conclusion

This chapter outlines structured interviews and measures available for the assessment of traumatic events and posttraumatic disorders. What becomes clear when reviewing most trauma interviews and inventories in the field is their inherent research focus, as opposed to being specific clinical tools. Some measures provide insufficient information on a given stressor, including its behavioral definition, whereas others access far more information than would be clinically indicated. Further work in this area will be most helpful to the extent that it produces trauma review measures that are validated and reliable and that are specifically developed for clinical practice.

Most of these measures also do not include behavioral definitions for interpersonal traumas. Furthermore, because of their schematic (if not rote) interrogatory style and potential to decrease interviewer–interviewee rapport, some trauma interviews may not be immediately acceptable to the general clinical interviewer. On the other hand, these protocols tend to evaluate the full range of trauma exposure and can decrease the subjectivity and limitations of informal trauma inquiry.

Chapter

# 5

# Diagnostic Interviews

T he vast majority of trauma-focused assessment in North America occurs in a diagnostic interview or opening psychotherapy session, as opposed to through formal psychological testing. In fact, the occasional suggestion that emergency room or crisis center personnel consider using "pencil and paper" trauma measures is usually greeted, at best, with amusement. This reaction is contextually appropriate, in the sense that (a) trauma work often occurs in a rapid, relatively intense environment where clinical impressions are quickly formed, (b) acute trauma victims are often too distraught or distracted to attend fully to reading and writing, and (c) many mental health emergency staff are psychiatrists or social workers—members of disciplines that typically have little training in psychological test administration and interpretation.

Although a central tenet of this volume is that psychological testing can be very helpful in trauma assessment, it is also true that no psychological test can replace the focused attention, visible empathy, and extensive clinical experience of a well-trained and seasoned trauma clinician. As a result, it is likely that both interview-based and—when timely and appropriate—formal psychological assessments are intrinsic to a complete trauma work-up. For this reason, this chapter focuses on issues and methodologies relevant to the face-to-face diagnostic interview. Because interview-based assessments are potentially less organized and focused however, two assessment approaches are presented here: the trauma-relevant (but informal) psychological interview and the structured diagnostic interview. As is noted in chapter 6, these procedures can assist in the accurate specification of relevant traumatic events and formal diagnostic outcomes; such interviews cannot provide the more in-depth and normative/comparative information generated from comprehensive psychological testing. Thus, it is recommended that structured, interview-based assessment be seen as an important tool but not as a procedure that necessarily obviates the (often later) need for psychological test data.

Finally, the description of structured interviews in this chapter is not meant to suggest that such instruments are necessary in all instances, or for all interviewers. Some clinical settings and situations do not require the detailed assessment provided by structured interviews, and some trauma-specialized clinicians feel themselves to be sufficiently conversant with the relevant criteria and issues that they do not require the prompts of a structured procedure. On the other hand, research suggests that routine clinical diagnosis (i.e., without a formal structured interview) may miss as much as half of all actual cases of posttraumatic stress disorder (PTSD; Zimmerman & Mattia, 1999). Even highly experienced trauma clinicians are likely to use structured interviews on occasion, such as in certain forensic or research contexts, or when diagnostic issues are especially complex.

## The Trauma-Relevant Psychological Interview

In most mental health clinics and psychiatric emergency rooms, the assessment of psychological disturbance occurs during the diagnostic interview or "mental status" examination. In the interview session, the client is typically evaluated for (a) altered consciousness or mental functioning (i.e., for evidence of dementia, confusion, delirium, cognitive impairment, or other organic disturbance), (b) psychotic symptoms (e.g., hallucinations, delusions, thought disorder, disorganized behavior, "negative" signs), (c) evidence of self-injurious or suicidal thoughts and behaviors,

(d) potential danger to others, (e) mood disturbance (i.e., depression, anxiety), (f) substance abuse or addiction, and (g) personality dysfunction. In combination with other information (e.g., from the client, significant others, and outside agencies), this interview data provides the basis for diagnosis and an intervention plan.

Because these clinical issues are frequently of immediate importance, assessment for other disorders or dysfunctional states often are postponed or deferred entirely. However, if the presenting problem is a posttraumatic reaction, these standard clinical screens miss important information. When there is a possibility of trauma-related disturbance, the interview should consider investigating the following additional components, if time allows and the client is sufficiently stable.

## Symptoms of posttraumatic stress

- ☐ Intrusive experiences such as flashbacks, nightmares, intrusive thoughts and memories, reliving experiences
- ☐ Avoidant symptoms such as behavioral or cognitive attempts to avoid trauma-reminiscent stimuli, as well as emotional numbing
- ☐ Hyperarousal symptoms such as decreased or restless sleep, muscle tension, irritability, jumpiness, or attention/concentration difficulties

## Dissociative responses

- ☐ Often ego-dystonic depersonalization or derealization experiences
- ☐ Fugue states
- ☐ "Spacing out" or cognitive–emotional disengagement
- ☐ Amnesia or missing time
- ☐ Identity alteration or confusion

## Somatic disturbance

- ☐ Conversion reactions (e.g., paralysis, anesthesia, blindness, deafness)
- ☐ Somatization (excessive preoccupation with bodily dysfunction)
- ☐ Psychogenic pain (e.g., pelvic pain, chronic pain)

## Sexual disturbance (especially secondary to a sexual assault)

- □ Sexual distress (including sexual dysfunction)
- □ Sexual fears and conflicts

## Trauma-related cognitive disturbance

- □ Low self-esteem
- □ Helplessness
- □ Hopelessness
- □ Overvalued ideas regarding the level of danger in the environment
- □ Irrational guilt

## Tension-reduction activities

- □ Self-mutilation
- □ Binging–purging
- □ Excessive or impulsive sexual behavior
- □ Compulsive stealing
- □ Impulsive aggression

## Transient posttraumatic psychotic reactions

- □ Trauma-induced cognitive slippage, loosened associations
- □ Trauma-induced hallucinations (often trauma-congruent)
- □ Trauma-induced delusions (often trauma-congruent, especially paranoia)

## Culture-specific trauma responses (e.g., *ataques de nervios*), if relevant, when

- □ Assessing individuals from other countries and cultures

Obviously, this list is more comprehensive than is indicated for certain posttraumatic presentations (e.g., a survivor of a motor vehicle accident), although most or all of the components may be relevant for certain chronic traumas (e.g., extended child abuse or torture). Some version of this examination is usually indicated, however, even if it is followed by a more structured diagnostic interview, because it evaluates specific symptoms and issues, as opposed to solely the presence or absence of psychological disorders.

# Structured Diagnostic Interviews

As noted, structured diagnostic interviews are used primarily to generate objectively determined *DSM* diagnoses. By providing the examiner with a list of diagnostic criteria and specific questions to tap those criteria, such interviews ideally decrease the chance of diagnostic error and increase the likelihood of covering all relevant symptoms. In the area of posttraumatic stress, there are several structured interviews for diagnosing PTSD, acute stress disorder (ASD), and the dissociative disorders.

As noted in chapter 2, in order for a *DSM–IV* stress disorder diagnosis to be made, the interviewer must establish that at least one trauma was specifically associated with all required diagnostic symptoms. In other words, it is not accurate to refer to the presence of PTSD or ASD if some required symptoms arise from one trauma and others arise from another. Unfortunately, a complete assessment of history–symptomatology links can be quite involved, especially if one examines the client's complete lifetime. As noted by Kessler et al. (1995),

> more than 10% of men and 6% of women in the [National Comorbidity Survey sample] reported four or more types of lifetime traumas, some of which involved multiple occurrences. . . . In some cases, a complete assessment of trauma history would involve an assessment of 20 more traumas. (p. 1058)

Given the number of traumas potentially experienced by the average client, as well as the need to link these traumas to specific PTSD or ASD symptoms, clinicians often either (a) diagnose PTSD or ASD if one or more Criterion A events can be found and the client presents with symptoms that meet diagnostic criteria for the disorder, or (b) determine which stressors the client views as most traumatic, and then evaluate the link between this smaller set and specific PTSD/ASD symptoms. Of these two, the latter strategy is preferable, because (unlike the former approach) it will not produce false positives.

# Posttraumatic Stress Disorder Interviews

There are several structured interviews that allow the clinician to render a diagnosis of PTSD with reasonable confidence. Presented are the best known and most validated of these.

## Structured Clinical Interview for DSM–IV–Posttraumatic Stress Disorder Module

The Structured Clinical Interview for DSM–IV–PTSD Module (SCID–IV–PTSD; Spitzer, Williams, Gibbon, & First, 1990) is one of the most widely used of diagnostic interview systems. The *DSM–IV* interview version (SCID–I; First, Spitzer, Gibbon, & Williams, 1997) includes a PTSD module, a component that was optional in the *DSM–III–R* version. The *DSM–IV* SCID–PTSD stressor definition has been changed from *DSM–III–R* (i.e., an "event outside normal human experience") to an approximate *DSM–IV* description of a qualifying A1 stressor (i.e., a traumatic, life threatening, or extremely upsetting event).[1] The 19 items of the SCID–PTSD inquire about the presence or absence of each PTSD diagnostic criterion, along with two items tapping guilt. The client's responses are coded as "absent," "present," or "subthreshold." PTSD status can be determined for the present (in the past month) or for the individual's lifetime (worse month ever).

The SCID has the advantage of screening for a variety of disorders in addition to PTSD, although, as with previous versions, it does not assess for the dissociative disorders. Its broad diagnostic range thus provides a more comprehensive clinical picture than is available with most trauma-specific measures. Clinical and research experience suggests that, other than the CAPS (Clinician-Administered Posttraumatic Stress Disorder Scale), the SCID–PTSD may be the most rigorous and accurate

---

[1] Although the SCID–IV screening question identifies fewer trauma histories than do more comprehensive trauma lists (Goodman et al., 1998), research by Franklin, Sheeran, and Zimmerman (2002) suggests that the SCID question identifies almost all of those with a PTSD-generating trauma.

interview assessment for PTSD. This is a subjective assessment, however, because the *DSM–IV* SCID–PTSD module has undergone little formal diagnostic utility evaluation.

## Diagnostic Interview Schedule–Posttraumatic Stress Disorder Module

The Diagnostic Interview Schedule–PTSD Module (DIS–PTSD; Robins et al., 2000) is a revision of the previous *DSM–III–R* version. The PTSD module asks about life experiences that might be traumatic and then inquires whether up to three of them led to each of 17 *DSM–III–R* PTSD symptoms.

Changes from the *DSM–III–R* version include greater attention to stressor specification, which probably improves its psychometric validity. However, until more data are available on these changes, it is recommended that the CAPS or SCID–IV PTSD module be used instead of the DIS–PTSD in most cases (see reviews by Lating, Zeichner, & Keane [1995] and Litz et al., [1992]). This caution is based on the performance of the *DSM–III–R* version. First, the earlier DIS, in general, has not proven to be especially sensitive to psychiatric disorders (Anthony et al., 1985; Burke, 1986). Second, data on the performance of the *DSM–III–R* DIS–PTSD module in the National Vietnam Veterans Readjustment Study was less than stellar (Kulka et al., 1988). Although the DIS–PTSD had fair sensitivity (.87), specificity (.73), and reliability (κ = .64) in the initial validation study, it had a sensitivity of only .22, a specificity of .98, and a κ of .26 in the community sample component.

## Anxiety Disorders Interview Schedule–IV

There has been almost no research on the diagnostic utility of the new Anxiety Disorders Interview Schedule–IV (ADIS–IV; Brown, DiNardo, & Barlow, 1994) PTSD module, although it has been used in several studies (e.g., Brown, Campbell, Lehman, Grisham, & Mancill, 2001; Erwin, Heimberg, Juster, & Mindlin, 2002). Research on the previous version (Blanchard, Gerardi, Kolb, & Barlow, 1986) suggested that the ADIS–R PTSD module was relatively reliable and valid. For example, it agreed with a clinical diagnosis of PTSD in 93% of 40 Veterans Administration patients, yielding a κ of .86.

## Structured Interview for Posttraumatic Stress Disorder

The Structured Interview for PTSD (SI–PTSD; Davidson, Kudler, & Smith, 1990) consists of 17 items designed to tap *DSM–IV* PTSD criteria. Items are rated on a five-point scale (0 = "absent," 4 = "extremely severe") and are endorsed for both current and lifetime ("worst ever") status. Symptoms have to be rated as a 2 ("moderate") or better to meet PTSD criteria. There are no descriptors for symptom items.

In a study of 116 veterans, the SI–PTSD had very good internal consistency (α = .94) and, in a subsample of 41 patients, good sensitivity and specificity with regard to the SCID–PTSD (.96 and .80, respectively, yielding a κ of .79). This measure is widely used in trauma research.

## Posttraumatic Stress Disorder Symptom Scale–Interviewer Version

The PTSD Symptom Scale–Interviewer Version (PSS–I; Foa, Riggs, Dancu, & Rothbaum, 1993) is a 17-item instrument that taps *DSM–III–R* symptoms of PTSD. Initially developed for sexual assault victims, the PSS–I can be easily modified for use with other traumas. Items are rated on a 0 ("not at all") to 3 ("5 or more times per week/very much") scale. A symptom is considered to be present (for diagnostic purposes) if it is rated a 1 or higher. It should be noted that, because the original PSS–I examines symptoms over a two-week period, instead of four weeks as required by *DSM–III–R* and *DSM–IV*, a formal *DSM* diagnosis cannot be made with this measure unless it is adjusted to the one-month *DSM* criterion.

In a sample of 118 female physical or sexual assault victims, the PSS–I had good internal consistency (α = .85) and excellent inter-rater reliability (r = .97). Using the SCID as a criterion, the PSS–I had fair sensitivity (.62) and excellent specificity (1.0). A second study (Foa & Tolin, 2000) compared the diagnostic efficacy of the PSS–I versus the CAPS in predicting SCID PTSD status in a sample of 64 civilian trauma victims. The CAPS and the PSS–I showed both high internal consistency (α's of .88 and .86, respectively) and high interrater reliability. Both instruments had good sensitivity and specificity vis-à-vis a SCID diagnosis, with the PSS–I having slightly better sensitivity (.86) and worse specificity (.78) than the various CAPS scoring rules.

## Clinician-Administered Posttraumatic Stress Disorder Scale

The CAPS (Blake et al., 1990; Blake et al., 1995) is considered by many to be the "gold standard" of structured interviews for PTSD. Initially, there were two versions of this interview: (a) the CAPS–1 (also known as the CAPS–DX), intended to evaluate PTSD symptoms and diagnosis over the last (or worst) month since the trauma, and (b) the CAPS–2 (also known as the CAPS–SX), used to measure PTSD symptom severity over the past week, primarily in the context of repeated assessment. These two versions have since been collapsed into a single measure, simply referred to as the CAPS (Weathers, Keane, & Davidson, 2001).

Based initially on *DSM–III–R*, and now revised for *DSM–IV* criteria, this measure was developed to address a variety of methodological problems with other trauma measures. As a result, the CAPS has several helpful features, including standard prompt questions and explicit, behaviorally anchored rating scales, and assesses both frequency and intensity of symptoms. The CAPS generates both dichotomous and continuous scores for current (one month) and lifetime ("worst ever") PTSD, as well as (optional) one-week symptom status. In addition to the standard 17 PTSD items, the CAPS also contains items tapping exposure to 17 Criterion A–level traumas (with associated A2 assessment), posttraumatic impacts on social and occupational functioning, overall response validity, and overall PTSD severity, as well as items addressing guilt and the dissociative symptoms of ASD (reduction in awareness, derealization, and depersonalization).

Items of the CAPS are rated on two 0 to 4 scales, one for frequency ("never" to "daily or almost daily") and one for intensity ("none" to "extreme," "overwhelming," or "incapacitating"). The specific anchors for individual items vary from item to item. There is also an option for the interviewer to indicate that any given client response is of "questionable validity." For diagnostic purposes, a symptom is considered endorsed if it is rated a 1 or greater in frequency (i.e., that it has occurred at least once in the previous month) and also rated a 2 or more in intensity (i.e., at least moderate in intensity). The authors also offer a more conservative scoring approach, considering a symptom endorsed only if the sum of frequency and intensity scales is 4 or higher. There is also a total scale scoring option (> 65 = PTSD), as described below, as well as a number of other, more experimental ones (Weathers, Ruscio, & Keane, 1999). One complaint about the CAPS is that its detail and length can extend administration time to 60 minutes or longer (Solomon, Keane, Newman, & Kaloupek, 1996).

Psychometric data on the CAPS is quite encouraging (Weathers et al., 2001). In a study of 60 combat veterans (Weathers, Blake, & Litz, 1991; Weathers et al., 1992), the CAPS had a two- to three-day test–retest reliability of .90 to .98 for the total score, and very good internal consistency ($\alpha$ = .94) for the composite severity score (frequency + intensity). Using the SCID as a criterion, a CAPS score of greater than 65 had a sensitivity of .84, a specificity .95, and a $\kappa$ of .78. Its correlation with the Mississippi Scale for Combat-Related PTSD was .91. A study of the CAPS in five veteran samples (ranging in Ns from 24 to 571) examined various scoring options, in addition to the greater than 65 rule (Weathers et al., 1999). Although the authors suggested several scoring rules, according the intended use of the CAPS, the greater than 65 rule yielded similar sensitivity (.82) and specificity (.91) vis-à-vis the SCID as was found in Weathers et al., 1991, 1992. Other findings of the Weathers et al. (1999) study were very good interrater reliability for the CAPS greater than 65 rule ($\kappa$'s of .86 and 1.0 in two samples), and evidence that the DSM–III–R and DSM–IV versions of the CAPS yield almost entirely equivalent results.

# Other Interviews

In addition to PTSD, structured clinical interviews are available to assess other posttraumatic outcomes. These include interviews for ASD, the dissociative disorders, and the non–*DSM–IV* construct of "disorders of extreme stress, not otherwise specified" (DESNOS).

## Acute Stress Disorder Interview

A relatively new diagnostic interview, the Acute Stress Disorder Interview (ASDI; Bryant, Harvey, Dang, & Sackville, 1998) consists of 19 items that evaluate the dissociative, reexperiencing, effortful avoidance, and arousal symptoms of ASD. Because symptoms are dichotomously scored, severity of ASD cannot be determined. Bryant et al. (1998) report very good sensitivity (.91) and specificity (.93) with reference to clinicians' ASD diagnoses using *DSM–IV* criteria. Test–retest reliability over two to seven days was also very good ($r$ = .88). The ASDI is one of only two published ASD interviews, the other being the Structured Clinical Interview for *DSM–IV* Dissociative Disorders (SCID–D; Steinberg, 1994a). However, there are little data on the SCID–D vis-à-vis its actual diagnostic utility for ASD. The stand-alone nature of the ASDI and its very good psychometric characteristics suggest that this interview will soon be considered the gold standard for assessing ASD.

## Dissociative Disorders Interview Schedule

The Dissociative Disorders Interview Schedule (DDIS; Ross et al., 1989) consists of 131 items, each of which is coded as "yes," "no," or "unsure." This inventory provides *DSM–III* (and now *DSM–IV*) diagnoses for major depressive episode, borderline personality disorder, psychogenic amnesia, psychogenic fugue, depersonalization disorder, multiple personality disorder (dissociative identity disorder [DID]), and dissociative disorder not otherwise specified (DDNOS), although there are little validity or diagnostic utility data available for diagnoses other than DID and DDNOS. In a sample of 80 patients, Ross, Joshie, and Currie

(1991) reported high sensitivity and specificity (.90 and 1.0, re-spectively) vis-à-vis clinical (*DSM–III*) diagnosis of multiple per-sonality disorder (DID). In a later study of psychiatric inpatients, Ross, Duffy, Ellason, and Weathersby (2002) found good chance-corrected agreement ($\kappa$ = .74) between the DDID and the SCID–D (described below) in identifying DID or DDNOS.

## Structured Clinical Interview for *DSM–IV* Dissociative Disorders

The Structured Clinical Interview for *DSM–IV* Dissociative Dis-orders (SCID–D; Steinberg, 1994a, 1994b) was developed in 1985, later undergoing revisions for *DSM–III–R* and *DSM–IV* dissocia-tive disorders. The SCID–D has more than 250 items, many of which are open-ended questions, although the use of branching options means the number of questions asked is variable by interview. It evaluates the existence and severity of five "core" dissociative symptoms (amnesia, depersonalization, derealiza-tion, identity confusion, and identity alteration) on scales ranging from 0 ("none") to 4 ("extremely"). These ratings are based on symptom frequency, duration, distress, and level of impairment or dysfunction. The SCID–D provides diagnoses for five *DSM–IV* dissociative disorders: dissociative amnesia, dissociative fugue, depersonalization disorder, DID, and DDNOS. ASD and the experimental (*DSM–IV* Appendix) dissociative trance disorder also can be assessed. Also provided in the SCID–D are helpful "intra-interview dissociative cues," such as alterations in de-meanor, spontaneous age regression, and trance-like appearance, which are coded in a postinterview section.

The reliability and validity of the SCID–D has been assessed in several studies (Steinberg et al., 1989–1993; Steinberg, Rounsa-ville, & Cicchetti, 1990). However, unlike PTSD measures (which are generally evaluated in terms of the CAPS or SCID), there is no widely recognized "gold standard" instrument that can be used as a criterion measure of dissociative disorder diagnoses. For this reason, little data are available on the sensitivity or specificity of the SCID–D.

Despite these difficulties, Steinberg et al. (1990) found the SCID–D to have very high interrater reliability (intraclass correlation coefficients, and κ's were in the .9s for presence of any dissociative disorder and ranged from .65 to .90 for the presence of a specific dissociative disorder). Although Steinberg et al. (1990) did not report on the sensitivity and specificity of the SCID–D with reference to clinician diagnoses of dissociative disorder, they did show that patients with dissociative disorders ($n$ = 18) scored significantly higher than patients with a nondissociative disorder ($n$ = 23) or a control group of nonclinical volunteers ($n$ = 7).

## Clinician-Administered Dissociative States Scale

The Clinician-Administered Dissociative States Scale (CADSS; Bremner et al., 1998) is a unique measure among dissociation tests, in that it evaluates current or *state* dissociation and because it includes both client and clinician or observer components. A typical client report item is "(At this time, in this room) . . . (d)o things seem to be moving in slow motion?" A representative observer item is "Did the subject blank out or space out, or in some other way appear to have lost track of what was going on?"

Psychometric analysis of the CADSS in a mixed group of participants indicated that interrater agreement on the observer items achieved an intraclass correlation coefficient of .92 and an internal consistency α of .90, whereas the client report items were internally consistent with an α of .94. Moderate correlations were found between the CADSS and the DES ($r$ = .48) and SCID–D ($r$ = .42). Although the clinical utility of measuring state dissociation may be less obvious than measurement of trait-level dissociation, the authors noted that "[state measures] are useful in measuring changes in symptoms, and can be applied . . . to psychotherapy or treatment trials" (Bremner et al., 1998, p. 126).

## Depersonalization Severity Scale

The Depersonalization Severity Scale (DSS; Simeon, Guralnik, & Schmeidler, 2001) is a brief, six-item clinician-administered scale that is read to the respondent. The clinician then assigns a severity value for each item (ranging from 0 [none] to 3 [severe]) based on the client's response. In a sample of 63 individuals, the DSS had low-moderate internal consistency ($\alpha$ = .59), but excellent interrater reliability ($r$ = .98 for the total score), good convergent validity, and evidence of sensitivity as a measure of treatment effects. Because there is only one published study on the psychometrics of the DSS, further investigation is probably indicated before this promising measure can be employed in clinical settings.

## Structured Interview for Disorders of Extreme Stress

The Structured Interview for Disorders of Extreme Stress (SIDES; Pelcovitz et al., 1997) was developed as a companion to existing interview-based rating scales for PTSD. This 45-item interview assesses for the current and lifetime presence of DESNOS criteria, for the total construct and each of six symptom clusters: Affect Dysregulation, Somatization, Alterations in Attention or Consciousness, Self-Perception, Relationships with Others, and Systems of Meaning. Item descriptors contain concrete behavioral anchors to facilitate clinician ratings. The SIDES interview has good interrater reliability ($\kappa$ = .81), internal consistency ($\alpha$ = .96), and construct validity (Pelcovitz et al., 1997; Zlotnick & Pearlstein, 1997). Because DESNOS does not represent a *DSM–IV* diagnosis, this interview is most relevant to research on complex non-PTSD outcomes of chronic developmental traumas and is useful as a detailed symptom review for such outcomes in clinical settings. Although the SIDES is typically employed as a measure of "complex PTSD," it should be noted that the SIDES does not evaluate PTSD-like symptoms (e.g., reliving, avoidance, and hyperarousal).

# Conclusion

As indicated in this chapter, a number of interviews are available to assist the clinician in the diagnosis of PTSD, ASD, and dissociative disorders. Several of these have only recently been converted from *DSM–III–R* criteria to *DSM–IV*, and thus there are not always substantial data regarding their diagnostic utility for current *DSM* diagnoses.

Most generally, it appears that the CAPS and SCID interviews are most helpful in diagnosing PTSD, with some slight trade-off between the two measures. The CAPS is probably the most accurate of the two vis-à-vis a *DSM–IV* diagnosis of PTSD, whereas the SCID is able to provide diagnostic information on other potentially comorbid disorders as well. If time is limited, research by Foa and Tolin (2000) suggests that the PSS–I is another good option. Those needing to assess for ASD have the option of using either the SCID–D or the ASDI. Of the two, the ASDI is more comprehensive and probably more accurate, although the SCID–D has the advantage of also evaluating dissociative disorders. Finally, the SIDES is currently the only valid structured interview to assess the notion of complex posttraumatic outcomes (e.g., DESNOS).

Despite these general recommendations, the "correct" interview usually is a function of the extent to which the client can tolerate detailed face-to-face assessment, the amount of time available, the specific goals of assessment, and, in some cases, the interviewer's level of expertise. When an accurate and defensible *DSM–IV* diagnosis is most important (e.g., in some research and forensic contexts), more highly structured and comprehensive interviews are usually, although not inevitably, best. When the assessment occurs in more general clinical contexts, however, the evaluator is advised to use whatever best fits the demands of the clinical situation. In some cases, this too will mean use of instruments such as the CAPS or SCID, whereas in others (e.g., when the client is especially stressed, easily overwhelmed, or time is of the essence) only a cursory diagnostic evaluation may be possible. When the level of evaluation is significantly reduced, however, the clinician should indicate in the assessment report any decreased confidence in the final assessment product that he or she might have.

Chapter

# 6

# General Objective and Projective Measures

I n contrast to interview-based measures, objective and projective tests rely on individuals' responses to stimuli that do not arise from the clinical interview process. In this chapter, several major objective tests and one projective instrument (the Rorschach) are described in terms of their sensitivity to posttraumatic states. In some instances, these tests contain no trauma-specific items or scales. In others, special items or scoring approaches have been added. Detailed information on the psychometric assessment of posttraumatic states can also be found in books by Carlson (1997), Stamm (1996), and Wilson and Keane (in press), as well as recent chapters by Briere (in press), Flack, Litz, Weathers, and Beaudreau (2002), Keane and Kaloupek (2002), Keane, Weathers, and Foa (2000), and Marsella (2001).

## Minnesota Multiphasic Personality Inventory and Minnesota Multiphasic Personality Inventor–2

The Minnesota Multiphasic Personality Inventory (MMPI; Hathaway & McKinley, 1943) and the more recent MMPI–2 (Butcher, Dahlstrom, Graham, Tellegen, & Kaemmer, 1989) have been used in a number of studies to assess posttraumatic states

and dysfunction. Generally, the same trauma-related scale eleva-
tions reported for the MMPI have been found to occur in the
MMPI–2 (Litz et al., 1991; Munley, Bains, Bloem, Busby, &
Pendziszewski, 1995).

**Posttraumatic stress disorder profiles.** One of the most common two-point profiles of posttraumatic stress disorder (PTSD)
sufferers on the MMPI and MMPI–2 is an 8–2 (elevated Sc and
D), along with an elevated F scale (Fairbank, Keane, & Malloy,
1983; Keane, Malloy, & Fairbank, 1984; Munley et al., 1995; Wilson & Walker, 1990). Other clinical scales are often elevated
above T65 or T70 as well, typically generating a variety of three-
point profiles (Forbes, Creamer, & McHugh, 1999; Munley et al.,
1995; Scheibe, Bagby, Miller, & Dorian, 2001). Munley et al. (1995)
noted in this regard that their findings

> highlight the complexity and variability of individual profile
> configurations in terms of a single scale high point and high
> 2-point code types within a group of PTSD patients. Although
> Scales 2 and 8 may frequently be elevated . . . , often they may
> not be found as the highest clinical scale or as one of the
> highest two clinical elevations in the profile, and may fre-
> quently occur in combinations with other clinical scale eleva-
> tions. (p. 176)

**Posttraumatic stress disorder scales.** It is not surprising that
a combination of standard MMPI scales—none of which were
developed with reference to traumatic stress—would be less
than definitive regarding the presence of posttraumatic stress.
Fortunately, the MMPI–2 has two scorable PTSD scales: the PS
(Schlenger & Kulka, 1989) and the PK (Keane et al., 1984). Although the PS has good internal consistency and discriminates
PTSD-positive from PTSD-negative research participants, the PK
is used more often, may be somewhat more predictive of PTSD
(e.g., Munley et al., 1995), and scores on the PK appear to be
generally equivalent for Black versus White respondents
(Fairbank, Caddell, & Keane, 1985), a phenomenon that has yet
to be demonstrated for the PS.

The PK scale, developed by Keane and colleagues in 1984 for the MMPI, has been revised slightly for the MMPI–2. The MMPI version was validated on a sample of 200 male combat veterans (100 with PTSD and 100 diagnosed with psychiatric disorders other than PTSD), wherein 49 items were found to maximally discriminate PTSD status. Based on visual inspection of the distribution of scores on this new scale, it was determined that a raw score of 30 was the best cutoff for discriminating PTSD from other psychiatric diagnoses. This cutoff score yielded a hit rate (i.e., correct prediction percentage) of 82% in the original validation sample. Other studies have since verified the predictive validity of the original PK scale (e.g., Koretzky & Peck, 1990; Litz et al., 1991; Orr et al., 1990; Watson et al., 1994), although cutoffs as low as 19 to 23 have been recommended (e.g., Herman, Weathers, Litz, Joaquim, & Keane, 1993; Koretsky & Peck, 1990). The PK scale appears to be valid even when administered as a stand-alone measure (Herman, Weathers, Litz, Keane, & Joaquim, 1993; Scotti, Sturges, & Lyons, 1996). The scale is probably most helpful, however, in the context of other MMPI scores.

The MMPI–2 version of the PK scale has 46 items, rather than the 49 contained in the MMPI version. This version was standardized on the MMPI–2 normative sample and thus generates T-scores based on 2,600 research participants from the general population (Lyons & Keane, 1992). In the normative sample analysis, the PK had $\alpha$ reliabilities of .86 and .89 for males and females, respectively. More recently, Herman et al. (1993) reported that the internal consistency of the MMPI–2 PK scale was even higher ($\alpha$ = .95). Because the MMPI–2 PK scale has three fewer items, Lyons and Keane suggests a cutoff of 28. Using this new cutoff score, Munley et al. (1995) found the PK to have a 76% hit rate for PTSD in a sample of 54 Veterans Administration patients.

Because of its relative newness, the MMPI–2 version has somewhat less research supporting it. However, a number of studies indicate that this PK scale also discriminates those with PTSD from those without PTSD (e.g., Forbes et al., 1999; Koretzky & Peck, 1990; Perrin, Van Hasselt, & Hersen, 1997).

There has been some criticism of the MMPI and MMPI–2 PK scales, however. Among the concerns are (a) their development and validation in primarily veteran samples (including the notion that they may be more sensitive to war-related PTSD than to that arising from civilian events), (b) the possibility that the 30- or 28-point PK scale cutoffs (MMPI and MMPI–2, respectively) are too high (see Norris & Hamblen, in press, for a review), (c) the possibility that the PK discriminates trauma exposure as much (or more) than PTSD, and (d) the wide variety of non-PTSD-like symptom items (as opposed to the small number of PTSD-specific items) contained in the scales, which may produce "false positives" when applied to depressed or highly symptomatic individuals (e.g., Wetzel et al. 2003). Regarding the last point, consider Graham's (1990) description of the MMPI–2 PK scale:

> The content of the PK scale items suggests great emotional turmoil. Some items deal with anxiety, worry, and sleep disturbance. Others suggest guilt and depression. In some items subjects are reporting the presence of unwanted and disturbing thoughts, and in others they are describing lack of emotional control. Feeling misunderstood and mistreated is also present in some item content. (p. 165)

Despite these and other potential issues, there is little question that the PK scale is a welcome addition to the MMPI–2 in terms of assessing posttraumatic stress.

**Dissociation scales.** Less developed than MMPI–2 PTSD scales are those attempting to measure dissociation. Part of the interest in assessing dissociation with the MMPI is the occasional study suggesting that scale 8, to some extent, taps dissociative responses (e.g., Elhai, Gold, Mateus, & Astaphan, 2001; Friedrich, Jaworski, Huxsahl, & Bengtson, 1997). Although several MMPI or MMPI–2 dissociation scales have been devised (e.g., Leavitt, 2001; Mann, 1995; Phillips, 1994; Sanders, 1986), however, few have sufficient psychometric data (especially evidence of cross-validation in other samples) to justify their general clinical use at this time. Part of the problem is that dissociation was not a focus of MMPI/MMPI–2 item writers, and thus few items may tap the construct sufficiently to warrant their inclusion in a dissociation scale. Nevertheless, several of these scales look promising and should be further tested.

**Assessment of child abuse effects.** Beyond PTSD and dissociation, the MMPI and MMPI–2 have been used to evaluate the long-term psychological effects of childhood maltreatment. The MMPI scores of sexual abuse survivors, for example, often produce a profile characterized by elevations in scales 4 (Pd) and 8 (Sc), frequently followed by lesser elevations on 2 (D), 7 (Pt), or 6 (Pa; e.g., Belkin, Greene, Rodriguez, & Boggs, 1994; Engles, Moisan, & Harris, 1994; Griffith, Myers, Cusick, & Tankersley, 1997; Goldwater & Duffy, 1990; Hunter, 1991; Lundberg-Love, Marmion, Ford, Geffner, & Peacock, 1992). The relationship between this two-point profile and a history of childhood sexual abuse has been documented for some time—for example, Caldwell and O'Hare (1975) noted almost three decades ago that women with elevated 4–8 profiles often report "a seductive and ambivalent father" and "a high frequency of incest" (p. 94).

Although a body of evidence suggests that sexual abuse survivors in therapy tend to present with a 4–8 MMPI profile (see, however, Carlin & Ward [1992], Elhai, Klotz Flitter, Gold, & Sellers [2001], and Follette, Naugle, & Follette [1997] for other scale clusters), it is not clear whether this configuration should be interpreted in the manner suggested by standard interpretive texts. Consider, for example, the following description by a well-known MMPI authority:

> 48/84 individuals do not seem to fit into their environment. They are seen by others as odd, peculiar, and queer. They are nonconforming and resentful of authority, and they often espouse radical religious or political views. Their behavior is erratic and unpredictable, and they have marked problems with impulse control. They tend to be angry, irritable, and resentful, and they act out in asocial or antisocial ways. (Graham, 1990, p. 99)

Although there is some overlap between what is known about clinically presenting abuse survivors and standard 4–8 interpretations, traditional approaches to MMPI interpretation can be misleading in the evaluation of abuse-related disturbance. Lundberg-Love et al. (1992) noted that

> Historically, clinically significant elevations on the Pd and Sc scales have been interpreted as evidence of sociopathy and schizophrenia, respectively. Indeed, Scott and Stone (1986) concluded that the results of their testing indicated that incest survivors possessed a general deviancy from societal standards and a tendency to act out in antisocial, immature, and egocentric ways. (p. 98)

Lundberg-Love et al. indicated that the sexual abuse survivors in their sample accomplished a 4–8 profile through the differential endorsement of certain Pd and Sc items (as measured by Harris & Lingoes [1968] subscales) over others. Specifically, abuse survivors' scale 4 elevations were primarily the result of endorsement of familial discord and current feelings of alienation, rather than the authority and social imperturbability Pd items often endorsed by more antisocial individuals. Similarly, their sexual abuse sample scored highest on the social alienation and reduced ego-mastery items of scale 8, as opposed to the clinical levels of bizarre sensory experiences and emotional alienation endorsements often found in schizophrenia.

It is not only clinical scale interpretation of the MMPI that may suffer when applied to abuse survivors. Also problematic, as described in chapter 3, is the F scale of this measure, which tends to be endorsed to a greater extent by former child abuse victims and others. Elliott (1993), for example, found that psychiatric inpatients with victimization histories had twice the likelihood of invalid MMPI profiles than their nonvictimized cohorts (30% vs. 15%). As noted in previous chapters, this may reflect the tendency for posttraumatic dissociative and intrusive symptomatology to produce unusual experiences and chaotic, disorganized internal states (Armstrong, 1995). Under such conditions, an elevated F scale does not represent a "fake bad" response or invalid protocol as much as an accurate portrayal of atypical experiences and extreme stress.

There are similar problems with traditional interpretations of the MMPI responses of domestic violence victims. In a study specifically examining the scale 4 (Pd) endorsements of battered women, for example, Rhodes (1992) found that although battered women scored significantly higher on 4 than did nonbattered women, the most elevated Harris and Lingoes subscale was Family Discord (T 69). Like Lundberg-Love, Rhodes drew on such findings to highlight the importance of content subscales in the interpretation of victims' MMPI scale scores. Similarly, Khan, Welch, and Zillmer (1993) found that battered women typically presented with an F–4–6–8 profile, but that traditional interpretations of this configuration could lead to misdiagnosis. This sample also had elevated PS and PK scale scores, thereby suggesting the potential posttraumatic basis of at least some of their MMPI–2 responses.

## Millon Clinical Multiaxial Inventory

The Millon Clinical Multiaxial Inventory (MCMI; Millon, 1983), MCMI–II (Millon, 1987), and MCMI–III (Millon, 1994) are among the most popular of personality tests (Choca, Shanley, & Van Denburg, 1992; Piotrowski & Lubin, 1990), yet they have only recently been applied to survivors of adult traumas. By contrast, there are a number of studies on the MCMI profiles of child abuse survivors, as noted later in this section. This differential attention is likely because of the frequent use of the MCMI to detect dysfunctional personality traits or frank personality disorders—outcomes now understood to arise, in many cases, from extended child abuse and neglect. The classic understanding of adult-onset PTSD, on the other hand, has stressed more acute, anxiety-related responses to overwhelming traumatic events, thereby potentially overlooking the more relational aspects of severe posttraumatic disturbance.

**Assessing posttraumatic stress disorder.** Another reason that the MCMI has been underapplied to trauma victims was the absence of a PTSD scale in the MCMI and MCMI–II. Lacking such a scale, PTSD symptoms were easily misinterpreted as evidence of personality dysfunction (e.g., borderline personality or, before the MCMI–III, the ill-conceived construct of "self-defeating" personality). Choca et al. (1992), for example, noted that individuals satisfying diagnostic criteria for PTSD often score in the clinical range on a variety of MCMI scales. They further noted that these scale elevations "do not exclusively identify individuals with PTSD because there may be individuals with other diagnoses who also fit the same pattern of scale elevations" (p. 128). The reverse also appears to be true: Individuals with PTSD are likely to appear to have other psychiatric disorders on the MCMI by virtue of the relevance of other scale items to posttraumatic symptomatology.

The absence of specific posttraumatic indicators on the MCMI and MCMI–II has been partially remedied with the advent of the MCMI–III. The MCMI–III contains a PTSD scale (the R scale, within the "clinical syndromes" group) that is loosely tied to some *DSM–IV* criteria. However, the content domain of this scale is somewhat problematic. Review of the R scale reveals a majority of items not directly associated with *DSM–IV* diagnostic criteria for PTSD. These include items examining sadness, worthlessness, having "strange" thoughts, rapid mood changes, repeated thoughts (content unstated), fears about the future, emptiness, and suicidality. In fact, there are only seven of 16 R scale items that actually evaluate current PTSD criteria: four address reexperiencing symptoms, two refer to hyperarousal, and one taps avoidance. Thus, this scale overvalues reexperiencing phenomena and substantially underestimates avoidance and hyperarousal.

As generally occurs with other MCMI–III scales, the R scale gives twice the weight to certain PTSD items, whereas other items are scored at face value. This differential weighing procedure is unique among trauma scales, and the psychometric effects of specifically doubling the value of some items but not others is unknown.

The base rate (BR) standardization method used by the MCMI–III may be affected by the contamination of the R scale with nontrauma-related (primarily depressive) items and its over-representation of reexperiencing symptoms. To the extent that these items do not represent the entire (or specific) content domain of PTSD, the MCMI's use of cutting scores to define the "presence" (BR > 75) or "prominence" (BR > 85) of PTSD is of questionable merit. Until sensitivity and specificity of these cutting scores can be assessed (ideally against a standard such as the CAPS), and in the absence of supporting interview data, it is not appropriate to state that an individual "has" PTSD by virtue of his or her MCMI–III R score, regardless of its BR elevation.

These various concerns do not mean that this scale is necessarily of lesser quality than the MMPI PK—a scale that also includes many depression and other nontrauma-related items. Rather, the fact that this scale was developed specifically to tap PTSD symptoms (as opposed to the PK, which used existing MMPI items) raises expectations that are only partially met. Ultimately, it may be that the R and PK scales are, to some extent, measures of "complex" PTSD (or PTSD with associated features) rather than pure PTSD, and thus may reflect more the sequelae of sustained or multi-event stressors, wherein depression and related difficulties are especially relevant.

Because the MCMI–III R scale is relatively new, relatively little data are available on its reliability or validity. The MCMI–III test manual reports that the R scale had an $\alpha$ of .89 in 398 cross-validation research participants and a test–retest coefficient of .94 in 87 research participants tested over a 5- to 14-day interval (Millon, 1994). The manual indicates that the R's BR score correlates at approximately the same levels (around .5 to .6) with the depression scales of the MMPI–2 and SCL–90–R, and the Beck Depression Inventory (BDI; Beck et al., 1961), as it does with a measure of traumatic stress (the Impacts of Event Scale [Horowitz, Wilner, & Alvarez, 1979]). Such data suggest that the R scale has less than optimal discriminant validity.

As noted, no data are available on the R scale's sensitivity or specificity with regard to a structured interview (e.g., Structured Clinical Interview for *DSM–IV* [SCID]) diagnosis of PTSD. Millon (1994) presented data, however, on the relationship between two dichotomous variables: a variable indicating whether the PTSD scale was the highest or second highest BR score on a MCMI–III profile, and another reflecting whether the clinician rated PTSD as the most prominent or second most prominent characteristic. Using this relatively broad criterion for diagnostic agreement,

Millon found R to have a sensitivity of only .37 and a specificity of .84 in a sample of 1,079 research participants evaluated by "several hundred" clinicians (p. 19). Millon noted, however, that "most clinical judges in our rating study saw the subject only once and usually without the benefit of clinical interviews or extensive readings of their histories" (p. 34). A second MCMI–III validity study (Millon, Davis, & Millon, 1997) revealed a considerable improvement in the diagnostic utility of the MCMI–III vis-à-vis PTSD, although it appears that the improvement was, in large part, the result of methodological problems associated with both the 1994 and 1997 studies (Hsu, 2002).

**Trauma profiles.** The few studies available on possible MCMI adult trauma profiles are, in most cases, limited to the MCMI and MCMI–II and deal almost exclusively with Vietnam veterans. These studies suggest that those suffering posttraumatic stress may have elevations on some combination of the Avoidant, Schizoid, Passive-Aggressive, and Borderline scales, along with, in many cases, Anxiety and Dysthymia clinical syndrome scales (e.g., Hyer Woods, Boudewyns, Bruno, & O'Leary, 1988; Hyer et al. Woods, Boudewyns, Harrison, & Tamkin, 1990; Munley et al., 1995). Two studies in this area also reported elevated scores on the Self-defeating Personality scale of the MCMI–II (Hyer et al. Davis, Woods, Albrecht, & Boudewyns, 1992; Hyer, Davis, Albrecht, Boudewns, & Woods, 1994), a scale that interprets suicidality and other detrimental behaviors as evidence of an unconscious desire to seek out negative outcomes and self-punishment. Perhaps apropos of its absence in the MCMI–III (although see the MCMI–III's Masochistic Personality scale), this scale and its underlying assumption is often misleading, if not victim-blaming, rather than clinically helpful.

As noted, the MCMI has been used to evaluate the lasting effects of child abuse on adults. At least three studies (Bryer et al., 1987; Busby, Glenn, Steggell, & Adamson, 1993; Fisher, Winne, & Ley, 1993) indicated that physical or sexual abuse survivors score in the clinical range on a variety of MCMI–I/ MCMI–II scales, most typically on the Avoidant, Dependent, Passive–Aggressive, and Borderline personality scales, along with elevated Anxiety, Somatoform, Thought Disorder, Major Depression, and Delusional Disorder scales.

As with the MMPI, a potential problem associated with interpreting child abuse survivors' responses to the MCMI is whether high scores on a given scale indicate that the survivor, in fact, "has" the relevant disorder or personality style. For example, although yet to be tested empirically, clinical experience suggests that most abuse survivors who have elevated scores on the MCMI Thought Disorder or Delusional Disorder scales do not have clinically significant psychotic symptoms, nor do all of those with an elevated Borderline scale score necessarily have borderline personality disorder. Instead, the MCMI psychotic scales (like the Rorschach in various trauma contexts) are likely to tap the posttraumatic symptoms (especially intrusion and avoidance) and chaotic internal experience of severe abuse survivors, whereas the Borderline scale may be affected by the greater tension-reduction activities and interpersonal difficulties of these individuals.

With the advent of the MCMI–III PTSD (R) scale, issues associated with misidentification of child abuse survivors and other trauma victims may be reduced. To the extent that the R scale operates as advertised, it may facilitate the interpretation of abuse survivors' MCMI scores by indicating the presence of posttraumatic stress. In such an instance, although other less relevant scales might also be elevated (e.g., Thought Disorder), the presence of a high PTSD score would alert the examiner to the possibility of alternate explanations for such scale elevations. The few studies using the MCMI–III in trauma victims suggests findings similar to the MCMI and MCMI–II data discussed, as well as suggesting that the R scale is, in fact, moderately associated with PTSD and other posttraumatic responses (Allen, Huntoon, & Evans, 1999; Craig & Olson, 1997; Hyer, Boyd, Stanger, Davis, & Walters, 1997).

Despite its potential limitations, the MCMI–III's broad coverage of Axis I and II, plus its inclusion of a PTSD-related scale, supports its application with trauma survivors—especially in instances where posttraumatic states coexist with dysfunctional personality traits, or where "complex PTSD" is a probable diagnostic issue. On such occasions, however, the clinician may have to translate MCMI descriptions of personality disorder into more accurate statements about personality styles, traits, or psychological defenses.

# Psychological Assessment Inventory

The Psychological Assessment Inventory (PAI; Morey, 1991) is a 344-item inventory consisting of four validity scales and 18 nonoverlapping clinical scales, many of which have scorable subscales. Because of its relative recency, the PAI has been less well studied in terms of its association with traumatic stress. It contains a PTSD subscale, however, evaluates both Axis I and several Axis II disorders, and—as one of the latest generation of psychological tests—has superior psychometric characteristics.

The PTSD subscale (ARD–T) of the PAI is one of three components of the full Anxiety-Related Disorders (ARD) scale. Five items of ARD–T tap reexperiencing phenomena, and three are concerned with, respectively, guilt, loss of interest, and avoidance of memory-triggering stimuli. In the beta stage of test development, ARD–T had an $\alpha$ of .89 in 325 research participants. In follow-up reliability studies, the $\alpha$ ranged from .81 to .89 in community, college student, and clinical samples. The ARD–T subscale correlated significantly ($r = .59$) with the Mississippi scale (Keane, Caddell, & Taylor, 1988) in 21 Veterans Administration patients, 11 of whom had diagnoses of PTSD (Morey, 1991). The PAI manual reported no concurrent validity with respect to the SCID–R or other structured interview. In a study of the PAI profiles of 53 clinical research participants with diagnoses of PTSD (diagnostic method not reported), Morey (1991) noted,

> the posttraumatic stress group had a more elevated profile [than those with other anxiety disorders], with mean scores above 70T on DEP [depression] and ARD [anxiety-related disorder]. The subscale configuration for the PTSD group was particularly interesting; marked ARD–T (traumatic stress), accompanied by indicators of confusion (SCZ–T), social estrangement (SCZ–S and BOR–N), and poor control over anger and aggression (BOR–A and AGG–P). (p. 104)

Although the ARD–T tends to prize posttraumatic reexperiencing over avoidance or hyperarousal, its moderate correlation
with the Mississippi and its specific elevation among PTSD sufferers suggests its potential usefulness when the PAI is applied
to traumatized individuals. Because its sensitivity and specificity
with reference to PTSD and other posttraumatic disorders are
unknown, however, it should not be used in isolation to make
a posttraumatic stress diagnosis. The PAI, itself, has wide content
coverage and very good psychometric characteristics—qualities
that may justify its frequent use in standard trauma assessment batteries.

## Symptom Checklist–90–Revised

The Symptom Checklist–90–Revised (SCL–90–R; Derogatis,
1977, 1983) is a widely used symptom checklist measure, based
on the earlier Hopkins Symptom Checklist (HSCL; Derogatis
et al., 1974; Lipman, Rickels, Ulenhuth, & Covi, 1974). Derogatis
has since developed the Brief Symptom Inventory (BSI, Derogatis
& Spencer, 1982), a shorter version of the SCL–90–R. The SCL–
90–R consists of nine subscales, as well an index of global distress.
The various subscales of the SCL–90–R appear to predict trauma-
related disturbance in a wide variety of individuals, including
disaster victims (e.g., Najarian, Goenjian, Pelcovitz, Mandel, &
Najarian, 2001), survivors of the Holocaust (e.g., Yehuda et al.,
1994), marital rape victims (e.g., Riggs, Kilpatrick, & Resick,
1992), war veterans (e.g., Wolfe,. Brown, & Bucsela, 1992), and
adults abused as children (e.g., Gold, Lucenko, Elhai, Swingle,
& Sellers, 1999). The SCL–90–R does not have a specific scale to
assess posttraumatic disturbance, however, and several scales
have items that may interpret trauma effects as, for example,
obsessive–compulsive or psychotic symptomatology, or as interpersonal sensitivity. As noted by Elliott (1994a):

> Although this instrument provides valuable information re-
> lated to psychological distress, its development without spe-
> cific reference to victimization may limit its usefulness in
> this regard. For example, some of the items thought to be

indicative of psychosis are consistent with long-term sexual abuse or battering relationships (such as feeling lonely even when you are with people and never feeling close to another person). Thus, as with other measures, item analysis is recommended when clinical elevations are reached on various scales. (p. 11)

Although the SCL–90–R does not have a specific posttraumatic stress scale, three SCL–PTSD scales have been developed *post-hoc*, one by Saunders and colleagues (Saunders, Arata, & Kilpatrick, 1990), one by Ursano et al. (1992), and one by Weathers et al. (1996). The Saunders et al. scale consists of the 28 SCL–90–R items that best discriminated PTSD status in a sample of 355 research participants from the general population. Saunders et al. found that the resultant subscale was internally consistent ($\alpha$ = .93) and could discriminate crime-related PTSD (CR–PTSD) in 89% of cases. Further analysis of this subscale was performed with a subsample of 266 female crime victims (Arata, Saunders, & Kilpatrick, 1991). The SCL–PTSD subscale was found to have incremental validity with respect to the IES and was able to discriminate CR–PTSD individuals from those without crime-related PTSD. Using the DIS as the PTSD criterion, the SCL–PTSD had a sensitivity of .75 and a specificity of .91. Because this subscale was validated in the same sample in which it was created, the authors correctly noted that the generalizability of these results is unknown. Further, the applicability of this subscale to noncrime-related PTSD is unclear, and there are no normative data available for this measure, as opposed to the full SCL–90–R. Nevertheless, if further tested and standardized, this scoring approach could provide clinicians with the opportunity to assess posttraumatic stress with the SCL–90–R, generally in a manner similar to the trauma scales of the MMPI–2, MCMI–III, and PAI.

A second SCL–90–R PTSD scale, created by Ursano et al. (1992), uses those 30 items from the SCL–90–R judged by a panel of experts to best represent the symptoms of PTSD, along with 12 new reexperiencing, avoidance, and hyperarousal items written in the SCL–90–R format. The resultant 42-item measure had a mean sensitivity of .67 and specificity of .91 in four disaster samples (total $N$ = 1,273) when compared to a cutoff score of 19 on the PK scale (Ursano et al., 1992; also described in Ursano et al., 1995). Like the CR–PTSD, there are no normative data for this scale.

A third measure, the War-Zone–PTSD scale (WZ–PTSD; Weathers et al., 1996), contains the 25 SCL–90–R items that best discriminated 202 Vietnam theater veterans with and without PTSD. The WZ–PTSD scale appears to have very good internal consistency ($\alpha$ = .97) and good diagnostic utility with reference to the SCID (Spitzer et al., 1990) or CAPS (Blake et al., 1990). Different WZ–PTSD cutoff scores are suggested for the determination of PTSD, based on whether sensitivity (identifying cases of PTSD) or specificity (identifying noncases of PTSD) is of greatest concern.

# Rorschach

As is true of the other standard measures reviewed here, the Rorschach (Rorschach, 1981/1921) has both positive and negative qualities with regard to the assessment of posttraumatic states. On one hand, this test provides an opportunity to avoid the constraints of objective testing, wherein the client is forced to respond to a specific test item and therefore to a specific minihypothesis regarding the structure of psychological disturbance. Instead, the Rorschach and other projective measures offer a set of relatively ambiguous stimuli, to which the client may respond in any manner he or she chooses. As a result, the client's responses are less predetermined and potentially more free to accurately reflect whatever trauma effects might be discoverable.

On the other hand, the interpretation systems used to classify Rorschach responses (especially non-Exnerian systems) are not entirely free of theoretical assumptions and are subject to whatever level of misinterpretation of posttraumatic states the underlying assessment perspective potentially entails. For example, some PTSD sufferers seemingly revealed signs of thought disorder or impaired reality testing in one Rorschach study of war veterans (van der Kolk & Ducey, 1984, 1989), despite the fact that these indicators "coexisted with an absence of psychotic thinking in clinical interviews, suggesting that the subjects possessed a basically intact reality orientation that was only overwhelmed by intrusive traumatic material in the context of unstructured tests" (Saunders, 1991, p. 50). Similar problems arise with reference to misdiagnosis of personality disorder in the Rorschach protocols of some trauma survivors (e.g., Luxenberg & Levin, in press; Saunders, 1991). The potential overlap between psychotic, personality disordered, and posttraumatic Rorschach presentations requires the clinician to be familiar with all three diagnostic scenarios and their Rorschach representations when evaluating posttraumatic dysfunction or disorder.

**Traumatic stress indicators.** A number of studies have reported a specific cluster of Rorschach indicators that appear to tap various aspects of posttraumatic stress. Although such indicators frequently make intuitive sense, the methodology of these studies often involved the mere comparison of a group of posttraumatic Rorschach scores to Exner's (1986) normative data. This procedure is not only potentially confounded by differences in background variables between the posttraumatic individuals and Exner's normative sample, it does not allow much discrimination between types of posttraumatic disturbance. For example, although a given study may find that dissociative disorder clients score higher on unstructured color or morbid content relative to norms, it is not clear whether this difference represents dissociation, differences in clinical acuity between samples, comorbid posttraumatic stress, or perhaps the generalized effects of a trauma history on affect regulation capacities. For this reason, the clinician is advised to use caution in making especially specific interpretations regarding what otherwise might be more general posttraumatic Rorschach responses.

Given these caveats, several studies outline potential Rorschach indicators of the reexperiencing, avoidant, and hypervigilant symptoms of acute stress disorder (ASD), PTSD, and other posttraumatic states. For example, protocols with unusually extratensive Erlebnistypus (Experience Balance [EB]), low human movement (M), and extensive unstructured color responses (CF and pure C > FC) have been interpreted as reflecting posttraumatic intrusion and reliving (e.g., van der Kolk & Ducey, 1984, 1989). Posttraumatic avoidance and psychic numbing, on the other hand, often covary with low affective ratios (Afr) and high Lambdas (Hartman et al., 1990; Kaser-Boyd, 1993). Hypervigilance in response to trauma often presents, as expected, as HVI (Luxenberg & Levin, in press). Also present in such protocols may be evidence of feelings of helpless and powerlessness, such as inanimate movement responses (m) and diffuse shading determinants (Y; Levin, 1993; van der Kolk & Ducey, 1984, 1989).

**Dissociation indicators.** Rorschach correlates of dissociation appear to parallel those of posttraumatic avoidance, along with potentially elevated form dimension responses (FD) and introversive–superintroversive EB styles (Armstrong, 1991; Lovitt & Lefkoff, 1985). Drawing on the work of Saunders (1991) and others, Leavitt and Labott (1996) also consider three Rorschach responses to be potential indicators of dissociation:

> (1) Reference to forms seen through obscuring media, such as veils, fog, or mist so that people or objects look unclear or blurry; (2) reference to unusual responses in which distance appears exaggerated such that objects or figures appear vague and far away from other specified objects; (3) reference to a sense of disorientation in which Rorschach stimuli are experienced as unstable, shifting, moving, or rapidly changing. (p. 488)

It should be noted, however, that this list has yet to be established as, in fact, definitive evidence of dissociation.

As is noted later in this chapter, Armstrong and Loewenstein (1990) also document especially frequent sex, blood, anatomy, and aggression content scores among those with dissociative identity disorder. However, this relationship may relate more to the traumatic etiology of dissociation than to dissociative symptomatology.

**Child abuse effects.** Survivors of chronic trauma, especially those experiencing the long-term effects of child abuse, tend to produce not only the unstructured color responses, poor form quality, and unusual content indicators described earlier, but also greater aggression, reduced texture, both more active and more passive movement, and greater bodily concerns (e.g., Kamphuis, Kugeares, & Finn, 2000; Leavitt, 2000; Meyers, 1988; Nash, Hulsey, Sexton, Harralson, & Lambert, 1993; Owens, 1984; Saunders, 1991). Also present may be elevated thought disorder and confabulation indicators (Cerney, 1990; Hartman et al., 1990; Levin, 1993; Sanders, 1991; van der Kolk & Ducey, 1984, 1989).

Many of these responses are considered to be evidence of personality disorder in traditional scoring approaches, perhaps especially borderline personality (e.g., Kwawer, Lerner, Lerner, & Sugarman, 1985). Trauma-specialized clinicians (e.g., Luxenberg & Levin, in press), however, noted that these same responses are provided by severely traumatized individuals and suggested that they need not represent characterologic difficulties as much as posttraumatic stress.

The presence of a childhood trauma history does not rule out the possibility of personality disorder, however. Although severe trauma can destabilize, affectively overwhelm, produce flashbacks, and lead to preoccupation with violent and sexual themes, it is also true that early traumas such as child abuse are risk factors for true personality-level symptoms and dysfunctions (e.g., Briere & Zaidi, 1989; Herman, Perry, & van der Kolk, 1989). As a result, although unstructured color responses in an abuse survivor may reflect the intrusion of flashbacks or other reliving experiences, they also may arise from more "borderline"-like difficulties in affect regulation that ultimately lead to externalizing tension reduction activities. Similarly, the presence of thought disorder or confabulation responses may signal a disorganized internal state arising from overwhelming trauma or may represent the more diffuse impairment in self functions found in some individuals with borderline personality disorder. As noted at various points in this book, this concatenation of posttraumatic stress and characterologic disturbance is especially salient in adult survivors of severe childhood abuse, where traditional distinctions between these two symptom clusters or axes may be difficult to make or even counterproductive in some instances (Briere, 1992a; Herman, 1992a; Kroll, 1993). Perhaps the "bottom line" with regard to this issue is one of interpretive balance: it is as wrong to misinterpret PTSD responses as psychosis or borderline personality disorder as it is to rule out the latter disorders solely because the individual has a child abuse history or other evidence of trauma exposure.

**Content indicators.** There is one area where traditional interpretive approaches to the Rorschach are particularly likely to misinterpret posttraumatic symptomatology as something else: that of ideographic (i.e., morbid, aggressive, blood, sex, and anatomy) content responses (e.g., Armstrong, 1991; Briere, 1996a; Leavitt & Labott, 1996; Levin, 1993; van der Kolk & Ducey, 1984, 1989). These responses, if excessive in frequency, are often seen as signs of thought disorder, primary process breakthrough, or primitive personality organization (e.g., Kissen, 1986). Yet, as noted by various authors (e.g., Armstrong, 1991; Riquelme & Perfetti, 2000; van der Kolk & Ducy, 1984, 1989), such responses do not necessarily suggest psychosis or personality disorder in traumatized individuals.

In an attempt to define the content responses of traumatized individuals, Armstrong and Loewenstein (1990) created a special Traumatic Content Index (TC/R), defined as "the sum of the sex, blood, and anatomy content scores plus the morbid and aggressive special scores divided by the total number of responses" and expressed as a percentage (p. 450). In a sample of 14 research participants, the authors found those with MPD (DID) had very high TC/R scores (a mean of 50%, with a range of 30% to 80%), which they attributed to "disruption by posttraumatic intrusions" (p. 453). Since its creation, this scale has been shown to discriminate traumatized from nontraumatized individuals in at least one other study (e.g., Kamphuis, Kugeares, & Finn, 2000).

In an approach similar to Armstrong and Loewenstein's, Leavitt and Labott (1996) compared the Rorschach responses of 29 psychiatric inpatient women with sexual abuse histories to 85 similar inpatients who reported no sexual abuse history. The authors found eight indicators that were (a) significantly more common among the sexual abuse group than the nonabuse group, and (b) occurred in the nonabused group infrequently (i.e., 5% or less of the time). These were sexual activity, sexual anxiety, sexual violence, damage to the body, imagery of adults as victims, imagery of children as victims, imagery of fearful adults, and imagery of fearful children. Using a "sexual abuse index" consisting of the number of signs present (ranging from zero to eight), the authors found that a cutoff score of two or more signs correctly classified 93% of the abused research participants and 98% of the nonabused research participants. This index also identified as abused 88% of a separate sample of women ($N = 26$) reporting recovered memories of sexual abuse who evidenced dissociative symptoms on the Rorschach. Leavitt (2000) essentially replicated these findings in a later study, finding that the "two or more signs" rule correctly identified 83% of women with continuous abuse memories, 52% of those with recovered memories for sexual abuse, and 96% of nonabused controls.

In light of the frequent relationship between trauma and certain content indicators, the sex, aggression, victimization, and anatomy responses of a rape victim or sexual abuse survivor are likely to reflect activation of victimization-related memories by the Rorschach (Briere, 1996a), just as a Vietnam veteran's frequent blood, violence, or morbid responses may arise from real wartime experiences. As first noted by Exner in 1979, "any excess of content should be regarded as a form of preoccupation, after which, the impact of that preoccupation should be judged" (p. 304). In the case of posttraumatic intrusion, the preoccupation often appears to arise from unresolved traumatic memories that are easily elicited or cued by Rorschach stimuli. Apropos of this, Carlson and Armstrong (1995) argue that

> for traumatized patients, tests like the Rorschach can cease to be a projective measure, and become instead a traumatic trigger. Unless the assessor is conversant with the PTSD literature . . . , traumatic reactions are likely to be misdiagnosed as indicators of psychotic or characterologically primitive function. (p. 169)

## Evaluation of Altered Self-Capacities

As noted in chapter 2, early and chronic psychological trauma can result in impaired *self-capacities* (Briere, 2002a; Briere & Runtz,

2002; McCann & Pearlman, 1990), involving chronic difficulties in identity and boundary awareness, interpersonal relatedness, and affect regulation. There are several multiscale tests that bear, to some extent, on the issue of self-capacities, including the MMPI–2, MCMI–III, and the PAI. Although the MMPI–2 does not have any clinical scales that directly evaluate self-functioning, there are supplementary scales (e.g., Ego Strength [ES]), scales (i.e., 4 [Pd]) and profile configurations (e.g., 4–8) that tap aspects of this domain. The MCMI–III assesses a variety of Axis-II concerns, although it generally conceptualizes them as disorders, as opposed to specific problems of self-capacity . The PAI, on the other hand, generates not only diagnostic information (e.g., the Borderline Features and Antisocial Features scales), but also four six-item Borderline subscales that tap certain self-capacity-related phenomena (i.e., Affective Instability, Identity Problems, Negative Relationships, and Self-Harm). In addition, the Trauma Symptom Inventory (discussed in the next chapter) has two scales (Impaired Self-reference and Tension-reduction Behavior) that tap identity and affect regulation symptoms.

In addition to these multiscale instruments, there are two standardized tests that limit their focus to some aspect of self-capacity alteration: the Bell Object Relations and Reality Testing Inventory (BORRTI; Bell, 1995) and the Inventory of Altered Self-Capacities (IASC; Briere, 2000a).

## Bell Object Relations and Reality Testing Inventory

The BORRTI is the only standardized test of what is referred to as *disturbed object relations*—a clinical construct that is, in some ways, similar to altered self-capacities. This instrument has scales that yield data on four object relations constructs: Alienation, Insecure Attachment, Egocentricity, and Social Incompetence. These scales have been shown by the test author to predict and potentially explain relational difficulties in individuals thought to have some form of personality disorder. BORRTI item content also reflects identity issues and affect regulation difficulties, although there are no scales specifically tapping those domains. Because the scales are linked to object relations theory, the results of this measure will be most directly applicable to clinicians who endorse that perspective. A very small literature in this area suggests that the BORRTI may be helpful in evaluating self-capacity and attachment issues in traumatized populations (e.g., Alpher, 1991; Santina, 1998).

### Inventory of Altered Self-Capacities

This measure contains seven scales that measure various types of "self-related" psychological disturbance common to survivors of sustained child abuse, neglect, and other early traumas. These are: Interpersonal Conflicts, Idealization–Disillusionment, Abandonment Concerns, Identity Impairment (with two subscales: Self-awareness and Diffusion), Susceptibility to Influence, Affect Dysregulation (with two subscales: Instability and Skills Deficits), and Tension Reduction Activities. Each symptom item is rated according to its frequency of occurrence over the previous six months, using a 4-point scale ranging from 1 (never) to 4 (often).

The IASC was standardized and normed on 620 general population participants and various clinical and university samples. It has been found to be reliable (with an average $\alpha$ across scales of .89) and to have convergent and discriminant validity in both normative and validation samples. The IASC scales have been shown to predict self-reported child abuse history (especially sexual and emotional maltreatment), attachment style, "borderline" and "antisocial" personality features, relationship problems, suicidality, dysfunctional sexual behavior, and substance abuse (Briere, 2000a; Briere & Runtz, 2002). The IASC is also designed to predict certain issues (e.g., abandonment fears, idealization or devaluation, and hypersusceptibility to interpretation) that otherwise might disrupt or derail the client–therapist relationship during treatment.

# Conclusion

As indicated in this chapter, traditional objective and projective psychological tests can be an important part of the trauma-focused assessment battery. First, generic tests provide important information on comorbid phenomena, such as the presence of anxiety, depression, personality disorder, or psychosis. Second, when trauma-specific scales or scoring procedures are available, such instruments may signal the possibility of one or more post-traumatic states. Finally, in most cases these scales are normed on general population samples, allowing the clinician to interpret specific scores in terms of their extremity, if not severity.

Unfortunately, almost none of the currently available generic measures, with or without trauma-specific features, are especially sensitive to posttraumatic stress. They typically include a variety of items that are not directly related to posttraumatic symptomatology, do not well represent the three components of PTSD, and do not assess symptoms within the one-month range required by *DSM–IV*. Equally important, almost none of these measures test for acute stress disorder or dissociative disorders. As a result, it is recommended that generic tests either be administered with—or followed up by—more specialized trauma measures whenever possible, rather than being used in isolation to index posttraumatic disturbance.

# 7

# Trauma-Specific
# Objective Measures

In additional to the generic psychological tests outlined in chapter 6, there are a number of more trauma-specific objective measures available to clinicians. These measures usually approach posttraumatic difficulties from one of two perspectives: diagnostic, criterion-based measures that tend to focus on *DSM–IV* diagnoses (although some also measure symptom intensity) and longer instruments that are more concerned with the degree of various posttraumatic symptoms (i.e., reexperiencing, avoidant, or dissociative responses). Both types of tests are reviewed in this chapter.

There are both strengths and weaknesses associated with trauma-specific objective measures. The primary advantages of such instruments are (a) their avoidance of the subjectivity sometimes associated with diagnostic interviews (trauma-based or otherwise), (b) the greater reliability they potentially offer, by virtue of multiple items addressing the same or related phenomena, (c) the reduced need for trained and qualified clinicians to be physically present during parts of the evaluation, and (d) the ease with which such tests can be administered, both in terms of the amount of time involved per test and the possibility of assessing multiple individuals simultaneously.

The growing availability of trauma-specific measures has been of critical importance in the development of effective research and treatment approaches to posttraumatic states. However, because of the relative youth of the field (especially in terms of assessing and treating noncombat-related traumatic stress) and the continuing changes in our understanding and categorization of posttraumatic states, problems continue.

First, research clinicians have tended to produce slightly different versions of essentially the same trauma measure. As discussed later in this chapter, a number of investigators have written measures that consist of 17 items reflecting the 17 diagnostic indicators of *DSM–III–R* (and then *DSM–IV*) posttraumatic stress disorder (Carlson, 1997). These measures differ primarily in terms of how these criteria are worded in lay language, with most differences in reliability and validity probably arising from the various levels of success associated with this endeavor and the samples used to test each measure. Not only is this approach somewhat redundant, it creates inherent limitations in the resultant instruments. Most important, such measures, by definition, provide only one item per posttraumatic stress disorder (PTSD) criterion. If the subject misinterprets or avoids that item, the underlying construct goes unassessed or is distorted. Furthermore, according to standard measurement theory, a single item is a far less reliable estimate of a construct than are several items—leading to error variation in the assessment of, for example, flashbacks or psychic numbing.

Second, most current trauma measures examine only three symptom clusters: posttraumatic reexperiencing, avoidance, and hyperarousal. Yet, as outlined in chapter 2 and elsewhere in this volume, there are a variety of other posttraumatic states or responses, ranging from acute stress disorder (ASD) to dissociation, somatization, and posttraumatic personality dysfunction. A comprehensive trauma assessment should evaluate these symptom clusters as well, perhaps especially the confluence of dissociation and more classic notions of posttraumatic stress.

Third, as noted in chapter 6, objective trauma measures that use a total score to reflect posttraumatic stress inappropriately collapse the three dimensions of posttraumatic stress into a single number. As a result, there may be several different ways for clients or research participants to achieve the same total PTSD score: for example, some primarily through reexperiencing, some through avoidance, some through hyperarousal, and some through moderate endorsement of all symptom items. Clearly, these different responses represent different clinical scenarios, each of which should be evaluated with separate scales.

Another problem for authors of trauma measures is whether to anchor the items in a specific, identified event, to leave the trauma unspecified, or to avoid any reference to a trauma altogether. Because ASD and PTSD are, by definition, linked to a single traumatic experience, it would seem that PTSD measures would have to directly refer to a specific stressor. However, this approach is difficult to accomplish in a measure that may be used to address different traumas for different people, as well as to assess those who have experienced multiple traumas. Some test authors have therefore included reference to the stressor but left it unspecified. This method is often an improvement but can easily confuse the victim of multiple traumas, who may not be sure whether flashback X is associated with stressor Y or Z, or whose dissociative numbing is not easily tied to any specific traumatic event. Based on this potential confusion, a few test developers (e.g., Briere, 1995; Carlson, 2001; Foy, Sipprelle, Rueger, & Carroll, 1984) measure the general level of intrusive reexperiencing or cognitive avoidance experienced by the individual, without reference to any specific stressor (e.g., "Upsetting thoughts about the past keep popping into my mind"). This approach has merit but produces a new problem: Does a person have PTSD if he or she has flashbacks from event A, avoidance associated with events B and C, and hyperarousal related to event D? Clearly, *DSM–IV* does not support this position, given its focus on a specific event. On the other hand, there appear to be few other ways that the clinician can assess the overall amount of posttraumatic stress a given client is experiencing, short of asking him or her to indicate for each symptom the specific trauma(s) on which it is based.

Finally, although a number of trauma-specific measures demonstrate reliability and validity in research contexts, fewer are developed to the point where they can be used unambiguously in clinical settings. Most importantly, many of these instruments are not accompanied by appropriate normative data. As a result, the clinician has almost no way of determining to what extent, if at all, the respondent's level of symptom endorsement is greater than what most people would endorse. In contrast, standardized measures allow the evaluator to compare the client's score with that of the general population and determine how deviant (i.e., clinically significant) it is.

In the case of solely diagnostic screening instruments, the absence of normative data generally is not a problem, because the only issue is whether a given set of symptoms are—or are not—present. For continuous measures of a clinical construct, however, the evaluator is left without knowing whether a score of X is normal or symptomatic. On occasion, this problem is partially addressed by cutting-scores, wherein a given score (or higher) is reported to be associated with a given diagnosis with a certain level of probability. However, the appropriate cutoff may vary from sample to sample, and this approach does not allow for interpretation of the entire range of scores below (or even above) the cutoff point.

Because of these concerns, the clinician is advised to limit his or her interpretation of scores on nonstandardized trauma-specific measures. In some cases, the best the examiner may be able to say is that approximately X% of research participants with Y disorder scored higher or lower than the respondent (based on available means and standard deviations) in a given sample in a given published study. In such cases, the examiner should also describe the extent to which the respondent matches the demographics and clinical status of that sample.

## Nonstandardized Tests

Despite these various issues, the trauma field has produced a number of instruments that provide a general assessment of posttraumatic stress, dissociative disturbance, and other posttraumatic responses, at least in research contexts. The following measures are presented here because they have been tested in at least one relevant sample and achieve some reasonable level of reliability and validity. In most cases, however, the absence of general population norms limits their regular use in clinical practice.

## Posttraumatic Stress Scales–Posttraumatic Stress Disorder–Related

The majority of nonstandardized posttraumatic stress scales were developed in the 1980s to early 1990s, in response to growing research interest in PTSD. Some of these tests consist of items reflecting the 17 possible symptoms of PTSD, whereas others include other symptoms often associated with PTSD, such as guilt, general distress, or suicidality.

**Impact of Events Scale and Impact of Events Scale–Revised.** The Impact of Events Scale (IES; Horowitz, Wilner, & Alvarez, 1979) is one of the earliest self-report measures of posttraumatic disturbance. This instrument specifically evaluates trauma-related intrusion and avoidance. Respondents are asked to rate IES symptom items according to how often each has occurred in the last seven days, on a scale marked 0 ("Not at all"), 1 ("Rarely"), 3 ("Sometimes") and 5 ("Often"). There are seven items evaluating intrusion and eight items tapping avoidance, yielding two subscale scores. The IES has been shown to discriminate a variety of traumatized groups from their nontraumatized cohorts (e.g., Alexander, 1993; Arata, Saunders, & Kilpatrick, 1991; Bryant & Harvey, 1996; Elliott & Briere, 1995; Lundin & Bodegard, 1993). Although the IES has not been normed by its authors, Briere and Elliott (1998) presented data on the normative responses of a large sample of the general population on this measure, using a nonspecific event as the reference trauma.

The original IES was developed to tap intrusive and avoidant symptomatology. As a result, it has no scale for the PTSD cluster of hyperarousal symptoms. In response, Weiss and colleagues have developed a revised version of the IES (IES–R; Weiss & Marmar, 1996; Weiss, Marmar, Metzler, & Ronfeldt, 1995), which contains six hyperarousal items and an additional item to parallel *DSM–IV* criteria.

**Los Angeles Symptom Checklist.** The Los Angeles Symptom Checklist (LASC; Foy et al., 1984; King, King, Leskin, & Foy, 1995) is a 43-item measure of posttraumatic stress, 17 items of which measure the reexperiencing, avoidance, and hyperarousal components of *DSM–IV* PTSD. Other items of the LASC tap physical status (e.g., appetite), social competence, general psychological distress, and suicidality. Individuals rate symptoms according to how much they are "a problem," ranging from 0 ("no problem") to 4 ("extreme problem"). In addition to a dichotomous PTSD indication, the LASC provides continuous measures of (a) general PTSD severity (sum of the 17 items); (b) three PTSD subscales (separate sums of the items representing reexperiencing, avoidance, and arousal; and (c) general distress and adjustment problems (the sum of all 43 items).

Originally named the Symptom Checklist (SCL; Foy et al., 1984), the LASC has been validated in a number of studies across a broad range of traumas (e.g., Berthold, 2000; Briere, 1995; Eriksson, Van de Kemp, Gorsuch, Hoke, & Foy, 2001; Lang, Kennedy, & Stein, 2002). In a review of similar (albeit earlier) studies, as well as based on a newer analysis of 874 mixed trauma research participants, King et al. (1995) concluded that the LASC has high internal and test–retest reliability, as well as acceptable convergent validity with respect to the Structured Clinical Interview for *DSM–IV–R* (SCID–R).

**Posttraumatic Stress Disorder Checklist.** The PTSD Checklist (PCL; Weathers, Litz, Herman, Huska, & Keane, 1993) is a 17-item measure that evaluates, on a 5-point scale, the extent to which respondents have been "bothered" by the symptoms of PTSD over the previous month. There are three versions of the PCL: two that do not refer to a specific stressor (the PCL–M for military service-related traumas, and the PCL–C for civilian trauma exposure), and one civilian version (the PCL–S) that links all symptoms to a specific event. The various versions of the PCL can be used as continuous measures of symptom severity by summing across the 17 items, or they can yield a possible diagnosis by considering items with a score of 3 or greater as symptoms and then applying *DSM–IV* PTSD criteria. In a sample of 123 Vietnam veterans, the PCL was very reliable ($\alpha = .97$, test–retest $r = .96$), demonstrated convergent validity, and had good sensitivity (.82) and specificity (.83) for a SCID diagnosis of PTSD (Weathers et al., 1993). An even higher diagnostic efficiency was found in the PCL's prediction of CAPS PTSD in a sample of 40 motor vehicle and sexual assault victims (Blanchard, Jones-Alexander, Buckley, & Forneris, 1996). A Spanish translation of the PCL has recently been developed (Orlando & Marshall, 2002). The PCL is widely used in posttraumatic stress research (e.g., Cordova, Studts, Hann, Jacobsen, & Andrykowski, 2000; Mueser et al., 2001).

**Mississippi Scale for Combat-Related Posttraumatic Stress Disorder.** The Mississippi Scale for Combat-Related PTSD (MSCRP; Keane, Caddell, & Taylor, 1988) is a 35-item instrument developed to measure PTSD in veterans of war. All items are anchored in war experiences, and respondents rate symptomatology that has occurred "since I was in the military" on 5-point Likert-like scales. This instrument is one of the most commonly used PTSD measure for veteran populations. It has been shown to have very good reliability (i.e., test–retest and internal consistency coefficients in the .90s; Keane et al., 1988; Kulka et al., 1990; McFall, Smith, McKay, & Tarver, 1990) and is generally felt to have among the higher correlation for combat-related PTSD among similar research measures (McFall et al., 1990; McFall, Smith, Roszell, Tarver, & Malas, 1990; Watson, 1990). For these reasons, the Mississippi Scale was chosen for use in the national survey component of the National Vietnam Veterans Readjustment Study (NVVRS).

**Civilian Mississippi Scale and Revised Mississippi Scale.** The Civilian Mississippi Scale (CMS), developed by Keane and colleagues, was used as an experimental scale in the NVVRS study as a way to evaluate the rate of PTSD in nonveterans (Vreven, Gudanowski, King, & King, 1995). The CMS contains 11 reexperiencing and situational avoidance items, 11 withdrawal and numbing items, 8 arousal items, and 5 guilt and suicidality items. Like the Mississippi Scale, this instrument does not yield subscale scores. All items of the CMS are rated on 5-point scales, enquiring about "the past," but the response anchors vary from item to item (e.g., "never true" to "always true" versus "never" to "very frequently" versus "not at all true" to "almost always true"). Lauterbach, Vrana, King, and King (1997) noted that although the CMS was internally consistent in their study ($\alpha = .89$) and could discriminate traumatized from non-traumatized respondents, "its relationship with measures of PTSD was weaker than its relationship with measures of depression and anxiety, suggesting that it may be more of a general measure of distress" (p. 499).

In response to some of the problems associated with the CMS, Norris and Perilla (1996) developed a Revised Civilian Mississippi Scale (RCMS). This measure consists of 28 items from the original CMS, as well as two items from Norris's (1990) Traumatic Stress Schedule. The RCMS is anchored in undetermined past trauma, referred to as "the event" (e.g., "Since the event, unexpected noises make me jump"). Also, in contrast to the CMS, all items are rated on the same 5-point scale (1 = "not at all true," 5 = "extremely true"). As opposed to the CMS, this measure has the expected three subscales (Reexperiencing, Avoidance, and Arousal), all of which are reasonably reliable.

**Posttraumatic Stress Disorder Symptom Scale–Self Report and Modified Posttraumatic Stress Disorder Symptom Scale–Self Report.** As noted, the rater version of the PSS was developed by Foa et al. (1993) to assess PTSD symptoms in rape victims. Similarly, each of the 17 PTSD Symptom Scale–Self Report (PSS–SR) items are anchored in rape experiences, although a revised version (described below) is usable for assessing the impacts of other traumatic events. Respondents rate each item in terms of its severity in the previous two weeks. Responses are made on four-point scales ranging from 0 (not at all) to 3 (very much). A rating of 1 or higher is required for the symptom to be considered present. In a sample of 44 rape victims, the three subscales of the PSS–SR (Reexperiencing, Avoidant, and Arousal) were reasonably reliable, demonstrated good concurrent validity with other measures, and had some convergent validity with the SCID (sensitivity of .62 and specificity of 1.0).

The PSS–SR has been modified by Falsetti, Resnick, Resick, and Kilpatrick (1993) for use with other trauma populations. This version, named the Modified PTSD Symptom Scale–Self Report (MPSS–SR), contains two rating scales per item: one for the frequency of each symptom over the last two weeks and one for how distressing it was.

**Screen for Posttraumatic Symptoms.** The Screen for Posttraumatic Symptoms (SPTSS; Carlson, 2001) was developed as a PTSD screening measure. In contrast to many other brief (i.e., 17-item) instruments, however, this test does not assess symptoms associated with a single traumatic event. Instead, like the PCL or TSI, it inquires about any PTSD-related symptoms experienced by the respondent, irrespective of its specific etiology. The SPTSS total score appears to be internally consistent, yielding an $\alpha$ of .91 in a sample of 136 psychiatric inpatients (Carlson, 2001). In addition, the total scale score correlates as expected with other brief trauma impact measures. Using the recommended cutoff of 4.0, the SPTSS had a sensitivity of .94 and a specificity of .60 in the prediction of PTSD, using as a criterion measure the Structured Interview for Posttraumatic Stress Disorder (SI–PTSD; Davidson, Kudler, & Smith, 1989). Although other cutoffs would have yielded a different balance of sensitivity and specificity, Carlson chose this score to maximize the likelihood that the SPTSS would identify most actual cases of PTSD in clinical groups. The low specificity of this score, of course, means that some non-PTSD cases will be identified as potentially PTSD-positive.

**Purdue Posttraumatic Stress Disorder Scale and Purdue Posttraumatic Stress Disorder Scale–Revised.** The Purdue PTSD Scale (PPS) was developed a number of years ago at Purdue University but rarely appeared in early published works (although see Figley, 1989). This 15-item measure of combat-related PTSD was designed to tap *DSM–III* criteria and thus is less relevant to *DSM–IV* diagnostic requirements. Of the 15 items, 11 relate to symptoms experienced within the last seven days, and four assess symptoms that have occurred since the respondents' war experience. Symptoms are rated on scales ranging from 1 ("not at all") to 4 ("extremely") (Hendrix, Anelli, Gibbs, & Fournier, 1994). Given the lack of concordance with *DSM–IV* PTSD criteria and its explicit focus on combat veterans, the PPS was revised by Lauterbach and Vrana (1996), who expanded the measure to tap *DSM–III-R* (and, later, *DSM–IV*) criteria in general trauma populations. In addition, the scales now uniformly examine symptoms over a four-week period, and use a 5-point scale ranging from "not at all" to "often."

**Penn Inventory for Posttraumatic Stress Disorder.** The Penn Inventory for PTSD (Hammarberg, 1992) is a 26-item scale that diverges somewhat from the approach used by most other PTSD scale developers. Items consist of four statements about a feeling or thought that represent increasing levels of symptom intensity. The respondent chooses the statement that best describes him- or herself, and the corresponding value of the statement (ranging from 0 to 3) is the item score. The scale generates a total PTSD score, without subscales. In two samples of Vietnam veterans and one mixed sample, Hammarberg (1992) found the Penn to have excellent reliability and stability over a five-day period. Unusually high hit rates with respect to PTSD diagnoses were found for this scale: sensitivities ranged from .90 to .98 across the three samples, and specificities were 1.0, .94, and .61, respectively. In a more recent study of 80 traumatized outpatients, the Penn Inventory had sensitivities of .90 and .89 for males and females, respectively, but relatively low specificities of .55 and .67 for males and female participants (Scragg, Grey, Lee, Young, & Turner, 2001). The authors concluded that the Penn Inventory may serve better as a screening instrument than a diagnostic test.

**Harvard Trauma Questionnaire.** The trauma section of the Harvard Trauma Questionnaire (HTQ) was described in chapter 4. This measure also has a symptom section, consisting of both PTSD and non-PTSD items. The PTSD component consists of 16 items that can be scored to suggest a *DSM–IV* diagnosis of PTSD. There are also 14 items that evaluate other stress symptoms. Although there are relatively little psychometric data available on this measure, the HTQ may be especially helpful when examining severe, politically motivated trauma, including torture (Kleijn, Hovens, & Rodenburg, 2001; Mollica et al., 1992; Smith Fawzi et al., 1997, and when applied to residents of Indo-China. When administered to individuals from other areas, only the 16 PTSD items may be directly applicable without significant further adaptation, because the remaining items of the HTQ are intended to be relatively specific to the culture in which it is applied.

## Posttraumatic Stress Scales–Acute Stress Disorder–Related

There are only two objective measures of ASD available to researchers, one that measures ASD symptoms on a continuum, and one that is used more frequently to generate a *DSM–IV* diagnosis. The relative dearth of tools in this area is no doubt related to the fact that ASD was introduced in *DSM–IV*, and thus is relatively new to researchers.

**Stanford Acute Stress Reaction Questionnaire.** The Stanford Acute Stress Reaction Questionnaire (SASRQ; Cardeña, Koopman, Classen, & Spiegel, 1996) was the first measure of ASD symptoms to appear in the traumatic stress literature. Unlike the only other measure of ASD, the Acute Stress Disorder Scale (ASDS; Bryant, Moulds, & Guthrie, 2000—reviewed later in this chapter), the SASRQ does not generate a dichotomous *DSM–IV* diagnosis of ASD. This measure consists of an open-ended question about the characteristics of the traumatic event, a 5-point item asking "How disturbing was this event to you," 30 items tapping the *DSM–IV* diagnostic criteria for ASD, and an item regarding the duration of "the worst symptoms of distress." There are both English and Spanish versions of this measure.

The current version of the SASRQ is undergoing psychometric evaluation. Preliminary analyses suggest that it is internally consistent and relatively stable across time when no traumas intervene (Cardeña, Koopman, Classen, Waelde, & Spiegel, 2000). The various versions of the SASRQ demonstrate predictive validity with respect to a variety of traumas, including earthquakes (Cardeña & Spiegel, 1993), fires (Koopman, Classen, & Spiegel, 1996), and witnessing an execution (Freinkel, Koopman, & Spiegel, 1994). As expected, this scale also predicts later PTSD (e.g., Birmes et al., 2001; Spiegel, Koopman, Cardeña, & Classen, 1996). Normative data on the SASRQ are not available at present but reportedly are being collected (Koopman et al., 1995; Cardeña et al., 2000).

## Dissociation Measures

Those studying dissociation have generally used the same measure (described below) since the mid-1980s, only recently broadening their measurement approach to take into account two newly considered forms of this construct (peritraumatic dissociation and somatoform dissociation). As a result, there are few nonstandardized measures of dissociation available to researchers.

**Dissociative Experiences Scale.** The Dissociative Experiences Scale (DES; Bernstein & Putnam, 1986) is the best known and most often used of the dissociation measures. The 28 items of the DES tap "disturbance in identity, memory, awareness, and cognitions and feelings of derealization or depersonalization or associated phenomena such as deja vu and absorption" (Bernstein & Putnam, 1986, p. 729). Various factor analytic studies suggest that the DES consists of three factors (amnesia, depersonalization and derealization, and absorption and imaginative involvement; e.g., Alper et al., 1997; Amdur & Liberzon, 1996; Ross, Joshi, & Currie, 1991).

The DES has been shown to have good internal consistency and test–retest reliabilities (Bernstein & Putnam, 1986; Dubester & Braun, 1995). Furthermore, DES scores discriminate trauma victims and those with dissociative disorders in a wide variety of studies (see Carlson & Armstrong [1994] and van IJzendoorm & Schuengel [1996] for reviews). In a study of 1051 psychiatric patients (Carlson et al., 1993), a score of 30 or higher on the DES correctly identified 74% of those with Multiple Personality Disorder (MPD; now Dissociative Identity Disorder) and 80% of those without MPD. In a comprehensive meta-analysis of DES studies, van IJzendoorm and Schuengel (1996) concluded that the DES has good to excellent reliability, convergent validity, and predictive validity, but that its discriminant validity suffers by virtue of the DES's moderate correlation with measures of general distress.

Because the DES is a popular and well-validated dissociation measure, trauma clinicians sometimes administer it in the context of a psychological test battery. If the inclusion of the DES is to determine the existence of dissociative identity disorder (DID), using the 30-point cutoff, the clinician should note in his or her report the only moderate sensitivity and specificity of that cutoff. Armstrong (1995) noted that it is not at all unusual for a person without DID to achieve a DES score of well above 30, and stated that

> no matter how high the [DES] score, we should never conclude that this score confirms that the patient has DID. We can only say that we have cause to suspect that the patient may have a dissociative disorder and that we need to investigate our hypothesis further. (p. 20)

**Peritraumatic Dissociative Experiences Questionnaire.** Unlike the DES, the Peritraumatic Dissociative Experiences Questionnaire (PDEQ; Marmar, Weiss, & Metzler, 1996) examines victims' self-reports of dissociation that occurred during the traumatic event. In support of the need for such a measure, Marmar, Weiss, Metzler, Ronfeldt, and Foreman (1996) cited research (e.g., Koopman, Classen, & Speigel, 1994) suggesting that dissociative response during trauma is a specific risk factor for later PTSD. As a result, the authors suggested that assessment of peritraumatic dissociative phenomena provides important information regarding longer-term psychological response to traumatic events.

The PDEQ was initially developed as a 9-item measure, although it now has 10 items. There are both rater and self-report versions. Victims are asked on the PDEQ to recall how they felt and what they experienced during a specific traumatic event. The self-report version has respondents rate each item on a four-point scale (ranging from "not at all" to "extremely"), whereas in the rater version responses are coded as "Don't know," "Absent or false," "Subthreshold," and "Threshold." Recent research with 9- and 10-item self-report and rater versions suggests that this instrument has good reliability, is associated with other measures of dissociation and posttraumatic stress, and increases with greater levels of exposure to traumatic events (Marmar et al., 1996). Recently, a reliable and valid 8-item version has been created by another group of investigators, modified to be more understandable to diverse ethnic and socioeconomic groups (Marshall, Orlando, Jaycox, Foy, & Belzberg, 2002).

As noted in chapter 2, although a number of studies have found a relationship between peritraumatic dissociation and subsequent PTSD (e.g., Birmes et al., 2001; Fullerton et al. , 2001; O'Toole, Marshall, Schureck, & Dobson, 1999; Tichenor, Marmar, Weiss, Metzler, & Ronfeldt, 1996), others (e.g., Briere, Scott, & Weathers, 2003; Holeva & Tarrier, 2001; Marshall & Schell, 2002; Mellman, David, Bustamante, Fins, & Esposito, 2001) found somewhat different results, especially at the multivariate level. Although the PDEQ appears to be a good measure of a statistical risk factor for ASD and subsequent PTSD, the causal relationship between these phenomena remains a focus of active study (Briere, Scott, & Weathers, 2003; Harvey & Bryant, 2002).

**Somatoform Dissociation Questionnaire.** The Somatoform Dissociation Questionnaire (SDQ; Nijenhuis, Spinhoven, Van Dyck, Van der Hart, & Vanderlinden, 1996) specifically evaluates "somatoform" dissociation (i.e., involving bodily perceptions and disturbance of a dissociative nature) and thus varies significantly from the other dissociation measures described in this chapter. There are two versions of the SDQ: the SDQ–20, which evaluates the severity of somatoform dissociative phenomena, and the SDQ–5—based on a logistic regression analysis of the SDQ–20 (Nijenhuis, Spinhoven, Van Dyck, Van der Hart, Vanderlinden, & Johan, 1997)—which is a screening instrument for the presence of a dissociative disorder. The SDQ–20 has good reliability and convergent validity and appears to measure a coherent latent domain (Nijenhuis, Spinhoven, Van Dyck, Van der Hart, & Vanderlinden, 1998). The SDQ–5 evidences predictive validity in two studies, with high sensitivity and specificity in discriminating dissociative disorders from other psychiatric disorders in a sample of 100 patients (.94 and .96, respectively), and DID patients from patients with a dissociative disorder not otherwise specified (DDNOS) in a smaller ($N = 31$) sample (.94 and .98 respectively; Nijenhuis et al., 1997, 1998).

## Trauma-Related Cognitive Measures

Growing awareness of the cognitive impacts of trauma exposure has lead to the development of several research measures of trauma-related helpless, hopelessness, self-blame, expectation of danger from others, and related constructs. Two of the best known of these measures are presented.

**World Assumptions Scale.** The 33-item World Assumptions Scale (WAS; Janoff-Bulman, 1989, 1992) measures perceived self-worth and the extent to which others and the world are seen as benevolent and meaningful. The subscales of the WAS (Benevolence of the World, Self-Worth, Benevolence of People, Justice, Controllability, Randomness, Self-Controllability, and Luck) are not linked to any given trauma, but several (Benevolence of People, Controllability, and Self-Controllability) have been shown to discriminate people with victimization histories from those without interpersonal trauma (Janoff-Bulman, 1989; Pyevich, Newman, & Daleiden, 2003; Solomon, Iancu, & Tyano, 1997). WAS subscales are moderately internally consistent, with α's ranging from .67 to .78 (Janoff-Bulman, 1989).

**Posttraumatic Cognitions Inventory.** The 33 items of the Posttraumatic Cognitions Inventory (PTCI; Foa, Ehlers, Clark, Tolin, & Orsillo, 1999) are linked to a single, unspecified traumatic event the respondent has experienced. The individual is asked to "tell us how much you agree or disagree with each statement" on a 1 (totally disagree) to 7 (totally agree) scale. A typical item is "The event happened because of the way I acted." The PTCI consists of three scales, Negative Cognitions About Self, Negative Cognitions About the World, and Self-Blame, which generally conform to the factor analytic results for this measure. Internal consistency for these scales range from .86 to .97. Scale test–retest reliabilities ranged from .74 to .89 across one week and, in a second sample, from .80 to .86 across three weeks. The PCTI scales exhibited convergent validity vis-à-vis other trauma-related cognition measures, correlated with PTSD severity, and were higher for traumatized individuals with PTSD than those who had experienced trauma but did not have PTSD or those with no trauma exposure (Foa et al., 1999).

## Trama-Related Grief Measures

As noted in chapter 2, the study of trauma-related grief is relatively new, only gaining its current level of attention since recent terrorist attacks on U.S. soil (e.g., the Oklahoma City bombing and the attacks on the World Trade Center). As a result, researchers have only recently undertaken the measurement of traumatic grief as a construct separate from depression, general loss, or posttraumatic stress. However, one nonstandardized measure (and its revision) is especially promising.

   **Inventory of Complicated Grief (and Inventory of Complicated Grief–Revised.** Measurement of complicated or traumatic grief is still at its early stages, and there are, as yet, no normed measures of this construct. However, the Inventory of Complicated Grief (ICG; Prigerson, Frank, Kasl, et al., 1995) and its subsequent revision (the ICG–R; Prigerson & Jacobs, 2001) have very good psychometric characteristics. Both the ICG and ICG–R are highly reliable, with ($\alpha$ values in the mid to high .90s for both instruments, and test–retest coefficients [for the ICG] of .80; Prigerson, Maciejewski, Reynolds, et al., 1995; Prigerson et al., 2002; Prigerson & Jacobs, 2001). Further, both measures have substantial content validity in the evaluation of complicated (as opposed to normal) grief responses. The 37-item ICG–R yields both a continuous total score and a dichotomous diagnosis of "Complicated Grief." The latter diagnosis was found in one study to have a sensitivity of .93 and a specificity of .93 in the detection of interview-determined complicated grief (Barry, Kasl, & Prigerson, 2002). In a study of friends of suicide victims (Prigerson, Bridge, Maciejewski, et al., 1999), an ICG–R determination of complicated grief was associated with five times greater likelihood of suicidal ideation than those without complicated grief, after controlling for depression. The ICG–R is a good example of a research measure that, were it to be normed and standardized, would be a useful clinical test.

## Multiscale Inventories

Multiscale trauma instruments allow measurement of a range of posttraumatic outcomes, rather than a single symptom cluster, and thus support the evaluation of more complex relationships to traumatic events. However, there is only one nonstandardized multiscale trauma measure commonly used in clinical research.

**Trauma Symptom Checklist–40.** The Trauma Symptom Checklist–40 (TSC–40; Briere & Runtz, 1989; Elliott & Briere, 1992) is a 40-item self-report research measure that evaluates symptomatology in adults arising from childhood and adult traumatic experiences. The TSC–40 is an expanded version of the Trauma Symptom Checklist–33 (TSC–33; Briere & Runtz, 1989). It consists of five scales (Dissociation, Anxiety, Depression, Post-Sexual Abuse Trauma–hypothesized [PSAT–h], and Sleep Disturbance) and a total score. Each TSC symptom item is rated according to its frequency over the previous two months, using a 4-point scale ranging from 0 ("never") to 3 ("often"). Studies using the TSC–33 and TSC–40 indicate that they are moderately reliable measures that are useful in the study of a variety of traumatic stressors (e.g., Classen et al., 2002; Elklit, 2002; Follette et al., 1996; Gold & Cardeña, 1998). Despite its frequent use as a measure of trauma impacts in clinical research, the TSC–40 does not include a number of symptoms associated with PTSD and thus should not be used as a measure of that disorder.

# Standardized Tests

As opposed to the tests described earlier, there are a number of relatively new measures that, by virtue of their standardization, psychometric qualities, and, in most cases, their normative data, are appropriate for general use in clinical settings. The small number of tests that meet these requirements, however, highlights the need to further instrument development in the psychological trauma field.

## Posttraumatic Stress Scales–Posttraumatic Stress Disorder–Related

Most standardized tests of posttraumatic stress are used in clinical settings to diagnose PTSD. Of the three major tests in this area, two are essentially 17-item measures, and one evaluates a broader range of outcomes.

**Posttraumatic Stress Diagnostic Scale.** The Posttraumatic Stress Diagnostic Scale (PDS; Foa, 1995) evaluates the presence of PTSD by examining four relevant domains: exposure to potentially traumatic events, characteristics of the most traumatic event, 17 symptoms corresponding to *DSM–IV* PTSD criteria, and extent of symptom interference in the individual's daily life. The frequency of each symptom is rated on a four-point scale, ranging from 0 ("not at all or only one time" to 3 ("5 or more times a week/almost always"). Although the measure described in the manual is named as above, the primary article describing this measure (Foa, Cashman, Jaycox, & Perry, 1997) refers to it as the "Posttraumatic Diagnostic Scale."

The PDS demonstrates high internal consistency ($\alpha$ = .92 for the 17 symptom items) and good test–retest reliability ($\kappa$ = .74 for PTSD diagnosis over a 10- to 22-day period). The PDS manual describes good sensitivity (.82) and specificity (.77) ($\kappa$ agreement = .59) with respect to a SCID PTSD diagnosis (Foa, 1995).[1] Because this instrument is criterion-based (i.e., evaluates whether a client meets *DSM–IV* diagnostic criteria for PTSD), general population norms are not required for its central function. The PDS does not yield standardized T-scores but rather defines PTSD symptom severity as "mild," "moderate," "moderate to severe," or "severe." The cutoff scores used to determine these severity levels were inferred from a sample of women with sexual or physical assault histories. Foa (1995) noted that these cutoffs are only estimates of PTSD severity, probably because the degree of assault-related posttraumatic stress in her female assault victim sample may or may not compare to those of female victims of other types of trauma or of males with trauma histories of any type.

**Davidson Trauma Scale.** The Davidson Trauma Scale (DTS; Davidson et al., 1997; Davidson, Tharwani, & Connor, 2002) is a 17-item scale measuring each *DSM–IV* symptom of PTSD on 5-point frequency and severity scales. Because it is a PTSD diagnostic test, there are no associated normative data for interpreting

---

[1] The later article on the "Posttraumatic Diagnostic Scale" (Foa et al., 1997) reports a sensitivity of .89, a specificity of .75, and a $\kappa$ of .65. According to the author, these postmanual statistics are more accurate, reflecting additional analyses (E. Foa, personal communication, September 28, 2003).

test scores. This measure yields a total score, as well as scales for Intrusion, Avoidance/Numbing, and Hyperarousal.

The DTS appears to have good test–retest reliability and internal consistency, as well as concurrent validity. Criterion validity has been assessed vis-à-vis the SCID, where the DTS was found to have a sensitivity of .69 and a specificity of .95. Although this agreement with positive SCID PTSD cases is less than stellar, the high specificity supports its use as a conservative measure of posttraumatic stress. In a recent study, Davidson et al. (2002) found that the sensitivity of the DTS in detecting medication (SSRI) effects on posttraumatic stress was equal to, or better than, those found for three other trauma measures, including the CAPS.

**Detailed Assessment of Posttraumatic Stress.** The Detailed Assessment of Posttraumatic Stress[2] (DAPS; Briere, 2001) is a 104-item inventory that provides information on an adult client's history of various types of trauma exposure (Trauma Specification and Relative Trauma Exposure), as well as scales that tap his or her immediate cognitive, emotional, and dissociative reactions (Peritraumatic Distress and Peritraumatic Dissociation), subsequent posttraumatic stress symptoms (Reexperiencing, Avoidance, and Hyperarousal), and level of experienced disability (Posttraumatic Impairment) in the context of a specific traumatic event. In addition to a narrative report, the DAPS interpretive program (Briere, Goldin, & Rodriguez, 2003) provides additional information on the Avoidance scale, yielding separate scores for Effortful Avoidance and Numbing symptom clusters. Like the PDS and DTS, the DAPS provides a potential *DSM–IV* diagnosis of PTSD. This measure has two validity scales that evaluate under- and overreport of symptoms (Positive Bias and Negative Bias, respectively), and three scales that measure common trauma/PTSD-related comorbidities (Trauma-specific Dissociation, Substance Abuse, and Suicidality).

---

[2]It should be noted that the author of this book has developed a number of the trauma-relevant tests described here and elsewhere. The reader should keep this proprietary connection in mind when considering his recommendations. That said, however, the author has endeavored to evaluate all tests objectively, including his own.

The DAPS was normed on 433 adults in the general population who had experienced at least one *DSM–IV* Criterion A trauma. The scales of this instrument are internally consistent, with an average clinical scale $\alpha$ of .82. In the validation sample, DAPS scales tapping posttraumatic stress symptoms (Reexperiencing, Avoidance, and Hyperarousal) were strongly associated with other measures of the same constructs (e.g., the IES and relevant scales of the CAPS). The associated features scales of the DAPS demonstrate evidence of discriminant validity: the DAPS Peritraumatic Dissociation scale correlates highest with the PDES, the Trauma-specific Dissociation scale is most related to the Multiscale Dissociation Inventory (MDI; Briere, 2002b) total score, Substance Abuse has the highest correlation with the PAI Alcohol and Drug scales, and Suicidality is most associated with the PAI Suicidal Ideation scale. The DAPS has good sensitivity (.88) and specificity (.86) in detecting CAPS PTSD status, with an associated $\kappa$ of .73.

## Posttraumatic Stress Scales–Acute Stress Disorder–Related

Because ASD was only introduced in *DSM–IV*, there are only two standardized instruments available for its clinical measurement. Both of these tests generates a potential diagnosis of ASD, although the first, described below, has more data supporting its validity thus far.

**Acute Stress Disorder Scale.** The Acute Stress Disorder Scale (ASDS; Bryant, Moulds, & Guthrie, 2000) is a 19-item instrument developed to assist in the diagnosis of ASD and to predict later PTSD. Although there are no normative data available for this measure, its adherence to *DSM–IV* ASD criteria and excellent diagnostic utility results justify its tentative inclusion here as a clinical measure. However, the ASDS has been validated only by one research project (Byant et al., 2000), albeit one that reports on five different studies, and thus further research is indicated to replicate the psychometrics reported here.

According to Bryant et al. (2000), the ASDS items correspond well with the ASD diagnostic criteria, as judged by a panel of five experts. Internal consistency of the ASDS was high (total score α = .96), and test–retest reliability of the total score was unusually good at r = .94 across two to seven days. ASDS reexperiencing, avoidance, and hyperarousal scale scores correlated as expected with equivalent scale scores on the IES and the Beck Anxiety Inventory (BAI; Beck, Epstein, Brown, & Steer, 1988), although the ASDS dissociation score did not correlate with the taxon score of the DES (DES–T; Waller, Putnam, & Carlson, 1996). Using a cutoff of greater than 9 for the dissociative scale, combined with a cutoff of greater than 28 on the sum of the reexperiencing, avoidance, and hyperarousal scales, the ASDS had a sensitivity of .95 and a specificity of .83 vis-à-vis a diagnosis of ASD on the ASDI. Although this is a very good result, the authors acknowledged that the items of the ASDS were modeled specifically on those of the ASDI and "therefore we would expect strong convergence between these two indexes" (p. 65).

**Detailed Assessment of Posttraumatic Stress.** The Detailed Assessment of Posttraumatic Stress (DAPS) yields a tentative ASD diagnosis, in addition to the PTSD assessment described earlier in this chapter. However, the ASD diagnosis is more advisory than definitive and has not yet been validated in terms of its agreement with an ASD interview such as the ASDI. The ASD decision rule (ASD1) presented in the professional manual is an approximation of the (somewhat complex) ASD criteria, reduced for easier scoring. The computerized interpretive algorithm for the DAPS (referred to as ASD2) uses the individual ASD diagnostic criteria of the DSM–IV and thus may be more accurate (Briere, Goldin, & Rodriguez, 2003).

## Dissociation Measures

Although dissociation is an important component of posttraumatic response, the vast majority of clinical assessment in this area has used the DES, as described. The only standardized and normed measure of dissociation is presented here.

**Multiscale Dissociation Inventory.** The Multiscale Dissociation Inventory (MDI; Briere, 2002b) is a 30-item self-report test of dissociative symptomatology. Each symptom is rated according to its frequency of occurrence over the previous month on a scale ranging from 1 (never) to 5 (very often). The MDI is normed on 444 trauma-exposed individuals from the general population, and has scales measuring six different type of dissociative responses: Disengagement, Depersonalization, Derealization, Emotional Constriction, Memory Disturbance, and Identity Dissociation. Scores on this measure can be converted to T-scores that allow for empirically based clinical interpretation of clients' level of dissociative disturbance. Because the different forms of dissociation are measured separately on the MDI, a "dissociation profile" is generated for each client, rather than the single dissociation score of other measures.

The MDI has been found to have good psychometric qualities in normative and validation samples. For example, Briere et al. (in press) factor analyzed the items of the MDI in a combined sample of 1,326 general population, clinical, and university participants and found five moderately intercorrelated (mean $r = .39$) factors that replicated the a priori scales of the MDI, except that the Depersonalization and Derealization scales formed a single factor. Differential relationships have been found between MDI scales and demographics, trauma history, clinical status, posttraumatic stress, and scores on other dissociation measures (e.g., Briere, 2002b; Dietrich, 2003). Further, a raw score of 15 or higher on the MDI's Identity Dissociation scale was found to identify 93% of those with diagnosis of DID[3] and 92% of those with no diagnosis of DID in a combined clinical/community sample (Briere, 2002b). However, this diagnostic utility has yet to be cross-validated in another sample.

## Trauma-Related Cognitive Measures

As noted at various points throughout this volume, research has increasingly revealed the importance of posttraumatic cognitions, both as a symptomatic response itself as well as an antecedent to negative emotional states and dysfunctional behavior. Although there are a number of clinical measures of general

---

[3] In all but two instances, diagnosis was based on the SCID–D.

cognitive disturbance available to the clinician, especially with regard to low self-esteem, there are few clinical tests of trauma-specific cognitive symptoms. Within the last several years, however, two standardized tests have become available.

**Trauma and Attachment Belief Scale.** Based on constructivist self-development theory (McCann & Pearlman, 1990; Pearlman, 1998; Pearlman & Saakvitne, 1995), the Trauma and Attachment Belief Scale (TABS; Pearlman, 2003) consists of 84 items that form 10 scales tapping internalized schema about self and others on five dimensions: Safety, Trust, Esteem, Intimacy, and Control. Quasi-normative values have been derived from 1,743 individuals, age 17 and older, based primarily on a regression-method interpolation of scores from the previous version of the TABS, then known as the Traumatic Stress Institute Belief Scale, Revision L (Pearlman, 1996). The TABS has good internal consistency and test–retest reliability (e.g., median values across scales of .79 and .75, respectively, in a sample of 260 college students). Previous versions of the TABS have been used to measure vicarious traumatization in therapists (e.g., Pearlman & Saakvitne, 1995), as well as to evaluate the effects of trauma (including childhood abuse) on college students, outpatients, battered women, and the homeless (Pearlman, 2003).

Although the TABS is a newly published clinical instrument with an unusual standardization approach, research on earlier versions of this test and a review of the specific scales and items of the TABS suggest that it is an important addition to existing measures of posttraumatic disturbance. In contrast to more symptom-based tests, the TABS measures the self-reported needs and expectations of trauma survivors and their perceptions of these phenomena in others. As a result, this measure is likely to be helpful in understanding important assumptions that the client carries in his or her relationships to others, including the therapist, and in formulating more relational (as opposed to solely symptom-focused) treatment goals.

**Cognitive Distortions Scale.** The Cognitive Distortions Scale (CDS; Briere, 2000b) is a 40-item test that measures five types of cognitive symptoms or distortions found among mental health clients and/or those who have experienced interpersonal victimization, including child abuse: Self-criticism, Self-blame, Helplessness, Hopelessness, and Preoccupation with Danger. Each item is rated according to its frequency of occurrence over the previous month, using a 5-point scale ranging from 1 ("never") to 5 ("very often"). CDS scales are internally consistent (with $\alpha$'s ranging from .89 to .97) and demonstrated convergent validity with other cognitive distortion measures in the standardization and validity samples. Validation studies reported in the manual indicate that CDS scales are predictive of interpersonal victimization history, suicidality, depression, and posttraumatic stress. Scales are normed separately for males and females, and can be expressed as T-scores.

## Multiscale Inventories

As described in chapter 6, broadband, multiscale inventories (e.g., the MMPI–2, PAI, and MCMI–III) are commonly used in clinical practice. However, there has been little equivalent development of such scales in the trauma field. This is unfortunate, because posttraumatic outcomes can range from PTSD to mood disturbance to dysfunctional behavior. The only standardized, multiscale trauma impacts measure currently available to the clinician is described next.

**Trauma Symptom Inventory.** The Trauma Symptom Inventory (TSI; Briere, 1995) contains 100 symptom-items, rated according to their frequency of occurrence on a four-point scale ranging from 0 ("never") to 3 ("often") over the previous six months. Because of the length of this time frame, the TSI identifies posttraumatic responses that may have occurred farther in the past and thus cannot generate a *DSM–IV* PTSD diagnosis.

The TSI has three validity scales and 10 clinical scales, all of which yield normative T-scores. The validity scales of the TSI are: Response Level, measuring a general underendorsement response style or a need to appear unusually symptom-free; Atypical Response, evaluating psychosis or extreme distress, a general overendorsement response set, or an attempt to appear especially disturbed or dysfunctional; and Inconsistent Response, measuring unusually inconsistent responses to similar TSI item-pairs. Although the validity scales have been shown to have convergent and discriminant validity vis-à-vis similar scales in other measures, one study suggested that the specific Atypical Response cutoff for invalidity may require a downward adjustment in forensic settings (Edens, Otto, & Dwer, 1998). The 10 clinical scales of the TSI are Anxious Arousal, Depression, Anger–Irritability, Intrusive Experiences, Defensive Avoidance, Dissociation, Sexual Concerns, Dysfunctional Sexual Behavior, Impaired Self Reference, and Tension Reduction Behavior.

The TSI was standardized on a random, mail-out sample of 828 adults whose demographics generally represent the U.S. general population. There are also normative data for military personnel, derived from a sample of 3,659 Navy recruits. Norms are available for four combinations of sex and age (males and females ages 18 to 54 and 55 or older). TSI scores vary slightly as a function of race (accounting for 2% to 3% of the variance in most scales), and minor adjustments for validity scale cutoffs are suggested for certain racial groups.

The clinical scales of the TSI are relatively consistent internally (mean α's ranging from .84 to .87 in general population, clinical, university, and military samples), and exhibit reasonable convergent, predictive, and incremental validity (Briere, 1995). In a standardization subsample, TSI scales demonstrated good convergent validity with independently assessed PTSD status (using Astin et al.'s, [1993] joint scoring of the IES and LASC), with a discriminant function specificity of .92 and sensitivity of .91. In a psychiatric inpatient sample, TSI scales identified 89% of those independently diagnosed with borderline personality disorder. Studies indicate that specific TSI scale elevations and configurations are associated with a variety of childhood and adult traumatic experiences (e.g., Briere et al., 1995; Green et al., 2000; Higgins & Follette, 2002; Runtz & Roche, 1999).

# Conclusion

This chapter has reviewed a number of trauma-specific instruments. Many of these tests are relatively new and thus have relatively short track records. Others are older but tend to have weaker psychometric characteristics or are limited to combat veterans. A number are more appropriately used as research measures than regular clinical tests. Even given these limitations, however, most of the instruments described in this chapter appear to be reliable and to have reasonably good sensitivity and specificity with regard to posttraumatic disturbance.

Despite the development of objective measures designed to yield a psychiatric diagnosis, a *DSM–IV* diagnosis of PTSD, ASD, or dissociative disorder should never be made based on paper-and-pencil measures alone. Instead, the diagnostic tests described in this chapter should be used to suggest the probability of a posttraumatic stress disorder, after which a diagnostic interview may be conducted to confirm or reject this finding.

Although the screening functions of the classic 17-item PTSD measures should not be discounted, especially in research contexts, a better use of trauma-specific tests ultimately may be to determine the relative type and level of posttraumatic stress or dissociation present for a given client. When the disorder of interest is PTSD, for example, the most helpful instruments should yield standardized, continuous scores on at least three different subscales, tapping posttraumatic reexperiencing, avoidance, and hyperarousal. If the associated features of PTSD are of interest, they should be expressed as separate subscales, rather than combining them with posttraumatic stress symptoms. An important psychometric goal for test authors or trauma researchers is to develop normative data for the best of the currently available research instruments and to ensure that future trauma-specific tests include full standardization data.

# 8

# Putting It All Together: Assessment of Pretrauma Functioning, Traumatic Events, Moderating Influences, and Posttraumatic States

The various chapters of this book have outlined a variety of assessment interviews and measures that are helpful in understanding posttraumatic states. The intent of this chapter is to integrate this (and additional) information into a practical form that can be applied to a comprehensive trauma assessment protocol. During this process, certain instruments will be highlighted as especially useful, although this will not mean that other measures are not acceptable. Based on the material outlined previously, the primary targets of assessment can be divided into six areas: (a) pretrauma functioning, (b) trauma exposure, (c) social supports, (d) comorbidity, (e) potential malingering or secondary gain, and (f) posttraumatic response. Whether each of these areas will be addressed in any given instance depends in part on the referral or assessment question, the amount of time or resources available to the assessor, and the extent to which the respondent can or will participate in evaluation. As a result, although each area will be reviewed in this chapter, it should not be assumed that all useful assessment reports will necessarily cover each of these areas in depth or at all.

# Pretrauma Psychological Functioning

It is often important to evaluate the client's pretrauma functioning to determine whether the client's current difficulties antedate the trauma or potentially arise from it. As well, knowledge of pretrauma psychological difficulties can provide insight into predisposing or exacerbating factors associated with a current posttraumatic state. For example, knowledge that a given client has a history of generalized anxiety disorder or prior posttraumatic stress disorder (PTSD) may help to explain why he or she develops seemingly "excessive" posttraumatic anxiety and hyperarousal in response to a moderately stressful event. Similarly, it would be helpful to know whether an individual who presents with a posttraumatic depression has had previous depressive episodes, grief reactions, or alcoholism, or that affective disorders "run in the family."

When possible and practical, the assessing clinician should investigate the following potential indicators of prior functioning:

- Previous psychological symptoms and disorders;
- Previous psychiatric or psychological treatment (including psychotherapy, prescribed psychoactive medications, electroconvulsive therapy, and any history of psychiatric hospitalization);
- Previous suicidality and history of suicide attempts
- Alcohol and drug abuse history;
- Previous occupational functioning (including its appropriateness to the client's intelligence level and education);
- Criminal and incarceration history;
- Premorbid social adjustment (e.g., living situation, number of friends, history of sustained sexual or romantic relationships);
- Evidence of pretrauma personality disturbance;
- Relevant medical history (e.g., history of brain injury or disorder); and
- Family history of depression, mania, psychosis, alcoholism, anxiety disorders, or other trauma-relevant disturbance.

Unfortunately, assessment of pretrauma functioning is not always easy. Individuals with ongoing psychological disturbance are sometimes poor historians—either underreporting previous symptoms because of memory problems or in an attempt to appear less chronically dysfunctional, or overstating previous disturbance in response to the distorting effects of current dysphoria or as a cry for help. Especially debilitating psychological states (e.g., psychosis, severe posttraumatic depression, or extreme dissociative withdrawal) or physical dysfunction (e.g., traumatic brain injury or physical disability) also may impede the client's ability to communicate with the evaluator regarding his or her previous level of functioning.

Because data gathered from the traumatized individual occasionally may be distorted or unreliable, information from collateral sources also should be collected when indicated and appropriate (Carlson & Dutton, 2003; Newman, Kaloupek, & Keane, 1996). These other sources of information may include spouses or cohabiting partners, family members, friends, coworkers, supervisors, teachers, and treating medical and psychological practitioners. When available, premorbid history may also be inferred from medical and psychotherapy files, police and prison records, and other institutional databases. However, the clinician should always be aware of confidentiality issues when consulting individuals other than the client regarding the client's psychological state, history, treatment status, and other relevant domains. The evaluator is advised to consult his or her professional ethics code (the 2002 APA code of ethics, in the case of psychologists) and both state and federal laws regarding his or her responsibilities in this area.

# Trauma Exposure

As has been discussed, it is not sufficient to know that an individual has been traumatized by an event. The evaluator should also ascertain the specific details of the stressor in terms of its type, duration, frequency, severity, and so on. as well as any significant prior traumatic events that the individual may have experienced.

Any of the "Criterion A" measures described in chapter 4 may assist the evaluator in assessing trauma exposure, as long as he or she ensures that there are behavioral definitions available for the various traumas listed by these instruments. As well, many of these interviews do not assess for the specific PTSD/acute stress disorder (ASD) A2 criteria of intense fear, horror, or helplessness, so the interviewer may have to independently inquire about these subjective responses before an ASD or PTSD diagnosis can be made.

Given these provisos, the most inclusive trauma exposure measures currently available appear to be the Potential Stressful Events Interview (PSEI; Falsetti et al., 1994) and the Traumatic Events Scale (TES; Elliott, 1992), either of which provides an extensive review of traumatic events and their specific characteristics. These measures also provide more definitional information than other similar instruments. In contrast to the TES, however, the PSEI requires additional inquiry regarding helplessness, horror, or terror. When a more brief measure is necessary, the clinician may wish to use the Traumatic Life Events Questionnaire (TLEQ; Kubany et al., 2000), which includes A2 and is much shorter than the PSEI or the TES. Alternatively, the Trauma Assessment for Adults (TAA; Resnick et al., 1993), or the revised version of the Traumatic Stress Schedule (TSS; Norris, 1992) may be helpful—in either case, however, A2 will have to be addressed through additional questions. If torture has occurred and the client is an Indochinese immigrant, the Harvard Trauma Questionnaire (HTQ; Mollica et al., 1992) may be especially useful. If previous combat experiences are relevant, use of one of the several combat exposure scales (e.g., the Combat Exposure Scale [CES; Keane et al., 1989]) is recommended.

When a detailed evaluation of childhood trauma is indicated, the most helpful measures appear to be the TES, the Childhood Trauma Questionnaire (CTQ; Bernstein et al., 1994), and the Child Maltreatment Interview Schedule (CMIS; Briere, 1992a). If psychological abuse is a major concern, the clinician should also consider the Childhood Maltreatment Questionnaire (CMQ; Demaré, 1993). Unfortunately, the CMIS and other maltreatment scales only evaluate childhood experiences of abuse and neglect, and thus cannot screen for non-abuse-related childhood traumas (e.g., neighborhood violence). For this reason, the TES may be preferable for rapid screening of general childhood trauma.

Finally, two trauma impacts measures, the Posttraumatic Stress Diagnostic Scale (PDS; Foa, 1995) and Detailed Assessment of Posttraumatic Stress (DAPS; Briere, 2001), also assess trauma exposure, and have the added benefit of addressing A2 issues. In the case of the PDS, however, only two of the three A2 criteria are investigated, and thus feeling "horrified" should be assessed as well.

For those clinicians who would rather use a more interview-based set of questions, the Initial Trauma Review–Revised (ITR–R; Briere, 1999) presented in the appendix may be helpful. If this entire interview is used, it will generate information on the client's overall trauma history as well as his or her A2 responses to each event. On other occasions, however, the clinician may choose a subset of these questions that are most relevant to the assessment issues at hand.

## Social Supports

As noted in chapter 1, social support after a stressful event is often associated with a more positive outcome. As a result, the level of social supports in the trauma victim's personal environment is an important assessment target. Although there are instruments available to measure social support, both in general and in the context of stress (see Meichenbaum, 1994, for a review), many clinicians evaluate this phenomenon more informally. For example, the client may be asked about the number and quality of friendships and family connections, their posttrauma availability, and whether they are perceived as, in fact, supportive.

Regarding the latter, it is useful to know whether the client is experiencing a "loss spiral" (Hobfoll, 1988), wherein his or her sustained need for support is draining social resources and producing further neediness and a growing sense of loss. The evaluator also should keep in mind that seemingly supportive individuals may, especially over time, communicate to the victim unhelpful messages—for example that he or she should "just get over it" or keep from expressing strong emotions associated with grief, despair, rage, or terror. Negative responses from one's social network in such contexts may be worse than no support at all (Andrews et al., 2003). As a result, the absolute number of potential social supports may be less relevant to trauma recovery than the quality and reliability of the victim's immediate interpersonal environment.

# Comorbidity

Because posttraumatic states often occur in the context of other psychological symptoms and disorders, comprehensive assessment of traumatized individuals also should include evaluation of less trauma-specific dysfunction. For this reason, it is recommended that one or more generic, multiscale measures of psychological disturbance be administered with more trauma-specific ones, and that test data be followed up with one or more clinical interviews.

Although there are many tests that yield important information on a broad range of psychological disturbance, clinical experience with trauma victims suggests the special validity of four: the Minnesota Multiphasic Personality Inventory–2 (MMPI–2; Millon, 1987), Psychological Assessment Inventory (PAI; Morey, 1991), Millon Clinical Multiaxial Inventory–III (MCMI–III; Millon, 1994), and Rorschach. The first two provide information on a variety of psychological disorders or symptom clusters, whereas the MCMI–III allows more detailed assessment of Axis II disturbance. The Rorschach, on the other hand, can yield data on more subtle and dynamic psychological processes that are unlikely to be accessed by objective tests. As well, all four have scales or special scores that address trauma-related symptomatology.

Which of these tests to use in a given circumstance is partially dependent on the amount of time and resources that are available, the client's overall level of tolerance for psychological testing, and the clinician's training or measure preference. If only a single generic test can be used, the MMPI–2 or PAI may be the best choice in many cases. If two tests can be administered, the MMPI or PAI can be augmented with the MCMI–III. If three generic tests are possible, the Rorschach can be added. Specific clinical situations may require different combinations of these and other tests, however. For example, clients with symptoms of bulimia or anorexia nervosa may benefit from the addition of the Eating Disorder Inventory (EDI–2; Garner, 1990).

Three additional comorbidity concerns relevant to posttraumatic states are suicidality, substance abuse, and medical and neurologic disorders. The first two are important coexisting problems for many of those experiencing significant posttraumatic disturbance. The third is often overlooked in trauma assessments despite its sometimes critical importance.

Suicidal thoughts and behaviors are relatively common among traumatized individuals, frequently arising from the depression, low self-esteem, loss, hopelessness, and overwhelming internal distress often associated with posttraumatic states. Elevated levels of suicidality have been documented in combat veterans (e.g., Adams, Barton, Mitchell, Moore, & Einagel, 1998; Centers for Disease Control, 1987) and victims of various forms of interpersonal violence (e.g., Brodsky et al., 2001; Ullman & Brecklin, 2002).

Although there are a number of instruments that tap suicidality (e.g., the Adult Suicidal Ideation Questionnaire [Reynolds, 1991]), the low base rate of actual suicidal behavior makes its psychometric prediction difficult (Bongar, 2002). Nevertheless, two tests that are frequently used in trauma assessment (the PAI and DAPS) each have suicidality scales that may alert the clinician to life threat issues. Above and beyond these scales, however, the clinician should always conduct a face-to-face suicide assessment interview with those suspected of suicidal intent. For excellent coverage of the various issues inherent in conducting such an interview, the reader is referred to Bongar (2002) and chapter 15 of Linehan's (1993) volume on treating borderline personality disorder.

Drug and alcohol abuse also is a well-known sequel of posttraumatic stress, as documented in studies of trauma victims (see Ouimette & Brown, 2003, for a review), perhaps especially child abuse survivors (e.g., Bulik, Prescott, & Kendler, 2001; Lisak & Miller, 2003). As a result, a detailed assessment of trauma victims usually includes evaluation of drug and alcohol use, either informally or through a structured interview or pencil and paper measure.

The advantage of a structured substance abuse evaluation, whether interview- or inventory-based, is that it provides comprehensive coverage of a wide variety of substances and typically quantifies the amount and frequency of use for each. This attention to detail is especially helpful because many substance abusers underestimate their consumption when asked global questions or have their own interpretations of what constitute psychoactive substances and their abuse. As a result, the clinician who only asks about alcohol and one or two drugs, or who inquires solely about "substance abuse," "alcoholism," or "addiction" may inadvertently facilitate client nondisclosure.

Fortunately for those using standardized diagnostic interviews, both the Structured Clinical Interview for DSM–IV (SCID; Spitzer et al., 1990) and the Diagnostic Interview Schedule (DIS; Robins & Heltzer, 1985) assess for substance use disorders. More detailed assessment is possible through the use of substance abuse measures such as the Michigan Alcoholism Screening Test (Selzer, 1971) or the Drug Abuse Screening Test (Skinner, 1992). For MMPI and MMPI–2 users, there is also the MacAndrews Scale (MacAndrew, 1965), which, although it contains no specific items regarding alcoholism or drug abuse, has reasonable sensitivity (but questionable specificity) in the detection of alcoholism (Jacobson, 1989). Unfortunately, scores on this measure may be confounded by race (Graham, 1987), as well as by criminality and legal substance use such as coffee or heavy cigarette smoking (Jacobson, 1989). Of the standardized self-report measures, both the PAI and DAPS assess substance abuse with specific scales. In general, significant elevations on either scale should trigger a face-to-face inquiry about drug or alcohol abuse.

A final comorbidity issue is that of medical or neurological disorder. Although not performed by nonmedical practitioners or, in some settings, psychiatrists, physical and laboratory examination of individuals presenting with significant posttraumatic disturbance is often indicated. As noted by Kudler and Davidson (1995)

> a number of physical disorders can mimic or exacerbate posttraumatic pathology. These include reactions to drugs (prescribed or abused), endocrine disorder (including hypo-

thalamic, pituitary, thyroid, adrenal, and diabetic dysfunction), neurologic disorders (including acute or chronic brain
injury endured in the trauma), cardiac, hepatic, and respira-
tory problems. (p. 76)

Especially relevant to posttraumatic presentations is the possibility of central nervous system pathology, such as seizure disorders, cognitive disorders arising from traumatic brain injury,
substance-induced mental disorders, and organic amnestic disorders due to head trauma (e.g., Kuyk, Spinhoven, Van Emde Boas,
& Van Dyck, 1999; Feinstein, Hershkop, Ouchterlony, Jardine,
& McCullagh, 2002; Harvey & Bryant, 2001). Because these conditions may arise from trauma or may mimic a variety of posttraumatic or dissociative symptoms, referral for a medical assessment
should occur whenever there is a significant possibility of a
physical etiology.

# Malingering or Secondary Gain

As described in chapter 3, malingering and potential secondary
gain can complicate the assessment of posttraumatic states. Although such behavior may be relatively rare in most clinical
contexts, the probability of malingering obviously increases in
certain situations. These include

□ Forensic settings where posttraumatic disturbance is being used as a defense against criminal prosecution or as
   a mitigating circumstance in sentencing;
□ In civil litigation, where a suit for psychological damages
   includes allegations of posttraumatic disturbance or
   dysfunction;
□ Instances where a finding of posttraumatic stress may
   result in financial compensation or wanted services (e.g.,
   in Veterans Administration settings, victim compensation
   hearings, Supplemental Social Security or disability applications); or
□ Where symptoms of posttraumatic stress or disorder
   would result in increased attention or support from the
   social milieu (e.g., in certain families or relationships).

It should be emphasized, however, that malingering is only a possible "rule out" in the these contexts, as opposed to an assured fact. For example, individuals claiming posttraumatic stress at disability hearings or in civil litigation often do suffer from posttraumatic difficulties. Although a person presenting with posttraumatic stress is as likely as anyone else to be misrepresenting, malingering, or seeking secondary gain, it should not be assumed beforehand that he or she is especially likely to be doing so.

When malingering is possible, the clinician should consider the client's general demeanor during the evaluation, the extent to which his or her symptoms correspond to what is known about posttraumatic states,[1] his or her past history of medical or mental health care (e.g., multiple brief admissions to a number of different treatment facilities, especially if records suggest malingering or factition) and, to some extent, the consistency of his or her reports of past history and previous symptoms.[2]

In addition to information gained from the assessment interview and review of records, chapter 3 outlines the potential utility of psychological tests in the evaluation of potential malingering. The two most common forms of test data in this regard are the results of instruments such as the Structured Interview of Reported Symptoms (SIRS; Rogers et al., 1992) and the interpretation of validity scales within inventories (e.g., the MMPI–2, PAI, MCMI–III, DAPS, or Trauma Symptom Inventory (TSI; Briere, 1995). Because the effects of traumatic stress on the SIRS (and related instruments) are not well documented, and traumatized individuals tend to have higher scores on "fake bad" validity scales, conclusions based on these data—in either direction— should be made with care and qualified when appropriate.

---

[1] PTSD-appropriate symptoms may be learned from reading books on trauma, however, and some lawyers have been accused of coaching their clients with regard to posttraumatic symptomatology.

[2] Although consistency of report is sometimes mentioned as a potential index of misrepresentation, some posttraumatic presentations (e.g., those involving significant dissociation or the normal waxing and waning of PTSD symptoms over time) can produce inconsistency that is not malingering.

# Posttraumatic Response

After considering the various precursors to and moderators of posttraumatic stress, the final issue is the specific measurement of posttraumatic response. As indicated in chapters 5 and 7, there are a variety of reliable and valid instruments and interviews in this area. As a result, the final choice of measures is often determined by the specific assessment goals at hand, along with relatively small differences between similar measures. In many cases, several instruments are administered simultaneously to tap both the specific posttraumatic responses of certain groups and general trauma-related dysfunction. For example, when combat-related trauma is being examined, many researchers and clinicians will want to add the Mississippi Scale for Combat-Related PTSD (Keane et al., 1988) to their test battery. Similarly, those evaluating the effects of torture and related trauma in Indochinese immigrants often administer the Harvard Trauma Questionnaire along with other measures.

## Structured Interviews

If a structured interview is required, a primary issue is whether posttraumatic stress, alone, is the focus, or whether other potentially comorbid disorders also are being assessed. In the latter case, the SCID probably is the most valid and useful, although it does not evaluate ASD or the dissociative disorders. The Structured Interview for Disorders of Extreme Stress (SIDES) also can yield useful information on more complex posttraumatic presentations, although the results it provides are not relevant to the *DSM–IV*. If only PTSD is being evaluated, one of the best measures appears to be the Clinician-Administered PTSD Scale (CAPS; Blake et al., 1995). This interview has very good psychometric characteristics and yields additional helpful data beyond the PTSD diagnosis. The extended time sometimes required to administer this measure (more than an hour in some cases), however, may make it less appealing when a quick diagnosis is needed. When ASD is the diagnostic issue, the Acute Stress Disorder Interview (ASDI; Bryant et al., 1998) is clearly superior to the SCID–D.

Several structured interviews are available for the evaluation of dissociative disorders. Of these, the SCID–D is most useful, because it is the only one to provide exact *DSM–IV* dissociative disorder diagnoses. Published psychometric data on the SCID–D are somewhat sparse thus far, although there is little reason to expect that this instrument does not perform as described.

## Inventories and Scales

As described in chapter 7, there are basically two kinds of objective measures that tap posttraumatic states: those that suggest a dichotomous *DSM–IV* diagnosis (primarily for PTSD or ASD) and those that measure the relative level of posttraumatic symptoms on one of more dimensions.

**Diagnostic measures.** The benefit of including a diagnostic measure in an assessment battery is that it provides a simple screen for the presence of PTSD or ASD and thus may prompt the evaluator to consider PTSD in his or her diagnostic formulation. The clinician should not overrely on these measures, however, especially those where each diagnostic criterion is tapped by a single item (i.e., in 17-item PTSD scales such as the PDS or PTSD Checklist [PCL; Weathers et al., 1993]). In such cases, a PTSD or ASD diagnosis may be inappropriately ruled in or out based on simple client errors (e.g., overlooking or misunderstanding one or two items). In fact, whenever using psychometric instruments, no diagnosis (or nondiagnosis) should be made on the basis of client response to written tests alone. Instead, diagnosis should arise from due consideration of test data *and* one or more diagnostic interviews.

Most of the measures in this group appear to operate in a similar fashion and probably work equally well in clinical practice. In fact, because they address the same diagnostic criteria (i.e., 17 items for the 17 PTSD criteria), the specific items of these various measures often are equivalent across instruments. One of these screens, the PDS, however, is likely to be superior for clinical applications, as long as the Criterion A issues described earlier are addressed. If a more detailed and comprehensive review of PTSD and related issues (e.g., trauma exposure, peritraumatic responses, substance abuse, suicidality, trauma-specific dissociation) is indicated, the DAPS may be the best choice. If the trauma has occurred within the last month, the ASDI is the best measure by virtue of its sensitivity and specificity to a *DSM–IV* diagnosis of ASD.

**Continuous trauma measures.** In contrast to diagnostic measures, there are a number of instruments whose primary function is to quantify the extent of a given posttraumatic state, rather than simply indicating the presence of a disorder. As noted in chapter 7, there are advantages and disadvantages of such measures. The primary benefit is that such tests allow the clinician to determine how traumatized or affected an individual actually may be, in the same way that a depression measure indicates the specific level of depression a person is experiencing. This information is often critical for the clinician, because it indicates the severity of the problem and the extent to which immediate intervention is indicated.

Unfortunately, some of the older instruments in this group have not been normed in the general population. As a result, the clinician who determines that his or her client has a given score on such tests often has little way of knowing the clinical significance of that score. Some researchers have partially addressed this problem by deriving cutting scores for what is likely to be disorder-level symptomatology. However, these scores often vary by sample and study, and such procedures still leave the clinician with dichotomous data rather than clinically meaningful continuous scores. Alternatively, clinicians may chose to compare a given client's test score to relevant means and standard deviations reported in published studies. This approach is not always ideal, however, because the study mean may be specific to the characteristics of that sample or may be an unstable estimate as a result of insufficient sample size. Finally, the use of "local" norms is sometimes a partial solution to nonstandardized tests. For example, if a clinic or trauma center has determined over time what a given score on instrument X means vis-à-vis a specific problem or symptom for their clientele, it may be possible to extrapolate clinical significance from scores on that test. This approach is more likely to be effective if (a) earlier data collection provides the mean, standard deviation, and standard error of test X in a representative sample of local clients, which is then used to assess the meaningfulness of "normal" versus "abnormal" scores, and (b) the client being tested "fits" the demographic and experiential profile of the sample of prior clients with which he or she is being compared.

The local norms solution may be generalized to broader applications on some occasions, primarily when a measure has been used so often with a certain type of client that clinicians have learned how to interpret a given scale with those individuals. Examples include use of the Mississippi with Vietnam veterans, the Dissociative Experiences Scale (DES; E. M. Bernstein & Putnam, 1986) with dissociative disorder clients, and the HTQ with immigrant torture survivors. Nevertheless, clinicians using this approach should be aware of the limitations of nonstandardized measures, and should interpret test scores on such measures with special care.

In contrast to nonstandardized measures, there are five normed posttraumatic stress-related self-report scales available to the clinician: three are PTSD scales of well-known psychological tests (the MMPI–2, PAI, and MCMI–III) and the other two are trauma-specific tests (the TSI and DAPS). The primary advantage of the former is that they can be used any time these general tests are used. Further, if at least two of these tests are included in the same battery, the clinician will have multiple sources of data on the same construct. The disadvantages of these scales are (a) the single "PTSD" score they render, as opposed to separate standardized scores for each PTSD cluster, (b) their tendency to weigh one component of PTSD over others (e.g., more intrusion items than avoidant or arousal ones), and (c) their only moderate sensitivity and specificity, partly due to the frequent inclusion of non-PTSD-related items in such scales. Nevertheless, the standardization of the MMPI, PAI, and MCMI allow quantitative interpretation of specific scale scores—an important requirement for modern psychological tests.

The TSI differs from the PTSD scales in that it assesses 10 separate types of posttraumatic responses, as well as three types of response validity. The wide range of symptoms tapped by the TSI, along with the fact that symptoms are not linked to a specific trauma, makes this measure a useful test of more complex posttraumatic outcomes, such as those associated with multiple interpersonal victimization experiences. In addition, the DAPS, although primarily a diagnostic test, also yield standardized continuous scores that provide information in a number of areas (e.g., peritraumatic distress, suicidality, substance abuse).

A full assessment of the trauma survivor will also involve evaluation of other phenomena closely linked to trauma exposure. Most importantly, these include self-capacities (i.e., the ability to regulate internal states, access a coherent sense of self, and develop and sustain meaningful interpersonal relationships) and dissociative symptoms.

There are few self-capacity measures available to the clinician, primarily the Inventory of Altered Self-Capacities (IASC; Briere, 2000a), Bell Object Relations and Reality Testing Inventory (BORRTI; Bell, 1995), and Trauma and Attachment Belief Scale (TABS; Pearlman, 2003), along with the Impaired Self-Reference (ISR) scale of the TSI. In most cases, the ISR will be a sufficient screen for self-difficulties, especially when the TSI is already being used. If the client is known to have significant problems with affect regulation, identity, or relationships, has distorted beliefs in the interpersonal domain, or carries a personality disorder diagnosis, more specific tests should be considered. These include the TABS, which evaluates relational cognitions associated with self and other, and the IASC, which surveys the range of self-capacity problems in depth. Clinicians with an object-relations perspective may prefer the BORRTI, which taps analytic constructs in the self domain. In addition, although not a self-report measure, the Rorschach is also useful in evaluating difficulties in the "self" area.

As indicated at various points in this book, dissociative symptomatology is a common effect of trauma exposure, especially if trauma began early in life and extended over time. Yet, many clinicians devote significantly less time to the evaluation of dissociative disturbance than they do to posttraumatic stress. This is unfortunate, because some dissociative symptoms can be quite debilitating, and the overuse of dissociative defenses can block trauma processing and, hence, recovery. As noted in chapter 7, the two most commonly used tests for dissociative symptoms are the DES and SCID–D. Although the DES is not normed on the general population, the oft-cited cutoff of 30 on this measure has moderate sensitivity (.74) and specificity (.80) in the detection of dissociative identity disorder (DID). This levels of accuracy, although reasonably high, nevertheless means that a significant number of DID-positive or -negative individuals will be misclassified (Armstrong, 1995). In addition, because it yields a single score, it is less informative about the range of dissociative symptom clusters or disorders. However, if the question is whether or not a given client has dissociative symptoms, per se, and the clinician is conversant with DES scores in clinical groups or will apply the Carlson et al. cutoff score, the DES can be an appropriate choice for a trauma test battery.

In contrast to the DES, the SCID–D and Multiscale Dissociation Inventory (MDI; Briere, 2002b) test provide data on the specific types of dissociation experienced by the client. In the case of the SCID–D interview, this information can provide a *DSM–IV* diagnosis for each of the dissociative disorders. The MDI, on the other hand, generally cannot provide diagnoses, although a raw score of 15 on its Identity Dissociation (IDDIS) scale identified more than 90% of those with or without a DID diagnosis in one study (Briere, 2002b). Instead, the MDI allows the clinician to evaluate a range of different types of dissociation, and yields standardized (*T*) scores that indicate how severe each type of dissociation is relative to the general population.

The decision of which dissociation measure to use in a given clinical situation depends on the goal of assessment. The DES is best used as a screener for the overall presence of dissociative symptoms, whereas the MDI provides information on the type and relative severity of six different symptom clusters. When it is important to know both the specific type(s) of dissociative symptoms experienced by a client and the likelihood that he or she has a specific *DSM–IV* disorder, the SCID–D interview is clearly indicated.

## Potential Instrument Choices Based on Common Trauma Presentations

The number of tests and interviews, both generic and trauma-specific, that are potentially applicable to the assessment of trauma survivors can be daunting. In an effort to assist the reader in choosing the appropriate tests in a given clinical situation, Table 8.1 presents a number of different trauma scenarios common to clinical practice, along with tests or interviews that might be most useful in each situation.

Tests are numbered within each category in terms of their general overall usefulness. Those with a (1) are often most useful, those with a (2) are also appropriate, but for whatever reason may be slightly less helpful than those ranked with a (1), and so on. Tests separated with a "/" are equally recommended, depending on availability, whether the goal is brevity or completeness, nuances of the clinical situation, and so on. In all cases, however, additional variables may lead the examiner to prefer a "lower" ranked test over a "higher" one, or he or she may correctly choose a measure not listed in this table.

The following section provides a narrative discussion of each trauma scenario. It must be emphasized, again, that this section is merely advisory; because there are many potential variables operating in any given clinical situation, the clinician should make his or her own determination of which actual tests to administer.

**Simple adult trauma, nonsexual (noncombat).** Individuals in this group include those who experienced one or two traumas in their adult life but were not significantly maltreated at any point early in life. Further, the trauma(s) in this scenario are physical (not sexual), sometimes not interpersonal, and did not arise in the context of combat. Such people may experience posttraumatic difficulties, including PTSD, but their general symptomatology often is not as extreme as for other groups.

As shown in Table 8.1, trauma exposure can be evaluated with the ITR–R, TES, PSEI, or, when the DAPS or PDS is already being administered, with the trauma specification sections of those measures. Other trauma exposure measures may be appropriate as well; these are chosen here for either their brevity (the ITR–R interview) or their comprehensiveness (the TES and PSEI).

Objective tests often helpful with this group include the PAI or MMPI, each of which evaluate a broad range of potential comorbidities and include PTSD scales. In general, the MCMI is

**TABLE 8.1**

*Suggested Instrument Options Based on Common Trauma Presentations*

| Trauma exposure type | Type of test | | | | | |
| --- | --- | --- | --- | --- | --- | --- |
| | Trauma exposure | Generic | | Broadband trauma | PTSD/ASD diagnosis (if indicated) | Other instruments (as needed) |
| | | Objective | Projective | | | |
| Simple adult trauma, nonsexual (noncombat) | (1) ITR–R/TES/PSEI (2) DAPS/ PDS (trauma sections) | (1) PAI/ MMPI | — | (1) TSI–A/TSI | (1) PDS/DAPS/ CAPS (ASDI if acute) | — |
| Simple adult trauma, sexual | (1) ITR–R/TES/PSEI (2) DAPS/ PDS (trauma sections) | (1) PAI/ MMPI | — | (1) TSI | (1) PDS/DAPS/ CAPS (ASDI if acute) | — |
| Simple adult trauma, combat | (1) CES/ITR–R (2) ITR–R/TES (3) DAPS/PDS (trauma sections) | (1) MMPI (2) PAI | — | (1) MSCRP (2) TSI–A/TSI | (1) DAPS (ASDI if acute) (2) PDS/CAPS (3) PCL–M | MDI/ SCID–D/ IASC/CDS/TSCS |

| | | | | | |
|---|---|---|---|---|---|
| Adult trauma, severe/complex (e.g., torture) | (1) ITR–R/TES/PSEI (2) HTQ if immigrant and tortured (3) DAPS/PDS (trauma sections) | (1) PAI/MMPI | (1) Rorschach (if indicated) | (1) TSI (2) SIDES | (1) DAPS (ASDI if acute) (2) PDS/CAPS | IASC/TABS/MDI/SCID–D/CDS/TSCS |
| Child abuse only | (1) CTQ/TES/ITR–R/CMIS | (1) PAI/MMPI | (1) Rorschach (if indicated) | (1) TSI (2) SIDES | (1) DAPS/PDS | IASC, TABS/MDI/SCID–D/CDS/TSCS |
| Both child abuse and adult trauma | (1) TES (2) CTQ/ITR–R | (1) PAI (2) MMPI (3) MCMI | (1) Rorschach (if indicated) | (1) TSI (2) SIDES | (1) DAPS (2) PDS/CAPS | (1) IASC/TABS/MDI/SCID–D (2) CDS/TSCS |

*Note.* ASDI = Acute Stress Disorder Inventory; CAPS = Clinician-Administered PTSD Scale; CDS = Cognitive Distortions Scale; CES = Combat Exposure Scale; CMIS = Child Maltreatment Interview Schedule; CTQ = Childhood Trauma Questionnaire; DAPS = Detailed Assessment of Posttraumatic Stress; HTQ = Harvard Trauma Questionnaire; IASC = Inventory of Altered Self-Capacities; ITR–R = Initial Trauma Review–Revised; MCMI = Millon Clinical Multiaxial Inventory; MDI = Multiscale Dissociation Inventory; MMPI = Minnesota Multiphasic Personality Inventory; MSCRP = Mississippi Scale for Combat-Related PTSD; PAI = Psychological Assessment Inventory; PCL = PTSD Checklist; PDS = Posttraumatic Stress Diagnostic Scale; PSEI = Potential Stressful Events Interview; SCID–D = Structured Clinical Interview for DSM–IV Dissociative Disorders; SIDES = Structured Interview for Disorders of Extreme Stress; TABS = Trauma and Attachment Belief Scale; TES = Traumatic Events Scale; TSCS = Tennessee Self-Concept Scale; TSI = Trauma Symptom Inventory; TSI–A = Trauma Symptom Inventory–Alternate.

seen by the current author as slightly less effective than the PAI or MMPI for traumatized people, although—clearly—those who prefer this measure may apply it effectively (see chapter 6). Even though the MMPI is listed along side the PAI under "Objective" measures throughout Table 8.1, generally the PAI is slightly preferable, based on its better psychometrics and the quality of its (directly scorable) subscales. On the other hand, the MMPI has a much more developed database, and those clinicians skilled in profile interpretation may derive more information from the MMPI than the PAI. No projective tests are specifically recommended for simple adult traumas, but those trained in the Rorschach may find it helpful.

Trauma-specific tests recommended for simple adult trauma include the TSI or TSI–A (the latter has no sexual symptom items and is sometimes preferred by those who have not experienced a sexual trauma or do not want to report on sexual issues). The TSI/TSI–A is the only standardized broadband trauma symptom test available, so it is recommended throughout Table 8.1 as a general screen of trauma-relevant symptomatology. If a *DSM–IV* diagnosis of PTSD is under consideration, any of three measures are recommended: the PDS, DAPS, or, if there is enough time, the CAPS interview. Other PTSD measures, such as the PCL, also are acceptable. When choosing between these various instruments, the PDS is most time-efficient, the DAPS is most comprehensive of self-report measures, and the CAPS is the "gold standard" when special precision is required. If the trauma occurred in the last month, the ASDI should be used in lieu of the PDS, DAPS, or CAPS.

Because simple adult trauma, without associated earlier trauma, is often less complicated in presentation, no "other instrument" is recommended here, although any given trauma survivor may require additional tests based on his or her particular situation and symptom presentation. For example, the traumatic loss of a loved one might easily produce psychological symptoms that would make the Inventory of Complicated Grief (ICG; Prigerson et al., 1995) an appropriate test.

**Simple adult trauma, sexual.** It is recommended that trauma survivors in this group be given the same general collection of measures used for simple nonsexual trauma, except that the full TSI should be given so that those sexual symptoms often correlated with rape or sexual assault (e.g., sexual conflicts, phobias, or concerns) can be assessed. As noted at various points throughout this book, a substantial number of adult sexual trauma victims also have a childhood sexual abuse history. If this is the case, refer to the "both child abuse and adult trauma" sections of Table 8.1.

**Simple adult trauma, combat.** This category label is a bit of a misnomer: those exposed to combat (e.g., in Korea, Vietnam, or Iraq Wars) rarely experience "simple" trauma exposure. Instead, war tends to involve a range of negative experiences that occur over a relatively extended period of time (see chapter 1). The world "simple" is used here primarily to indicate that no other major traumas, above and beyond those associated with combat, are present—or at least that they are noncontributory to the central combat response. Trauma exposure can be evaluated with the same instruments used in the other groups but, in many cases, should include the Combat Exposure Scale or other measure of war-specific traumas. Recommended generic objective measures are the same as the other groups, except that the considerable research on the MMPI profiles of combat veterans may support the use of this inventory over the PAI in some instances, all other things being equal.

Broadband trauma measures include the TSI, although some veterans may prefer the TSI–A. The TSI is preferable to the TSI–A, however, for combat veterans who were sexually assaulted during their tour of duty. The combat version of the Mississippi should be considered as well, given the tremendous amount of research available on this measure for combat veterans. PTSD measure recommendations for combat trauma are similar to other adult traumas, except that the military version of the PCL is also an option, given its regular application with combat veterans.

Because combat is potentially quite traumagenic, some survivors experience psychological outcomes well beyond those tapped by specific trauma measures, especially in cases of extended battle, horrific loss, or capture and imprisonment. For this reason, a number of other instruments are also recommended in Table 8.1. These generally include tests evaluating dissociation (i.e., the MDI or SCID–D), relational disturbance (i.e., the IASC or TABS), and cognitive distortions (i.e., the Cognitive Distortions Scale [CDS; Briere, 2000b] or Tennessee Self-Concept Scale [TSCS; Roid & Fitts, 1994]).

**Adult trauma, severe/complex (e.g., torture).** Some adult trauma experiences are of sufficient severity or complexity that, although there may be no history of child abuse, the outcomes are nevertheless extreme and pervasive. Examples of this are torture victims, chronically battered domestic violence victims, and some of those taken hostage by criminals or combatants. The recommendations for assessment with this group generally parallel those for combat veterans, except that combat exposure usually is not an issue, specialized trauma exposure tests such as the HTQ may be required, and there may be a need for complex trauma symptom measures such as the Structured Interview for Disorders of Extreme Stress (SIDES; Pelcovitz et al., 1997). Assessment with other, less trauma-specific instruments is often indicated. This is especially true when treatment will be provided for such individuals, during which time information on affect regulation capacity, identity issues, and relationality can be helpful. Those trained and qualified to use the Rorschach often find this instrument especially helpful in examining the more complex and pervasive impacts of severe adult trauma (see Luxenberg & Levin, in press, for more information in this area).

**Child abuse only.** As suggested by the accumulating trauma literature, extended or severe child abuse is associated with significant psychological disturbance in many victims—in some cases more than what is found in those solely traumatized in adulthood. Typically, these effects, in turn, increase the likelihood of revictimization as adults. As a result, the assessment of many survivors of major child maltreatment is covered by the next category (i.e., child abuse and adult trauma). Nevertheless, a substantial minority of clinically presenting individuals were maltreated in childhood, yet have not been victimized in adulthood. As shown in Table 8.1, these individuals ideally should be evaluated with a measure that examines childhood maltreatment experiences, such as the CTQ or CMIS. However, given that revictimization is a significant issues for those abused as children, these measures are best augmented with (or even replaced by) the TES or ITR–R, because they allow the clinician to assess whether, in fact, child abuse was the only trauma experienced by the individual. Other test recommendations are similar to those for complex adult trauma, except that, of course, the ASDI would not be relevant.

**Both child abuse and adult trauma.** This group comprises those individuals who, on average, have the most complex and pervasive psychological difficulties of all the categories presented in Table 8.1. Not all of those with both childhood and adult trauma exposure are necessarily highly symptomatic, but, nevertheless, a significant proportion are. Evaluation of these people requires trauma exposure measures that tap both childhood and adult events, and impact measures that evaluate the full range of potential trauma-related disturbance and dysfunction. For highly symptomatic individuals in this group, the "other instruments" has its first specific recommendation—indicated by the (1) in that column. In this regard, the self-capacities of multiply-traumatized should be assessed when possible. This may be done using some combination of the IASC, TABS, and (if indicated) BORRTI. Other measures in the column (i.e., those measuring dissociation and cognitive distortions) also are important considerations.

# Conclusion

This chapter highlights a central principle of assessment in the area of posttraumatic stress: a complete psychological evaluation in this area relies on the use of multiple psychological tests in the context of one or more detailed psychological interviews. Reliance on test data alone, for example, is insufficient to produce a *DSM–IV* diagnosis, let alone a reasonably complete clinical picture, and an interview alone (structured or otherwise) is unlikely to provide the wealth of data and normative comparisons potentially available from objective psychological testing.

The inclusion of multiple psychological tests within a given battery is paramount, given the breadth of potential posttraumatic responses and the limitations of any one psychological measure. Test choice will necessarily revolve around the specific assessment goals and those instruments best able to address those goals. As suggested in the last section, for example, a full trauma-relevant psychological test battery might include one of the traumatic events measures (e.g., the ITR–R or TES), either the PAI or MMPI–2, a diagnostic measure (for PTSD, the PDS or DAPS, and for ASD the Acute Stress Disorder Scale [ASDS; Bryant et al., 2000]) and each of the following: the Rorschach, TSI, MDI, and the TABS. If the trauma was early or associated with "Axis II" issues, the IASC (or the BORRTI) and MCMI–III would be added. On the other hand, a briefer battery might consist solely of the TES or ITR–R, MMPI–2 or PAI, and the TSI, PDS, or DAPS, depending on the diagnostic issue and complexity of the clinical picture.

Whatever the choice of instruments, the trauma-focused test battery should be considered a tool to assist in the complex task of clinical judgment, not as replacement for that judgment. Ultimately, clinical evaluation and diagnosis arise from as many sources of information as possible, ranging from review of records and interviews with family or friends, to the application of focused psychological tests and the results of one or more empathic and attuned clinical interviews.

Chapter

# 9

# Conclusion

A s the front page of almost any urban newspaper will suggest, interpersonal violence, war, transportation accidents, and disasters are a normal part of modern human existence. In fact, recent mass traumas in New York, Washington, DC, Pennsylvania, and Oklahoma City; the wars in Afghanistan and Iraq; daily atrocities in Liberia; the ongoing Israel–Palestine conflicts; and the deluge of recently discovered clergy sexual abuse cases have ensured that psychological trauma is now widely acknowledged and discussed in the general population, let alone in clinical circles. Yet, as noted in this volume, the concept of posttraumatic stress was relatively unknown to both the person on the street and the mental health professional before *DSM–III*. This book documents the rapid growth of trauma-related research and clinical practice once posttraumatic stress disorder (PTSD) became a valid concept. Since the publication of *DSM–III* in 1980, many thousands of articles, chapters, and books have been written on the etiology, incidence, assessment, and treatment of posttraumatic states—more than 13,850 for PTSD alone (PILOTS database search, October 17, 2003). At the same time, a new—albeit informal—mental health specialty has come into existence, with its primary focus being the diagnosis and clinical resolution of posttraumatic states and disorders. Some of these specialists have come from academic psychology departments, others from U.S. Veterans Administration hospitals, rape crisis centers, child

211

abuse programs, torture treatment centers, and battered women's shelters, while yet others are employed by disaster-oriented agencies such as the Red Cross.

What these researchers and clinicians have found is a collection of psychological disorders and conditions that are intrinsically related to traumatic events yet have been largely overlooked in the past. These include acute stress disorder (ASD), PTSD, brief psychotic disorder, a variety of dissociative disorders, and a number of other symptom clusters (e.g., involving somatization or disturbed relatedness) that arise at least partially from traumatic events. With each additional iteration of our diagnostic system (i.e., the progression from *DSM–I* to *DSM–IV*), these disorders and states have become more clearly defined, although there may have been some errors along the way. So, too, has our understanding grown of the complex interaction between person, history, stressor, and environment in the genesis of posttraumatic distress and disorder.

This volume has considered one small piece of this growing knowledge base: the accurate assessment of posttraumatic states. Examination of the literature in this area highlights the tension between two phenomena: the primacy of those pre–*DSM–III* psychological tests and interviews used to assess basically non-trauma-based psychological disturbance, and, yet, the rapidly growing post–*DSM–II* need for tests of a whole new realm of psychological dysfunction. Traditional psychological instruments have tended to misinterpret what mental health professionals now understand to be posttraumatic states, often repackaging them as psychosis, personality disorder, and other less relevant psychological conditions. The net effect of this misinterpretation has been to provide clinicians with erroneous information, potentially leading to inadequate treatment outcomes.

As noted in this volume, however, researchers and clinicians are beginning to understand the phenomenology of posttraumatic disturbance and are increasingly able to provide assessment approaches that accurately reflect the internal experience of the trauma survivor. Clinicians have begun to adapt traditional psychological tests to the assessment of posttraumatic states, often by developing new scoring systems and interpretation approaches, and by creating more trauma-sensitive scales for these measures. Perhaps even more important, however, is the development of a host of new standardized psychological tests and structured interviews that directly tap posttraumatic stress and disorder.

Because all of this movement has been relatively recent, not all available tests have optimal sensitivity and specificity with regard to posttraumatic stress, and most older trauma-specific tests lack the normative data necessary for full-fledged clinical use. This transitional period is nearly over, however, given the speed at which researchers and clinicians are working in this field. As a result, trauma survivors in both mental health and emergency-outreach populations are increasingly likely to be understood clinically—an outcome that can only lead to improved intervention and a better likelihood of recovery.

# Appendix

# Initial Trauma Review–Revised (ITR–R)

## CHILDHOOD QUESTIONS:

1. [Physical abuse questions] *"Before you were age 18, did a parent or another adult ever hurt or punish you in a way that left a bruise, cut, scratches, or made you bleed?"*
   Yes ___   No ___   [Yes = physical abuse]
   *If yes:*
   - *"When this happened, did you ever feel very afraid, horrified, or helpless?"*
     Yes ___   No ___
   - *"Did you ever think you might be injured or killed?"*
     Yes ___   No ___

2. [Sexual abuse questions] *"Before you were age 18, did anyone who was 5 or more years older than you ever do something sexual with you or to you?"*
   Yes ___   No ___   [Yes = sexual abuse]
   *If yes:*
   - *"Did the person ever put their penis, a finger, or an object into your vagina, or anus, or a penis in your mouth?"*
     Yes ___   No ___   [Yes = sexual abuse with penetration]

- *"Was this ever done against your will or when you couldn't defend yourself (for example when you were asleep or intoxicated)?"*
  Yes __ No __ [Yes = sexual abuse]
- *"When this happened, did you ever feel very afraid, horrified, or helpless?"* [NOTE: For sexual abuse only, this part is not necessary for PTSD Criterion A.]
  Yes __ No __
- *"Did you ever think you might be injured or killed?"* [NOTE: For sexual abuse only, this part is not necessary for PTSD Criterion A.]
  Yes __ No __

3. [Peer sexual assault questions] *"Before you were age 18, did anyone who was less than 5 years older than you ever do something sexual to you that was against your will or that happened when you couldn't defend yourself (for example when you were asleep or intoxicated)?"*
   Yes __ No __ [Yes = peer child sexual assault]

   *If yes:*
   - *"Did the person ever put their penis, a finger, or an object into your vagina, anus, or mouth?"*
     Yes __ No __ [Yes = peer child rape if any insertion in vagina or anus, or penile insertion in mouth]
   - *"When this happened, did you ever feel very afraid, horrified, or helpless?"*
     Yes __ No __
   - *"Did you ever think you might be injured or killed?"*
     Yes __ No __

4. [Disaster questions] *"Before you were age 18, were you ever involved in a serious fire, earthquake, flood, or other disaster?"*
   Yes __ No __ [Yes = childhood exposure to disaster]

*If yes:*
- *"When this happened, did you ever feel very afraid, horrified, or helpless?"*
  Yes __    No __
- *"Did you ever think you might be injured or killed?"*
  Yes __    No __

5. [Motor vehicle accident (MVA) questions] *"Before you were age 18, were you ever involved in a serious automobile accident?"*

    Yes __    No __    [Yes = childhood exposure to MVA]

*If yes:*
- *"When this happened, did you ever feel very afraid, horrified, or helpless?"*
  Yes __    No __
- *"Did you ever think you might be injured or killed?"*
  Yes __    No __

6. [Witnessing trauma questions] *"Before you were age 18, did you ever see someone else get killed or badly hurt?"*

    Yes __    No __    [Yes = childhood witness to trauma]

*If yes:*
- *"When this happened, did you ever feel very afraid, horrified, or helpless?"*
  Yes __    No __
- *"Did you ever think you might be injured or killed?"*
  [NOTE: Not required for PTSD Criterion A.]
  Yes __    No __

# ADULTHOOD QUESTIONS:

1. [Adult sexual assault questions] *"Since you were 18 or older, has something sexual ever been done to you against your will or when you couldn't defend yourself (for example when you were asleep or intoxicated)?"*

    Yes __    No __    [Yes = adult sexual assault]

*If yes:*
- *"Did the person ever put their penis, a finger, or an object into your vagina or anus, or a penis in your mouth?"*
  Yes ___ No ___ [Yes = adult rape]
- *"When this happened, did you ever feel very afraid, horrified, or helpless?"*
  Yes ___ No ___
- *"Did you ever think you might be injured or killed?"*
  Yes ___ No ___
- *"Did this ever happen on a date, or with a sexual/romantic partner or spouse?*
  Yes ___ No ___ [Yes = date/partner/
  marital sexual
  assault or rape]

2. [Spouse/partner abuse questions] *"Since you were 18 or older, have you*
   - *ever been slapped, hit, or beaten in a sexual or marital relationship?"*
     Yes ___ No ___ [Yes = partner battering]
   - *ever been shot, shot at, stabbed, or nearly strangled in a sexual or marital relationship?"*
     Yes ___ No ___ [Yes = partner battering and
     possible attempted
     murder]

   *If yes to either:*
   - *"When this happened, did you ever feel very afraid, horrified, or helpless?"*
     Yes ___ No ___
   - *"Did you ever think you might be injured or killed?"*
     Yes ___ No ___

3. [Nonintimate assault questions] *"Since you were 18 or older, have you ever been physically attacked, assaulted, stabbed, or shot at by someone who wasn't a sex partner or husband/wife?"*
   Yes ___ No ___ [Yes = nonintimate assault
   and possible
   attempted murder]

*If yes:*
- *"When this happened, did you ever feel very afraid, horrified, or helpless?"*
  Yes ___   No ___
- *"Did you ever think you might be injured or killed?"*
  Yes ___   No ___

4. [War questions] *"Since you were 18 or older, have you ever experienced combat or fought in a war?"*
   Yes ___   No ___   [Yes = combat exposure]
   *If yes:*
   - *"When this happened, did you ever feel very afraid, horrified, or helpless?"*
     Yes ___   No ___
   - *"Did you ever think you might be injured or killed?"*
     Yes ___   No ___

5. [Motor vehicle accident questions] *"Since you were 18 or older, were you ever involved in an serious automobile accident?"*
   Yes ___   No ___   [Yes = motor vehicle accident]
   *If yes:*
   - *"When this happened, did you ever feel very afraid, horrified, or helpless?"*
     Yes ___   No ___
   - *"Did you ever think you might be injured or killed?"*
     Yes ___   No ___

6. [Disaster questions] *"Since you were 18 or older, were you ever involved in a serious fire, earthquake, flood, or other disaster?"*
   Yes ___   No ___   [Yes = disaster exposure]
   *If yes:*
   - *"When this happened, did you ever feel very afraid, horrified, or helpless?"*
     Yes ___   No ___

- *"Did you ever think you might be injured or killed?"*
  Yes ___    No ___

7. [Torture questions—If client is an immigrant from another country] *"In the country where you used to live, were you ever tortured by the government or by people against the government?"*
   Yes ___    No ___    [Yes = torture]
   *If yes:*
   - *"When this happened, did you ever feel very afraid, horrified, or helpless?"*
     Yes ___    No ___
   - *"Did you ever think you might be injured or killed?"*
     Yes ___    No ___

8. [Police and trauma questions] *"In this country, have you ever been hit, beaten, assaulted, or shot by the police or other law enforcement officials, during or after an arrest, or at some other time?"*
   Yes ___    No ___    [Yes = police trauma]
   *If yes:*
   - *"When this happened, did you ever feel very afraid, horrified, or helpless?"*
     Yes ___    No ___
   - *"Did you ever think you might be injured or killed?"*
     Yes ___    No ___

9. [Witnessing questions] "Since you were 18 or older, did you ever see someone else killed or badly hurt?
   Yes ___    No ___    [Yes = adult witness to trauma]
   *If yes:*
   - *"When this happened, did you ever feel very afraid, horrified, or helpless?"*
     Yes ___    No ___
   - *"Did you ever think you might be injured or killed?"* [NOTE: For witnessing trauma, this part is not necessary for *DSM–IV* Criterion A.]
     Yes ___    No ___

# References

Acierno, R., Brady, K. L., Gray, M., Kilpatrick, D. G., Resnick, H. S., & Best, C. L. (2002). Psychopathology following interpersonal violence: A comparison of risk factors in older and younger adults. *Journal of Clinical Geropsychology, 8*, 13–23.

Adams, D. P., Barton, C., Mitchell, G., Moore, A. L., & Einagel, V. (1998). Hearts and minds: Suicide among United States combat troops in Vietnam, 1957–1973. *Social Science and Medicine, 47*, 1687–1694.

Affleck, G., Tennen, H., Croog, S., & Levine, S. (1987). Causal attribution, perceived benefits, and morbidity after a heart attack: An 8-year study. *Journal of Consulting and Clinical Psychology, 55*, 29–35.

Aldridge, M. R. (1993). Professional skepticism towards multiple personality disorder [letter]. *British Journal of Psychiatry, 163*, 569–570.

Alexander, D. (2001). Nairobi terrorist bombing: The personal experience of a mental health adviser. *International Journal of Emergency Mental Health, 3*, 249–257.

Alexander, P. C. (1993). The differential effects of abuse characteristics and attachment in the prediction of long-term effects of sexual abuse. *Journal of Interpersonal Violence, 8*, 346–362.

Allen, J. G. (2001). *Traumatic relationships and serious mental disorders.* Chichester, England: Wiley.

Allen, J. G., Huntoon, J., & Evans, R. B. (1999). Complexities in complex posttraumatic stress disorder in inpatient women: Evidence from cluster analysis of MCMI–III personality disorder scales. *Journal of Personality Assessment, 73*, 449–471.

Alper, K., Devinsky, O., Perrine, K., Luciano, D., Vazquez, B., Pacia, S., et al. (1997). Dissociation in epilepsy and conversion nonepileptic seizures. *Epilepsia, 38*, 991–997.

Alpher, V. S. (1991). Assessment of ego functioning in multiple personality disorder. *Journal of Personality Assessment, 56*, 373–387.

Amdur, R. L., & Liberzon, I. (1996). Dimensionality of dissociation in subjects with PTSD. *Dissociation, 9*, 118–124.

American Psychiatric Association. (1952). *Diagnostic and statistical manual of mental disorders.* Washington, DC: Author.

American Psychiatric Association. (1968). *Diagnostic and statistical manual of mental disorders* (2nd ed.). Washington, DC: Author.

American Psychiatric Association. (1980). *Diagnostic and statistical manual of mental disorders* (3rd ed.). Washington, DC: Author.

American Psychiatric Association. (1987). *Diagnostic and statistical manual of mental disorders* (3rd ed., rev.). Washington, DC: Author.

American Psychiatric Association. (2000). *Diagnostic and statistical manual of mental disorders* (4th ed., text rev.). Washington, DC: Author.

Amnesty International. (2002). *Amnesty International, Report 2002*. Retrieved February 3, 2004 from http:/web.amnesty.org/web/ar2002.nsf/home

Anderson, M. C., Ochsner, K. N., Huhl, B., Cooper, J., Robertson, E., Gabrieli, S. W., et al. (in press). Neural systems underlying the suppression of unwanted memories. *Science.*

Andrews, B., Brewin, C. R., & Rose, S. (2003). Gender, social support, and PTSD in victims of violent crime. *Journal of Traumatic Stress, 16,* 421–427.

Andrews, B., Brewin, C. R., Rose, S., & Kirk, M. (2000). Predicting PTSD symptoms in victims of violent crime: The role of shame, anger, and childhood abuse. *Journal of Abnormal Psychology, 109,* 69–73.

Anthony, J. C., Folstein, M., Romanoski, A. J., Vonkorff, M. R., Nestadt, C. R., Merchant, A., et al. (1985). Comparison of lay Diagnostic Interview Schedule and a standardized psychiatric diagnosis. *Archives of General Psychiatry, 42,* 667–676.

Arata, C. M., Saunders, B. E., & Kilpatrick, D. G. (1991). Concurrent validity of a crime-related Post-Traumatic Stress Disorder Scale for women within the Symptom Checklist–90–Revised. *Violence and Victims, 6,* 191–199.

Arbisi, P. A., & Ben-Porath, Y. S. (1997). Characteristics of the MMPI–2 $F(p)$ scale as a function of diagnosis in an inpatient sample of veterans. *Psychological Assessment, 9,* 102–105.

Armenian, H. K., Morikawa, M., Melkonian, A. K., Hovanesian, A. P., Akiskal, K., & Akiskal, H. S. (2002). Risk factors for depression in the survivors of the 1988 earthquake in Armenia. *Journal of Urban Health: Bulletin of the New York Academy of Medicine, 79,* 373–382.

Armstrong, J. (1991). The psychological organization of multiple personality disordered patients as revealed in psychological testing. *Psychiatric Clinics of North America, 14,* 533–546.

Armstrong, J. (1995). Psychological assessment. In J. L. Spira (Ed.), *Treating dissociative identity disorder* (pp. 3–37). San Francisco: Jossey-Bass.

Armstrong, J., & Loewenstein, R. J. (1991). The psychological organization of multiple personality disordered patients as revealed in psychological testing. *Psychiatric Clinics of North America, 14,* 533–546.

Armstrong, J. A., & High, J. (1999). Guidelines for differentiating malingering from PTSD. *National Center for PTSD Clinical Quarterly, 8,* 46–48.

Asmundson, G. J. G., Frombach, I., McQuaid, J. R., Pedrelli, P., Lenox, R., & Stein, M. B. (2000). Dimensionality of posttraumatic stress symptoms: A confirmatory factor analysis of DSM–IV symptom clusters and other symptom models. *Behaviour Research and Therapy, 38,* 203–214.

Astin, M. C., Ogland-Hand, S. M., Coleman, E. M., & Foy, D. W., (1995). Post-traumatic stress disorder and childhood abuse in battered women: Comparisons with maritally distressed women. *Journal of Consulting and Clinical Psychology, 63*, 308–312.

Atkeson, B., Calhoun, K., Resick, P., & Ellis, E. (1982). Victims of rape: Repeated assessment of depressive symptoms. *Journal of Consulting and Clinical Psychology, 50*, 96–102.

Baggaley, M. R. (1998). "Military Munchausen's": Assessment of factitious claims of military service in psychiatric patients. *Psychiatric Bulletin, 22*, 153–154.

Bagley, C. (1991). The prevalence and mental health sequels of child sexual abuse in a community sample of women aged 18 to 27. *Canadian Journal of Community Mental Health, 10*, 103–116.

Bagley, C., & Young, L. (1987). Juvenile prostitution and child sexual abuse: A controlled study. *Canadian Journal of Community Mental Health, 6*, 5–26.

Baker, R. (1992). Psychosocial consequences for tortured refugees seeking asylum refugee status in Europe. In M. Basoglu (Ed.), *Torture and its consequences: Current treatment approaches* (pp. 83–106). Cambridge: Cambridge University Press.

Barry, L. C., Kasl, S. V., & Prigerson, H. G. (2002). Psychiatric disorders among bereaved persons: The role of perceived circumstances of death and preparedness for death. *American Journal of Geriatric Psychiatry, 10*, 447–457.

Bartone, P. T., & Wright, K. M. (1990). Grief and group recovery following a military air disaster. *Journal of Traumatic Stress, 3*, 523–539.

Bassuk, E. L., Dawson, R., Perloff, J. N., & Weinreb, L. F. (2001). Post-traumatic stress disorder in extremely poor women: Implications for health care clinicians. *Journal of the American Medical Women's Association, 56*, 79–85.

Bassuk, E. L., Melnick, S., & Browne, A. (1998). Responding to the needs of low-income and homeless women who are survivors of family violence. *Journal of the American Medical Women's Association, 53*, 57–64.

Basoglu, M., Salcioglu, E., & Livanou, M. (2002). Traumatic stress responses in earthquake survivors in Turkey. *Journal of Traumatic Stress, 15*, 269–276.

Beck, A. T., Epstein, N., Brown, G., & Steer, R. A. (1988). An inventory for measuring clinical anxiety: Psychometric properties. *Journal of Consulting and Clinical Psychology, 56*, 893–897.

Beck, A. T., Ward, C. H., Mandelson, M., Mock, J., & Erbaugh, J. (1961). An inventory for measuring depression. *Archives of General Psychiatry, 4*, 561–571.

Beckham, J. C., Moore, S. D., Feldman, M. E., Hertzberg, M. A., Kirby, A. C., & Fairbank, J. A. (1998). Health status, somatization, and severity of posttraumatic stress disorder in Vietnam combat veterans with posttraumatic stress disorder. *American Journal of Psychiatry, 155*, 1565–1569.

Belkin, D. S., Greene, A. F., Rodriguez, J. R., & Boggs, S. R. (1994). Psychopathology and history of sexual abuse. *Journal of Interpersonal Violence, 9*, 535–547.

Bell, M. D. (1995). *Bell Object Relations and Reality Testing Inventory*. Los Angeles: Western Psychological Services.

Bennett, P., Conway, M., Clatworthy, J., Brooke, S., & Owen, R. (2001). Predicting post-traumatic symptoms in cardiac patients. *Heart and Lung: The Journal of Acute and Critical Care, 30*, 458–465.

Berah, E. F., Jones, H. J., & Valent, P. (1984). The experience of a mental health team involved in the early phase of a disaster. *Australia and New Zealand Journal of Psychiatry, 18*, 354–358.

Berg, S. H. (2001). *Everyday sexism and post-traumatic stress disorder in women: A correlational study*. Unpublished doctoral dissertation, City University of New York, New York.

Berger, A. M., Knutson, J. F., Mehm, J. G., & Perkins, K. A. (1988). The self-report of punitive childhood experiences of young adults and adolescents. *Child Abuse and Neglect, 12*, 251–262.

Berliner, L., & Briere, J. (1998). Trauma, memory, and clinical practice. In L. Williams (Ed.), *Trauma and memory* (pp. 3–18). Thousand Oaks, CA: Sage.

Berliner, L., & Elliott, D. M. (2002). Sexual abuse of children. In J. E. B. Myers, L. Berliner, J. Briere, C. T. Hendrix, T. Reid, & C. Jenny (Eds.), *The APSAC handbook on child maltreatment* (2nd ed., pp. 55–78). Thousand Oaks, CA: Sage.

Bernstein, D. P., Ahluvalia, T., Pogge, D., & Handelsman, L. (1997). Validity of the Childhood Trauma Questionnaire in an adolescent psychiatric population. *Journal of the American Academy of Child and Adolescent Psychiatry, 36*, 340–348.

Bernstein, D. P., Fink, L., Handelsman, L., Foote, J., Lovejoy, M., Wenzel, K., et al. (1994). Initial reliability and validity of a new retrospective measure of child abuse and neglect. *American Journal of Psychiatry, 151*, 1132–1136.

Bernstein, E. M., & Putnam, F. W. (1986). Development, reliability, and validity of a dissociation scale. *Journal of Nervous and Mental Diseases, 174*, 727–734.

Berthold, S. M. (2000). War traumas and community violence: Psychological, behavioral, and academic outcomes among Khmer refugee adolescents. *Journal of Multicultural Social Work, 8*, 15–46.

Birmes, P., Arrieu, A., Payen, A., Warner, B. A., & Schmitt, L. (1999). Traumatic stress and depression in a group of plane crash survivors. *Journal of Nervous and Mental Disease, 187*, 754–755.

Birmes, P., Carreras, D., Ducasse, J. L., Charlet, J. P., Warner, B. A., Lauque, D., et al. (2001). Peritraumatic dissociation, acute stress, and early posttraumatic stress disorder in victims of general crime. *Canadian Journal of Psychiatry, 46*, 649–651.

Blake, D. D., Weathers, F. W., Nagy, L. M., Kaloupek, D. G., Gusman, F. D., Charney, D. S., et al. (1995). The development of a clinician-administered PTSD scale. *Journal of Traumatic Stress, 8*, 75–90.

Blake, D. D., Weathers, F. W., Nagy, L. M., Kaloupek, D. G., Klauminzer, G., Charney, D. S., et al. (1990). A clinician rating scale for assessing current and lifetime PTSD: The CAPS–1. *Behavior Therapist, 13*, 187–188.

Blanchard, E. B., Gerardi, R. J., Kolb, L. C., & Barlow, D. H. (1986). The utility of the Anxiety Disorders Schedule (ADIS) in the diagnosis of post-traumatic stress disorder (PTSD) in Vietnam veterans. *Behavior Research and Therapy, 24*, 2701–2707.

Blanchard, E. B., & Hickling, E. J. (2004). *After the crash: Psychological assessment and treatment of motor vehicle survivors* (2nd ed.). Washington, DC: American Psychological Association.

Blanchard, E. B., Jones-Alexander, J., Buckley, T. C., & Forneris, C. A. (1996). Psychometric properties of the PTSD Checklist (PCL). *Behaviour Research and Therapy, 34*, 669–673.

Bleich, A., Gelkopf, M., & Solomon, Z. (2003). Exposure to terrorism, stress-related mental health symptoms, and coping behaviors among a nationally representative sample in Israel. *Journal of the American Medical Association, 290*, 612–620.

Boelen, P. A., Van Den Bout, J., & de Keijser, J. (2003). Traumatic grief as a disorder distinct from bereavement-related depression and anxiety: A replication study with bereaved mental health care patients. *American Journal of Psychiatry, 160*, 1339–1341.

Bongar, B. (2002). *Suicidal patient: Clinical and legal standards of care* (2nd ed.). Washington, DC: American Psychological Association.

Boudarene, M. (2002). Terrorisme en Algerie: Quel devenir pour les liens filial et social? [Terrorism in Algeria: What future to filial and social binds?] *Revue Francophone du Stress et du Trauma, 2*, 213–217.

Brabin, P. J., & Berah, E. F. (1995). Dredging up past traumas: Harmful or helpful? *Psychiatry, Psychology, and the Law, 2*, 165–171.

Brady, K. T., Killeen, T., Brewerton, T. D., & Lucerini, S. (2000). Comorbidity of psychiatric disorders and posttraumatic stress disorder. *Journal of Clinical Psychiatry, 61* (Suppl. 7), 22–32.

Brauer, R., Harrow, M., & Tucker, G. (1970). Depersonalization phenomena in psychiatric patients. *British Journal of Psychiatry, 117*, 509–515.

Bremner, J. D., Krystal, J. H., Putnam, F. W., Southwick, S. M., Marmar, C. R., Charney, D. S., et al. (1998). Measurement of dissociative states with the Clinician–Administered Dissociative States Scale (CADSS). *Journal of Traumatic Stress, 11*, 125–136.

Bremner, J. D., Southwick, S., Brett, E., Fontana, A., Rosenheck, R., & Charney, D. S. (1992). Dissociation and posttraumatic stress disorder in Vietnam combat veterans. *American Journal of Psychiatry, 149*, 328–332.

Bremner, J. D., Steinberg, M., Southwick, S. M., Johnson, D. R., & Charney, D. S. (1993). Use of the Structured Clinical Interview for DSM–IV Dissociative Disorders for systematic assessment of dissociative symptoms in posttraumatic stress disorder. *American Journal of Psychiatry, 150*, 1011–1014.

Brennan, K. A., & Shaver, P. R. (1995). Dimensions of adult attachment, affect regulation, and romantic relationship functioning. *Personality and Social Psychology Bulletin, 21,* 267–283.

Breslau, N., Chilcoat, H. D., Kessler, R. C., & Davis, G. C. (1999). Previous exposure to trauma and PTSD effects of subsequent trauma: Results from the Detroit Area Survey of Trauma. *American Journal of Psychiatry, 156,* 902–907.

Breslau, N., & Davis, G. C. (1992). Posttraumatic stress disorder in an urban population of young adults: Risk factors for chronicity. *American Journal of Psychiatry, 149,* 671–675.

Breslau, N., Davis, G. C., & Andreski, P. (1995). Risk factors for PTSD-related traumatic events: A prospective analysis. *American Journal of Psychiatry, 152,* 529–535.

Breslau, N., Davis, G. C., Andreski, P., & Peterson, E. L. (1991). Traumatic events and post-traumatic stress disorder in an urban population of young adults. *Archives of General Psychiatry, 48,* 216–222.

Brewin, C. R., Andrews, B., & Rose, S. (2000). Fear, helplessness, and horror in posttraumatic stress disorder: Investigating DSM–IV criterion A2 in victims of violent crime. *Journal of Traumatic Stress, 13,* 499–509.

Brewin, C. R., Andrews, B., Rose, S., & Kirk, M. (1999). Acute stress disorder and posttraumatic stress disorder in victims of violent crime. *American Journal of Psychiatry, 156,* 360–366.

Brewin, C. R., Andrews, B., & Valentine, J. D. (2000). Meta-analysis of risk factors for posttraumatic stress disorder in trauma-exposed adults. *Journal of Consulting and Clinical Psychology, 68,* 748–766.

Briere, J. (1992a). *Child abuse trauma: Theory and treatment of the lasting effects.* Newbury Park, CA: Sage.

Briere, J. (1992b). Medical symptoms, health risk, and history of childhood sexual abuse (Editorial). *Mayo Clinic Proceedings, 67,* 603–604.

Briere, J. (1995). *Trauma Symptom Inventory professional manual.* Odessa, FL: Psychological Assessment Resources.

Briere, J. (1996a). *Therapy for adults molested as children* (2nd ed.). New York: Springer.

Briere, J. (1996b). *Trauma Symptom Checklist for Children (TSCC).* Odessa, FL: Psychological Assessment Resources.

Briere, J. (1999). *Initial Trauma Review.* Unpublished psychological test. Los Angeles: University of Southern California.

Briere, J. (2000a). *Inventory of Altered Self Capacities (IASC).* Odessa, FL: Psychological Assessment Resources.

Briere, J. (2000b). *Cognitive Distortions Scale (CDS).* Odessa, FL: Psychological Assessment Resources.

Briere, J. (2001). *Detailed Assessment of Posttraumatic Stress (DAPS).* Odessa, FL: Psychological Assessment Resources.

Briere, J. (2002a). Treating adult survivors of severe childhood abuse and neglect: Further development of an integrative model. In J. E. B. Myers, L. Berliner, J. Briere, C. T. Hendrix, T. Reid, & C. Jenny (Eds.), *The APSAC handbook on child maltreatment* (2nd ed., pp. 175–202). Newbury Park, CA: Sage.

Briere, J. (2002b). *Multiscale Dissociation Inventory.* Odessa. FL: Psychological Assessment Resources.

Briere, J. (in press). Psychological assessment of child abuse effects in adults. In J. P. Wilson & T. M. Keane (Eds.), *Assessing psychological trauma and PTSD: A handbook for practitioners* (2nd ed.). New York: Guilford Press.

Briere, J., & Elliott, D. M. (1997). Psychological assessment of interpersonal victimization effects in adults and children. *Psychotherapy: Theory, Research and Practice, 34,* 353–364.

Briere, J., & Elliott, D. M. (1998). Clinical utility of the Impact of Event Scale: Psychometrics in the general population. *Assessment, 5,* 135–144.

Briere, J., & Elliott, D. M. (2000). Prevalence, characteristics, and long-term sequelae of natural disaster exposure in the general population. *Journal of Traumatic Stress, 13,* 661–679.

Briere, J., & Elliott, D. M. (2003). Prevalence and symptomatic sequelae of self-reported childhood physical and sexual abuse in a general population sample of men and women. *Child Abuse and Neglect, 27,* 1205–1222.

Briere, J., Elliott, D. M., Harris, K., & Cotman, A. (1995). Trauma Symptom Inventory: Psychometrics and association with childhood and adult trauma in clinical samples. *Journal of Interpersonal Violence, 10,* 387–401.

Briere, J., & Gil, E. (1998). Self-mutilation in clinical and general population samples: Prevalence, correlates, and functions. *American Journal of Orthopsychiatry, 68,* 609–620.

Briere, J., Goldin, J. N., & Rodriguez, M. M. (2003). *Detailed Assessment of Posttraumatic Stress Interpretive Report for Windows® (DAPS–IR)™.* Odessa, FL: Psychological Assessment Resources.

Briere, J., & Jordan, C. (in press). Violence against women: Outcome complexity, "assault syndromes," and implications for treatment. *Journal of Interpersonal Violence.*

Briere, J., & Runtz, M. (1988). Symptomatology associated with childhood sexual victimization in a nonclinical adult sample. *Child Abuse and Neglect, 12,* 51–59.

Briere, J., & Runtz, M. (1989). The Trauma Symptom Checklist (TSC-33): Early data on a new scale. *Journal of Interpersonal Violence, 4,* 151–163.

Briere, J., & Runtz, M. (1990a). Augmenting Hopkins SCL scales to measure dissociative symptoms: Data from two nonclinical samples. *Journal of Personality Assessment, 55,* 376–379.

Briere, J., & Runtz, M. (1990b). Differential adult symptomatology associated with three types of child abuse histories. *Child Abuse and Neglect, 14,* 357–364.

Briere, J., & Runtz, M. (2002). The Inventory of Altered Self-Capacities (IASC): A standardized measure of identity, affect regulation, and relationship disturbance. *Assessment, 9,* 230–239.

Briere, J., & Scott, C. (in press). *Principles of trauma therapy: A practical guide to symptoms, evaluation, and therapy.* Thousand Oaks, CA: Sage.

Briere, J., Scott, C., & Weathers, F. (2003). *Peritraumatic and persistent dissociation in the presumed etiology of PTSD.* Unpublished manuscript.

Briere, J., & Spinazzola, J. (in press). Phenomenology and psychological assessment of complex posttraumatic states. *Journal of Traumatic Stress.*

Briere, J., Weathers, F. W., & Runtz, M. (in press). Is dissociation a multidimensional construct? Data from the Multiscale Dissociation Inventory. *Journal of Traumatic Stress.*

Briere, J., Woo, R., McRae, B., Foltz, J., & Sitzman, R. (1997). Lifetime victimization history, demographics, and clinical status in female psychiatric emergency room patients. *Journal of Nervous and Mental Disease, 185,* 95–101.

Briere, J., & Zaidi, L. Y. (1989). Sexual abuse histories and sequelae in female psychiatric emergency room patients. *American Journal of Psychiatry, 146,* 1602–1606.

Brodsky, B. S., Oquendo, M. A., Ellis, S. P., Haas, G. L., Malone, K. M., & Mann, J. J. (2001). The relationship of childhood abuse to impulsivity and suicidal behavior in adults with major depression. *American Journal of Psychiatry, 158,* 1871–1877.

Brown, T. A., Campbell, L. A., Lehman, C. L., Grisham, J. R., & Mancill, R. B. (2001). Current and lifetime comorbidity of the DSM–IV anxiety and mood disorders in a large clinical sample. *Journal of Abnormal Psychology, 110,* 585–599.

Brown, T. A., DiNardo, P. A., & Barlow, D. H. (1994). *Anxiety Disorders Interview Schedule for DSM–IV (ADIS–IV).* San Antonio, TX: Psychological Corporation.

Brown, E. J., & Heimberg, R. G. (2001). Effects of writing about rape: Evaluating Pennebaker's paradigm with a severe trauma. *Journal of Traumatic Stress, 14,* 781–790.

Bryant, R. A., & Harvey, A. G. (1996). Posttraumatic stress reactions in volunteer firefighters. *Journal of Traumatic Stress, 9,* 51–62.

Bryant, R. A., & Harvey, A. G. (1999). Acute stress disorder following motor vehicle accidents. In E. J. Hickling & E. B. Blanchard (Eds.), *The international handbook of road traffic accidents and psychological trauma: Current understanding, treatment and law* (pp. 29–42). Amsterdam, Netherlands: Elsevier Science.

Bryant, R. A., & Harvey, A. G. (2000). *Acute stress disorder: A handbook of theory, assessment, and treatment.* Washington, DC: American Psychological Association.

Bryant, R. A., & Harvey, A. G. (2002). Delayed-onset posttraumatic stress disorder: A prospective evaluation. *Australian and New Zealand Journal of Psychiatry, 36,* 205–209.

Bryant, R. A., Harvey, A. G., Dang, S. T., & Sackville, T. (1998). Assessing acute stress disorder: Psychometric properties of a structured clinical interview. *Psychological Assessment, 10,* 215–220.

Bryant, R. A., Moulds, M. L., & Guthrie, R. M. (2000). Acute Stress Disorder Scale: A self-report measure of acute stress disorder. *Psychological Assessment, 12,* 61–68.

Bryer, J. B., Nelson, B. A., Miller, J. B., & Krol, P. A. (1987). Childhood sexual and physical abuse as factors in adult psychiatric illness. *American Journal of Psychiatry, 144,* 1426–1430.

Bulik, C. M., Prescott, C. A., & Kendler, K. S. (2001). Features of childhood sexual abuse and the development of psychiatric and substance use disorders. *British Journal of Psychiatry, 179,* 444–449.

Burgess, A. W., & Holstrom, L. L. (1974). Rape trauma syndrome. *American Journal of Psychiatry, 133,* 981–986.

Burke, J. (1986). Diagnostic categorization by the Diagnostic Interview Schedule (DIS): A comparison with other measures of assessment. In J. E. Barrett & R. M. Rose (Eds.), *Mental disorder in the community: Progress and challenge.* New York: Guilford Press.

Bury, A. S., & Bagby, R. M. (2002). The detection of feigned uncoached and coached posttraumatic stress disorder with the MMPI–2 in a sample of workplace accident victims. *Psychological Assessment, 14,* 472–484.

Busby, D. M., Glenn, E., Steggell, G. L., & Adamson, D. W. (1993). Treatment issues for survivors of physical and sexual abuse. *Journal of Marital and Family Therapy, 19,* 377–391.

Butcher, J. N., Dahlstrom, W. G., Graham, J. R., Tellegen, A., & Kaemmer, B. (1989). *Minnesota Multiphasic Personality Inventory (MMPI–2). Manual for administration and scoring.* Minneapolis: University of Minnesota Press.

Caldwell, A. B., & O'Hare, C. (1975). *A handbook of MMPI personality types.* Santa Monica, CA: Clinical Psychological Services.

Calhoun, P. S., Earnst, K. S., Tucker, D. D., Kirby, A. C., & Beckham, J. C. (2000). Feigning combat-related posttraumatic stress disorder on the Personality Assessment Inventory. *Journal of Personality Assessment, 75,* 338–350.

Campbell, J. C., & Soeken, K. L. (1999). Forced sex and intimate partner violence: Effects on women's risk and women's health. *Violence Against Women, 5,* 1017–1035.

Cardeña, E., Classen, C., & Spiegel, D. (1991). *Stanford Acute Stress Reaction Questionnaire (SASRQ).* Unpublished manuscript, Department of Psychiatry and Behavioral Sciences, Stanford University, Palo Alto, CA.

Cardeña, E., Holen, A., McFarlane, A., Solomon, Z., Wilkenson, C., & Spiegel, D. (1998). A multi-site study of acute stress reactions to a disaster. In American

Psychiatric Association (Ed.), *DSM–IV sourcebook, Volume IV*. Washington, DC: American Psychiatric Association.

Cardeña, E., Koopman, C., Classen, C., & Spiegel, D. (1996). Review of the Stanford Acute Stress Reaction Questionnaire. In B. H. Stamm (Ed.), *Measurement of stress, trauma and adaptation*. Lutherville, MD: Sidran Press.

Cardeña, E., Koopman, C., Classen, C. C., Waelde, L. C., & Spiegel, D. (2000). Psychometric properties of the Stanford Acute Stress Reaction Questionnaire (SASRQ): A valid and reliable measure of acute stress. *Journal of Traumatic Stress, 13,* 719–734.

Cardeña, E., Lewis-Fernandez, R., Bear, D., Pakianathan, I., & Spiegel, D. (1996). Dissociative disorders. In American Psychiatric Association (Ed.), *DSM–IV sourcebook, Volume 2*. Washington, DC: American Psychiatric Association.

Cardeña, E., & Speigel, D. (1993). Dissociative reactions to the San Francisco Bay Area Earthquake of 1989. *American Journal of Psychiatry, 150,* 474–478.

Carlin, A. S., & Ward, N. G. (1992). Subtypes of psychiatric inpatient women who have been sexually abused. *Journal of Nervous and Mental Disease, 180,* 392–397.

Carlson, E. B. (1997). *Trauma assessments: A clinician's guide*. New York: Guilford Press.

Carlson, E. B. (2001). Psychometric study of a brief screen for PTSD: Assessing the impact of multiple traumatic events. *Assessment, 8,* 431–441.

Carlson, E. B., & Armstrong, J. (1994). Diagnosis and assessment of dissociative disorders. In S. J. Lynn & J. L. Rhue (Eds.), *Dissociation: Theoretical, clinical, and research perspective* (pp. 159–174). New York: Guilford Press.

Carlson, E. B., & Dalenberg, C. J. (2000). A conceptual framework for the impact of traumatic experiences. *Trauma, Violence, and Abuse: A Review Journal, 1,* 4–28.

Carlson, E. B., Dalenberg, C. J., Armstrong, J. G., Daniels, J. W., Loewenstein, R. J., & Roth, D. (2001). Multivariate prediction of posttraumatic symptoms in psychiatric inpatients. *Journal of Traumatic Stress, 14,* 549–567.

Carlson, E. B., & Dutton, M. A. (2003). Assessing experiences and responses of crime victims. *Journal of Traumatic Stress, 16,* 133–148.

Carlson, E. B., Putnam, F. W., Ross, C. A., Torem, M., Coons, P., Dill, D., et al. (1993). Validity of the Dissociative Experiences Scale in screening for multiple personality disorder: A multicenter study. *American Journal of Psychiatry, 150,* 1030–1036.

Cattell, J. P., & Cattell, J. R. (1974). Depersonalization: Psychological and social perspectives. In S. Arieti (Ed.), *American handbook of psychiatry* (pp. 767–799). New York: Basic Books.

Center for Victims of Torture. (2004). *National outreach*. Retrieved February 3, 2004 from http://www2.cvt.org/main.php/BuildingHealing Communities/NationalOutreach

Centers for Disease Control. (1987). Postservice mortality among Vietnam veterans. *Journal of the American Medical Association, 257*, 790–795.

Cerney, M. (1990). The Rorschach and traumatic loss: Can the presence of traumatic loss be detected from the Rorschach? *Journal of Personality Assessment, 55*, 781–789.

Chakraborty, A. (1991). Culture, colonialism, and psychiatry. *Lancet, 337*, 1204–1207.

Chan, C. S. (1987). Asian-American women: Psychological responses to sexual exploitation and cultural stereotypes. *Women and Therapy, 6*, 33–38.

Choca, J. P., Shanley, L. A., & Van Denburg, E. (1992). *Interpretative guide to the Millon Clinical Multiaxial Inventory.* Washington, DC: American Psychological Association.

Chu, J. A., & Dill, D. L. (1990). Dissociative symptoms in relation to childhood physical and sexual abuse. *American Journal of Psychiatry, 147*, 887–892.

Chu, J. A., Frey, L. M., Ganzel, B. L., & Matthews, J. A. (1999). Memories of childhood abuse: Dissociation, amnesia, and corroboration. *American Journal of Psychiatry, 156*, 749–755.

Chung, M. C., Farmer, S., Werrett, J., Easthope, Y., & Chung, C. (2001). Traumatic stress and ways of coping of community residents exposed to a train disaster. *Australian and New Zealand Journal of Psychiatry, 35*, 528–534.

Classen, C. C., Koopman, C., Hales, R. E., & Spiegel, D. (1998). Acute stress disorder as a predictor of posttraumatic stress symptoms. *American Journal of Psychiatry, 155*, 620–624.

Classen, C. C., Nevo, R., Koopman, C., Nevill-Manning, K., Gore-Felton, C., Rose, D. S., et al. (2002). Recent stressful life events, sexual revictimization, and their relationship with traumatic stress symptoms among women sexually abused in childhood. *Journal of Interpersonal Violence, 17*, 1274–1290.

Cloitre, M., Cohen, L. R., Edelman, R. E., & Han, H. (2001). Posttraumatic stress disorder and extent of trauma exposure as correlates of medical problems and perceived health among women with childhood abuse. *Women and Health, 34*, 1–17.

Cloitre, M., Tardiff, K., Marzuk, P. M., Leon, A. C., & Portera, L. (1996). Childhood abuse and subsequent sexual assault among female inpatients. *Journal of Traumatic Stress, 9*, 473–482.

Coe, M. T., Dalenberg, C. J., Aransky, K. M., & Reto, C. S. (1995). Adult attachment style, reported childhood violence history and types of dissociative experiences. *Dissociation: Progress in the Dissociative Disorders, 8*, 142–154.

Coker, A. L., Smith, P. H., Thompson, M. P., McKeown, R. E., Bethea, L., & Davis, K. E. (2002). Social support protects against the negative effects of partner violence on mental health. *Journal of Women's Health and Gender-Based Medicine, 11*, 465–476.

Cole, P. M., & Putnam, F. W. (1992). Effect of incest on self and social functioning: A developmental psychopathology perspective. *Journal of Consulting and Clinical Psychology, 60,* 174–184.

Cooper, B. S., Kennedy, M. A., & Yuille, J. C. (2001). Dissociation and sexual trauma in prostitutes: Variability of responses. *Journal of Trauma and Dissociation, 2,* 27–36.

Cordova, M. J., Studts, J. L., Hann, D. M., Jacobsen, P. B., & Andrykowski, M. A. (2000). Symptom structure of PTSD following breast cancer. *Journal of Traumatic Stress, 13,* 301–319.

Courtois, C. (1995). Assessment and diagnosis. In C. Classen (Ed.), *Treating women molested in childhood* (pp. 1–34). San Francisco: Jossey-Bass.

Courtois, C. A. (1999). *Recollections of sexual abuse: Treatment principles and guidelines.* New York: Norton.

Craig, R. J., & Olson, R. (1997). Assessing PTSD with the Millon Clinical Multiaxial Inventory–III. *Journal of Clinical Psychology, 53,* 943–952.

Culbertson, K. A., & Dehle, C. (2001). Impact of sexual assault as a function of perpetrator type. *Journal of Interpersonal Violence, 16,* 992–1007.

Currier, G., & Briere, J. (2000). Trauma orientation and detection of violence histories in the psychiatric emergency service. *Journal of Nervous and Mental Disease, 188,* 622–624.

Dalenberg, C. J. (1999). The management of dissociative symptoms in PTSD patients. *National Center for PTSD Clinical Quarterly, 8,* 27–29.

Dancu, C. V., Riggs, D. S., Hearst-Ikeda, D., Shoyer, B. G., & Foa, E. B. (1996). Dissociative experiences and posttraumatic stress disorder among female victims of criminal assault and rape. *Journal of Traumatic Stress, 9,* 253–267.

David, D., Kutcher, G. S., Jackson, E. I., & Mellman, T. A. (1999). Psychotic symptoms in combat-related posttraumatic stress disorder. *Journal of Clinical Psychiatry, 60,* 29–32.

Davidson, J., Kudler, H., & Smith, R. (1990). *The Structured Interview for PTSD (SI–PTSD).* Unpublished manuscript, Department of Psychiatry, Duke University, Durham, NC.

Davidson, J. R. T. (1994). Issues in the diagnosis of posttraumatic stress disorder. In R. S. Pynoos (Ed.), *Posttraumatic stress disorder: A clinical review* (pp. 1–15). Lutherville, MD: Sidran Press.

Davidson, J. R. T., Book, S. W., Colket, J. T., Tupler, L. A., Roth, S. H., David, D., et al. (1997). Assessment of a new self-rating scale for posttraumatic stress disorder. *Psychological Medicine, 27,* 153–160.

Davidson, J. R. T., & Foa, E. B. (1991). Diagnostic issues in posttraumatic stress disorder: Considerations for the DSM–IV. *Journal of Abnormal Psychology, 100,* 346–355.

Davidson, J. R. T., & Foa, E. B. (Eds.). (1993). *Posttraumatic Stress Disorder: DSM–IV and beyond.* Washington, DC: American Psychiatric Press.

Davidson, J. R. T., Tharwani, H. M., & Connor, K. M. (2002). Davidson Trauma Scale (DTS): Normative scores in the general population and effect sizes in placebo-controlled SSRI trials. *Depression and Anxiety, 15,* 75–78.

De Jong, J. T. V. M., Komproe, I. H., Van Ommeren, M., El Masri, M., Araya, M., Khaled, et al. (2001). Lifetime events and posttraumatic stress disorder in 4 postconflict settings. *Journal of the American Medical Association, 286,* 555–562.

Demaré, D. (1993). *The Childhood Maltreatment Questionnaire.* Unpublished manuscript, University of Manitoba, Winnipeg, Manitoba, Canada.

Demaré, D., & Briere, J. (1994, Aug.). *Childhood maltreatment and current symptomatology in 1,179 university students.* Paper presented at the annual meeting of the American Psychological Association, Los Angeles, CA.

Derogatis, L. R. (1977). *SCL–90: Administration, scoring, and procedure manual–I for the R (revised) version.* Baltimore: Johns Hopkins University School of Medicine.

Derogatis, L. R. (1983). *SCL–90–R administration, scoring, and procedures manual II for the revised version* (2nd ed.). Towson, MD: Clinical Psychometrics Research.

Derogatis, L. R., Lipman, R. S., Rickels, K., Ulenhuth, E. H., & Covi, L. (1974). The Hopkins Symptom Checklist (HSCL): A self-report symptom inventory. *Behavioral Science, 19,* 1–15.

Derogatis, L. R., & Spencer, P. M. (1982). *The Brief Symptom Inventory administration, scoring, and procedures.* Baltimore: Clinical Psychometric Research Institute.

Desivilya, H. S., Gal, R., & Ayalon, O. (1996). Extent of victimization, traumatic stress symptoms, and adjustment of terrorist assault survivors: A long-term follow-up. *Journal of Traumatic Stress, 9,* 881–889.

De Zulueta, F. I. S. (1998). Human violence: A treatable epidemic. *Medicine, Conflict and Survival, 14,* 46–55.

Dietrich, A. M. (2003). Characteristics of child maltreatment, psychological dissociation, and somatoform dissociation of Canadian inmates. *Journal of Trauma and Dissociation, 4,* 81–100.

DiTomasso, M. J., & Routh, D. K. (1993). Recall of abuse in childhood and three measures of dissociation. *Child Abuse and Neglect, 17,* 477–485.

Drossman, D. A., Lesserman, J., Nachman, G., Li, Z., Gluck, H., Toomey, T. C., & Mitchell, C. M. (1990). Sexual and physical abuse in women with functional or organic gastrointestinal disorders. *Annuals of Internal Medicine, 113,* 828–833.

Dougall, A. L., Herberman, H. B., Delahanty, D. L., Inslicht, S. S., & Baum, A. S. (2000). Similarity of prior trauma exposure as a determinant of chronic stress responding to an airline disaster. *Journal of Consulting and Clinical Psychology, 68,* 290–295.

Dubester, K. A., & Braun, B. G. (1995). Psychometric properties of the dissociative experiences scale. *Journal of Nervous and Mental Disease, 183,* 231–235.

Dutton, D. G. (1992). Theoretical and empirical perspectives on the etiology and prevention of wife assault. In R. D. Peters, R. J. McMahon, & V. L. Quinsey (Eds.), *Aggression and violence throughout the life span*. Newbury Park, CA: Sage.

Dutton, M. A., Hohnecker, L. C., Halle, P. M., & Burghardt, K. J. (1994). Traumatic responses among battered women who kill. *Journal of Traumatic Stress, 7*, 549–564.

Dutton, M. A., Kilpatrick, D. G., Friedman, M., & Patel, V. (2003). Violence against women. In B. L. Green, M. J. Friedman, J. T. V. M. De Jong, S. D. Solomon, T. M. Keane, J. A. Fairbank, et al. (Eds.), *Trauma interventions in war and peace: Prevention, practice, and policy* (pp. 155–184). New York: Kluwer Press.

Edens, J. F., Otto, R. K., & Dwyer, T. J. (1998). Susceptibility of the Trauma Symptom Inventory to malingering. *Journal of Personality Assessment, 71*, 379–392.

Edwards, G., & Angus, J. (1972). Depersonalization. *British Journal of Psychiatry, 120*, 242–244.

Eisenman, D. P., Gelberg, L., Liu, H., & Shapiro, M. F. (2003). Mental health and health-related quality of life among adult Latino primary care patients living in the United States with previous exposure to political violence. *Journal of the American Medical Association, 290*, 627–634.

Ekblad, S., Prochazka, H., & Roth, G. (2002). Psychological impact of torture: A 3-month follow-up of mass-evacuated Kosovan adults in Sweden, lessons learnt for prevention. *Acta Psychiatrica Scandinavica, 106*, 30–36.

El-Bassel, N., & Schilling, R. (1997). Sex trading and psychological distress among women recruited from the streets of Harlem. *American Journal of Public Health, 87*, 66–70.

Elhai, J. D., Gold, P. B., Frueh, B. C., & Gold, S. N. (2000). Cross-validation of the MMPI–2 in detecting malingering posttraumatic stress disorder. *Journal of Personality Assessment, 75*, 449–463.

Elhai, J. D., Gold, S. N., Mateus, L. F., & Astaphan, T. A. (2001). Scale 8 elevations on the MMPI–2 among women survivors of childhood sexual abuse: Evaluating posttraumatic stress, depression, and dissociation as predictors. *Journal of Family Violence, 16*, 47–57.

Elhai, J. D., Gold, S. N., Sellers, A. H., & Dorfman, W. I. (2001). The detection of malingered posttraumatic stress disorder with MMPI–2 fake bad indices. *Assessment, 8*, 221–236.

Elhai, J. D., Klotz Flitter, J. M., Gold, S. N., & Sellers, A. H. (2001). Identifying subtypes of women survivors of childhood sexual abuse: An MMPI–2 cluster analysis. *Journal of Traumatic Stress, 14*, 157–175.

Elhai, J. D., Ruggiero, K. J., Frueh, B. C., Beckham, J. C., Gold, P. B., & Feldman, M. E. (2002). The Infrequency-Posttraumatic Stress Disorder Scale (FPTSD) for the MMPI–2: Development and initial validation with veterans presenting with combat-related PTSD. *Journal of Personality Assessment, 79,* 531–549.

Elklit, A. (2002). Victimization and PTSD in a Danish national youth probability sample. *Journal of the American Academy of Child and Adolescent Psychiatry, 41,* 174–181.

Ellason, J. W., Ross, C. A., & Fuchs, D. L. (1996). Lifetime axis I and II comorbidity and childhood trauma history in dissociative identity disorder. *Psychiatry, 59,* 255–266.

Elliott, D. M. (1992). *Traumatic Events Survey.* Unpublished psychological test. Los Angeles: Harbor–UCLA Medical Center.

Elliott, D. M. (1993, Nov.). *Assessing the psychological impact of recent violence in an inpatient setting.* Paper presented at the meeting of the International Society for Traumatic Stress Studies, San Antonio, TX.

Elliott, D. M. (1994a). Assessing adult victims of interpersonal violence. In J. Briere (Ed.), *Assessing and treating victims of violence.* New Directions for Mental Health Services series (MHS #64, 5–16). San Francisco: Jossey-Bass.

Elliott, D. M. (1994b). Impaired object relations in professional women molested as children. *Psychotherapy, 31,* 79–86.

Elliott, D. M. (1997). Traumatic events: Prevalence and delayed recall in the general population. *Journal of Consulting and Clinical Psychology, 65,* 811–820.

Elliott, D. M., & Briere, J. (1992). Sexual abuse trauma among professional women: Validating the Trauma Symptom Checklist–40 (TSC–40). *Child Abuse and Neglect, 16,* 391–398.

Elliott, D. M., & Briere, J. (1994). Forensic sexual abuse evaluations of older children: Disclosures and symptomatology. *Behavioral Sciences and the Law, 12,* 261–277.

Elliott, D. M., & Briere, J. (1995). Posttraumatic stress associated with delayed recall of sexual abuse: A general population study. *Journal of Traumatic Stress, 8,* 629–647.

Elliott, D. M., & Briere, J. (in press). Prevalence and symptomatic sequelae of physical and sexual domestic violence in a general population sample of women. *Psychotherapy: Theory, Research and Practice.*

Elliott, D. M., Mok, D., & Briere, J. (in press). Adult sexual assault: Prevalence, symptomatology, and sex differences. *Journal of Traumatic Stress.*

El Sarraj, E., Punamaki, R., Salmi, S., & Summerfield, D. (1996). Experiences of torture and ill-treatment and posttraumatic stress disorder symptoms among Palestinian prisoners. *Journal of Traumatic Stress, 9,* 595–606.

Engdahl, B. E., & Eberly, R. E. (1990). The effects of torture and other maltreatment: Implications for psychology. In P. Suedfeld (Ed.), *Psychology and torture* (pp. 31–47). New York: Hemisphere.

Engles, M. L., Moisan, D., & Harris, R. (1994). MMPI indices of childhood trauma among 110 female outpatients. *Journal of Personality Assessment, 63,* 135–147.

Engelhard, I. M., van den Hout, M. A., & Arntz, A. (2001). Posttraumatic stress disorder after pregnancy loss. *General Hospital Psychiatry, 23,* 62–66.

Enns, C. Z., McNeilly, C. L., Corkery, J. M., & Gilbert, M. S. (1995). The debate about delayed memories of child sexual abuse: A feminist perspective. *Counseling Psychologist, 23,* 181–279.

Epstein, M. A., & Bottoms, B. L. (2002). Explaining the forgetting and recovery of abuse and trauma memories: Possible mechanisms. *Child Maltreatment, 7,* 210–225.

Epstein, R. S. (1993). Avoidant symptoms cloaking the diagnosis of PTSD in patients with severe accidental injury. *Journal of Traumatic Stress, 6,* 451–458.

Epstein, R. S., Fullerton, C. S., & Ursano, R. J. (1998). Posttraumatic stress disorder following an air disaster: A prospective study. *American Journal of Psychiatry, 155,* 934–938.

Eriksson, C. B., Van de Kemp, H., Gorsuch, R., Hoke, S., & Foy, D. W. (2002). Trauma exposure and PTSD symptoms in international relief and development personnel. *Journal of Traumatic Stress, 14,* 205–212.

Erwin, B. A., Heimberg, R. G., Juster, H. R., & Mindlin, M. (2002). Comorbid anxiety and mood disorders among persons with social anxiety disorder. *Behaviour Research and Therapy, 40,* 19–35.

Exner, J. E. (1979). *The Rorschach: A comprehensive system.* New York: Wiley.

Exner, J. E. (1986). *The Rorschach: A comprehensive system* (2nd ed.). New York: Wiley.

Fairbank, J. A., Caddell, J. M., & Keane, T. M. (1985, Aug.). *Black–White differences on the MMPI and PTSD subscale.* Paper presented at the annual meeting of the American Psychological Association, Los Angeles.

Fairbank, J. A., Hansen, D. J., & Fitterling, J. M. (1991). Patterns of appraisal and coping across different stressor conditions among former prisoners of war with and without posttraumatic stress disorder. *Journal of Consulting and Clinical Psychology, 59,* 274–281.

Fairbank, J. A., Keane, T. M., & Malloy, P. F. (1983). Some preliminary data on the psychological characteristics of Vietnam veterans with post-traumatic stress disorder. *Journal of Consulting and Clinical Psychology, 51,* 912–919.

Fairbank, S. A., McCaffrey, R. J., & Keane, T. M. (1985). Psychometric detection of fabricated symptoms of post-traumatic stress disorder in Vietnam veterans. *Journal of Clinical Psychology, 43,* 44–55.

Falsetti, S. A., & Resnick, H. S. (1995). Helping the victims of violent crime. In J. R. Freedy & S. E. Hobfoll (Eds.), *Traumatic stress: From theory to practice* (pp. 263–285). New York: Plenum.

Falsetti, S. A., & Resnick, H. S. (1997). Frequency and severity of panic attack symptoms in a treatment seeking sample of trauma victims. *Journal of Traumatic Stress, 10,* 683–689.

Falsetti, S. A., Resnick, H. S., Kilpatrick, D. G., & Freedy, J. R. (1994). A review of the "Potential Stressful Events Interview": A comprehensive assessment instrument of high and low magnitude stressors. *Behavior Therapist, 17,* 66–67.

Falsetti, S. A., Resnick, H. S., Resick, P. A., & Kilpatrick, D. G. (1993). The Modified PTSD Symptom Scale: A brief self-report measure of post-traumatic stress disorder. *Behavior Therapist, 17,* 66–67.

Farley, M. (Ed.). (in press). *Prostitution, trafficking, and traumatic stress.* Binghamton, NY: Hayworth.

Farley, M., Baral, I., Kiremire, M., & Sezgin, U. (1998). Prostitution in five countries: Violence and post-traumatic stress disorder. *Feminism and Psychology, 8,* 405–426.

Farley, M., & Barkan, H. (1998). Prostitution, violence and posttraumatic stress disorder. *Women and Health, 27,* 37–49.

Farley, M., Cotton, M., Lynne, J., Zumbeck, S., Spiwak, F., Reyes, M. E., Alvarez, D., et al. (in press). Prostitution and trafficking in nine countries: An update on violence and posttraumatic stress disorder. In M. Farley (Ed.), *Prostitution, trafficking, and traumatic stress.* Binghamton, NY: Hayworth.

Farley, M., & Kelly, V. (2000). Prostitution: A critical review of the medical and social sciences literature. *Women and Criminal Justice, 11,* 29–64.

Fauerbach, J. A., Richter, L., & Lawrence, J. W. (2002). Regulating acute post-trauma distress. *Journal of Burn Care and Rehabilitation, 23,* 249–257.

Fear, C. F. (1996). Factitious post-traumatic stress disorder revisited. *Irish Journal of Psychological Medicine, 13,* 116–118.

Feinstein, A., Hershkop, S., Ouchterlony, D., Jardine, A., & McCullagh, S. (2002). Posttraumatic amnesia and recall of a traumatic event following traumatic brain injury. *Journal of Neuropsychiatry and Clinical Neurosciences, 14,* 25–30.

Feldman-Summers, S., & Pope, K. S. (1994). The experience of "forgetting" childhood abuse: A national survey of psychologists. *Journal of Consulting and Clinical Psychology, 62,* 636–639.

Figley, C. R. (1989). *Helping traumatized families.* San Francisco: Jossey-Bass.

Finkelhor, D. (1990). Early and long-term effects of child sexual abuse: An update. *Professional Psychology: Research and Practice, 21,* 325–330.

Finkelhor, D., Hotaling, G., Lewis, I. A., & Smith, C. (1989). Sexual abuse and its relationship to later sexual satisfaction, marital status, religion, and attitudes. *Journal of Interpersonal Violence, 4,* 279–399.

Finkelhor, D., Hotaling, G., Lewis, I. A., & Smith, C. (1990). Sexual abuse in a national survey of adult men and women: Prevalence, characteristics, and risk factors. *Child Abuse and Neglect, 14,* 19–28.

Finkelhor, D., & Yllo, K. (1985). *License to rape: Sexual abuse of wives.* New York: Holt, Rinehart, & Winston.

Finnsdottir, T., & Elklit, A. (2002). Posttraumatic sequelae in a community hit by an avalanche. *Journal of Traumatic Stress, 15,* 479–485.

First, M. B., Spitzer, R. L., Gibbon, M., & Williams, J. B. W. (1997). *Structured clinical interview for DSM–IV Axis I (SCID–I), Clinician version.* Washington, DC: American Psychiatric Press.

Fisher, P. M., Winne, P. H., & Ley, R. G. (1993). Group therapy for adult women survivors of child sexual abuse: Differentiation of completers versus dropouts. *Psychotherapy, 30,* 616–624.

Flack, W. F., Litz, B. T., Weathers, F. W., & Beaudreau, S. A. (2002). Assessment and diagnosis of PTSD in adults: A comprehensive psychological approach. In M. B. Williams & J. F. Sommer (Eds.), *Simple and complex posttraumatic stress disorder: Strategies for comprehensive treatment in clinical practice* (pp. 9–22). Binghamton, NY: Haworth Press.

Flett, R. A., Kazantzis, N., Long, N. R., MacDonald, C., & Millar, M. (2002). Traumatic events and physical health in a New Zealand community sample. *Journal of Traumatic Stress, 15,* 303–312.

Foa, E. B. (1995). *Posttraumatic Stress Diagnostic Scale.* Minneapolis, MN: National Computer Systems.

Foa, E. B., Cashman, L., Jaycox, L. H., & Perry, K. J. (1997). The validation of a self-report measure of posttraumatic stress disorder: The Posttraumatic Diagnostic Scale. *Psychological Assessment, 9,* 445–451.

Foa, E. B., Ehlers, A., Clark, D. M., Tolin, D. F., & Orsillo, S. M. (1999). The Posttraumatic Cognitions Inventory (PTCI): Development and validation. *Psychological Assessment, 11,* 303–314.

Foa, E. B., Riggs, D. S., Dancu, C. V., & Rothbaum, B. O. (1993). Reliability and validity of a brief instrument assessing post-traumatic stress disorder. *Journal of Traumatic Stress, 6,* 459–474.

Foa, E. B., & Tolin, D. F. (2000). Comparison of the PTSD Symptom Scale-Interview Version and the Clinician-Administered PTSD Scale. *Journal of Traumatic Stress, 13,* 181–191.

Foa, E. B., Zinbarg, R. E., & Rothbaum, B. O. (1992). Uncontrollability and unpredictability in post-traumatic stress disorder: An animal model. *Psychological Bulletin, 112,* 218–238.

Follette, V. M., Polusney, M. A., Bechtle, A. E., & Naugle, A. E. (1996). Cumulative trauma: The impact of child sexual abuse, adult sexual assault, and spouse abuse. *Journal of Traumatic Stress, 9,* 25–35.

Follette, W. C., Naugle, A. E., & Follette, V. M. (1997). MMPI–2 profiles of adult women with child sexual abuse histories: Cluster-analytic findings. *Journal of Consulting and Clinical Psychology, 65,* 858–866.

Fontana, A., & Rosenheck, R. A. (1998). Duty-related and sexual stress in the etiology of PTSD among women veterans who seek treatment. *Psychiatric Services, 49,* 658–662.

Forbes, D., Creamer, M., & McHugh, T. (1999). MMPI–2 Data for Australian Vietnam veterans with combat-related PTSD. *Journal of Traumatic Stress, 12,* 371–378.

Forman, B. D. (1982). Reported male rape. *Victimology, 7,* 235–236.

Forster, P. (1992). Nature and treatment of acute stress reactions. In L. S. Austin (Ed.), *Responding to disaster: A guide for mental health professionals.* Washington, DC: American Psychiatric Press.

Foy, D. W., Resnick, H. S., Sipprelle, R. C., & Carroll, E. M., (1987). Premilitary, military, and postmilitary factors in the development of combat-related Posttraumatic Stress Disorder. *Behavior Therapist, 10,* 3–9.

Foy, D. W., Sipprelle, R. C., Rueger, D. B., & Carroll, E. M. (1984). Etiology of posttraumatic stress syndrome in Vietnam veterans: Analysis of premilitary, military, and combat exposure influences. *Journal of Consulting and Clinical Psychology, 52,* 79–87.

Franklin, C. L., Sheeran, T., & Zimmerman, M. (2002). Screening for trauma histories, posttraumatic stress disorders (PTSD) and subthreshold PTSD in psychiatric outpatients. *Psychological Assessment, 14,* 467–471.

Freinkel, A., Koopman, C., & Spiegel, D. (1994). Dissociative symptoms in media execution witnesses. *American Journal of Psychiatry, 151,* 1335–1339.

Friedman, M. J., & Jaranson, J. M. (1994). The applicability of the PTSD concept to refugees. In A. J. Marsella, T. H. Borneman, S. Ekblad, & J. Orley (Eds.), *Amid peril and pain: The mental health and well-being of the world's refugees* (pp. 207–228). Washington, DC: American Psychological Association.

Friedrich, W. N. (1994). Assessing children for the effects of sexual victimization. In J. Briere (Ed.), *Assessing and treating victims of violence* (pp. 17–27). New Directions for Mental Health Services series (MHS #64). San Francisco: Jossey-Bass.

Friedrich, W. N. (2002). *Psychological assessment of sexually abused children and their families.* Thousand Oaks, CA: Sage.

Friedrich, W. N., Jaworski, T. M., Huxsahl, J. E., & Bengtson, B. S. (1997). Dissociative and sexual behaviors in children and adolescents with sexual abuse and psychiatric histories. *Journal of Interpersonal Violence, 12,* 155–171.

Finnsdottir, T., & Elklit, A. (2002). Posttraumatic sequelae in a community hit by an avalanche. *Journal of Traumatic Stress, 15,* 479–485.

Frueh, B. C., Hamner, M. B., Cahill, S. P., Gold, P. B., & Hamlin, K. L. (2000). Apparent symptom overreporting in combat veterans evaluated for PTSD. *Clinical Psychology Review, 20,* 853–885.

Fullerton, C. S., Ursano, R. J., Epstein, R. S., Crowley, B., Vance, K., Kao, T. C., et al. (2001). Gender differences in posttraumatic stress disorder after motor vehicle accidents. *American Journal of Psychiatry, 158,* 1486–1491.

Galea, S., Ahern, J., Resnick, H. S., Kilpatrick, D. G., Bucuvalas, M. J., Gold, J., & Vlahov, D. (2002). Psychological sequelae of the September 11 terrorist attacks in New York City. *New England Journal of Medicine, 346,* 982–987.

Galloucis, M., Silverman, M. S., & Francek, H. M. (2000). The impact of trauma exposure on the cognitive schemas of a sample of paramedics. *International Journal of Emergency Mental Health, 2,* 5–18.

Ganley, A. L. (1981). *Court mandated counseling for men who batter: Participants' and trainers' manuals*. Washington, DC: Center for Women's Policy Studies.

Garner, D. M. (1990). *Eating Disorder Inventory–2 professional manual*. Odessa, FL: Psychological Assessment Resources.

Gautam, S., Gupta, I. D., Batra, L., Sharma, H., & Khandelwa, R. (1998). Psychiatric morbidity among victims of a bomb blast. *Indian Journal of Psychiatry, 40*, 41–45.

Gidron, Y. (2002). Posttraumatic stress disorder after terrorist attacks: A review. *Journal of Nervous and Mental Disease, 190*, 118–121.

Gilbert, B. (1994). Treatment of adult victims of rape. In J. Briere (Ed.), *Assessing and treating victims of violence* (pp. 67–78; NDMHS #64). San Francisco: Jossey-Bass.

Gold, J. W., & Cardeña, E. (1998). Convergent validity of three posttraumatic symptoms inventories among adult sexual abuse survivors. *Journal of Traumatic Stress, 11*, 173–180.

Gold, P. B., & Frueh, B. C. (1999). Compensation-seeking and extreme exaggeration of psychopathology among combat veterans evaluated for posttraumatic stress disorder. *Journal of Nervous and Mental Disease, 187*, 680–684.

Gold, S. N., Lucenko, B. A., Elhai, J. D., Swingle, J. M., & Sellers, A. H. (1999). A comparison of psychological/psychiatric symptomatology of women and men sexually abused as children. *Child Abuse and Neglect, 23*, 683–692.

Goldberg, J., True, W. R., Eisen, S. A., & Henderson, W. G. (1990). A twin study of the effects of the Vietnam war on posttraumatic stress disorder. *Journal of the American Medical Association, 263*, 1227–1232.

Goldwater, L., & Duffy, J. F. (1990). Use of the MMPI to uncover histories of childhood abuse in adult female psychiatric patients. *Journal of Clinical Psychology, 46*, 392–398.

Goodman, G. S., Ghetti, S., Quas, J. A., Edelstein, R. S., Alexander, K. W., Redlich, A. D., et al. (2003). A prospective study of memory for child sexual abuse: New findings relevant to the repressed-memory controversy. *Psychological Science, 14*, 113–118.

Goodman, L. A., Corcoran, C. B., Turner, K., Yuan, N., & Green, B. L. (1998). Assessing traumatic event exposure: General issues and preliminary findings for the Stressful Life Events Screening Questionnaire. *Journal of Traumatic Stress, 11*, 521–542.

Goodman, L. A., Saxe, L., & Harvey, M. R. (1991). Homelessness as psychological trauma: Broadening perspectives. *American Psychologist, 46*, 1219–1225.

Goto, T., Wilson, J. P., Kahana, B., & Slane, S. (2002). PTSD, depression and help-seeking patterns following the Miyake Island volcanic eruption. *International Journal of Emergency Mental Health, 4*, 157–171.

Graham, J. R. (1987). *The MMPI: A practical guide* (2nd ed.). New York: Oxford University Press.

Graham, J. R. (1990). *MMPI–2 assessing personality and psychopathology*. New York: Oxford University Press.

Gray, G. C., Reed, R. J., Kaiser, K. S., Smith, T. C., & Gastanaga, V. M. (2002). Self-reported symptoms and medical conditions among 11,868 Gulf War–era veterans: The Seabee Health Study. *American Journal of Epidemiology, 155*, 1033–1044.

Green, B. L. (1994). Traumatic stress and disaster: Mental health effects and factors influencing adaptation. In F. Liehmac & C. C. Nadelson (Eds.), *International Review of Psychiatry* (Vol. 2, pp. 177–210). Washington, DC: American Psychiatric Press.

Green, B. L., Goodman, L. A., Krupnick, J. L., Corcoran, C. B., Petty, R. M., Stockton, P., et al. (2000). Outcomes of single versus multiple trauma exposure in a screening sample. *Journal of Traumatic Stress, 13*, 271–286.

Green, B. L., Grace, M. C., Lindy, J. D., & Gleser, G. C. (1990). War stressor and symptom persistence in posttraumatic stress disorder. *Journal of Anxiety Disorder, 4*, 31–39.

Green, B. L., Grace, M. C., Lindy, J. D., Gleser, G. C., & Leonard, A. C. (1990). Risk factors for PTSD and other diagnoses in a general sample of Vietnam veterans. *American Journal of Psychiatry, 147*, 729–733.

Green, B. L., Krupnick, J. L., Stockton, P., Goodman, L. A., Corcoran, C. B., & Petty, R. M. (2001). Psychological outcomes associated with traumatic loss in a sample of young women. *American Behavioral Scientist, 44*, 817–837.

Green, B. L., Lindy, J. D., Grace, M. C., & Gleser, G. C. (1989). Multiple diagnosis in post-traumatic stress disorder: The role of war stressors. *Journal of Nervous and Mental Disease, 177*, 329–335.

Green, B. L., Lindy, J. D., Grace, M. C., Gleser, G. C., Leonard, A. C., Korol, M. S., et al. (1990). Buffalo Creek survivors in the second decade: Stability of stress symptoms. *American Journal of Orthopsychiatry, 60*, 45–54.

Green, B. L., & Solomon, S. D. (1995). The mental health impact of natural and technological disasters. In J. R. Freedy & S. E. Hobfoll (Eds.), *Traumatic stress: From theory to practice* (pp. 163–180). New York: Plenum Press.

Griffith, P. L., Myers, R. W., Cusick, G. M., & Tankersley, M. J. (1997). MMPI–2 profiles of women differing in sexual abuse history and sexual orientation. *Journal of Clinical Psychology, 53*, 791–800.

Grilo, C. M., Martino, S., Walker, M. L., Becker, D. F., Edell, W. S., & McGlashan, T. H. (1997). Controlled study of psychiatric comorbidity in psychiatrically hospitalized young adults with substance use disorders. *American Journal of Psychiatry, 154*, 1305–1307.

Guarnaccia, P., Rivera, M., Franco, F., & Neighbors, C. (1996). The experiences of ataques de nervios: Towards an anthropology of emotions in Puerto Rico. *Culture, Medicine and Psychiatry, 20*, 343–367.

Hammarberg, M. (1992). Penn Inventory for Posttraumatic Stress Disorder: Psychometric properties. *Psychological Assessment, 4*, 67–76.

Hamner, M. B., Frueh, B. C., Ulmer, H. G., & Arana, G. W. (1999). Psychotic features and illness severity in combat veterans with chronic posttraumatic stress disorder. *Society of Biological Psychiatry, 45,* 846–852.

Hanneke, C. R., Shields, N. M., & McCall, G. J. (1986). Assessing the prevalence of marital rape. *Journal of Interpersonal Violence, 1,* 350–362.

Hanson, R. F., Kilpatrick, D. G., Falsetti, S. A., & Resnick, H. S. (1995). Violent crime and mental health. In J. R. Freedy & S. E. Hobfoll (Eds.), *Traumatic stress: From theory to practice* (pp. 129–161). New York: Plenum Press.

Hardesty, L., & Greif, G. L. (1994). Common themes in a group for female IV drug users who are HIV positive. *Journal of Psychoactive Drugs, 26,* 289–293.

Harris, R., & Lingoes, J. (1968). *Subscales for the Minnesota Multiphasic Personality Inventory* (mimeographed materials). Department of Psychology, University of Michigan, Ann Arbor.

Hartman, W. L., Clark, M. E., Morgan, M. K., Dunn, V. K., Fine, A. D., Perry, G. G., et al. (1990). Rorschach structure of a hospitalized sample of Vietnam veterans with PTSD. *Journal of Personality Assessment, 54,* 149–159.

Harvey, A. G., & Bryant, R. A. (1998a). Acute stress disorder following mild traumatic brain injury. *Journal of Nervous and Mental Disease, 186,* 333–337.

Harvey, A. G., & Bryant, R. A. (1998b). Relationship of acute stress disorder and posttraumatic stress disorder following motor vehicle accidents. *Journal of Consulting and Clinical Psychology, 66,* 507–512.

Harvey, A. G., & Bryant, R. A. (1999). Acute stress disorder across trauma populations. *Journal of Nervous and Mental Disease, 187,* 443–446.

Harvey, A. G., & Bryant, R. A. (2001). Reconstructing trauma memories: A prospective study of "amnesic" trauma survivors. *Journal of Traumatic Stress, 14,* 277–282.

Harvey, A. G., & Bryant, R. A. (2002). Acute stress disorder: A synthesis and critique. *Psychological Bulletin, 128,* 886–902.

Hathaway, S. R., & McKinley, J. C. (1943). *The Minnesota Multiphasic Personality Inventory* (rev. ed.). Minneapolis: University of Minnesota Press.

Hazzard, A., Weston, J., & Gutterres, C. (1992). After a child's death: Factors related to parental bereavement. *Journal of Developmental and Behavioral Pediatrics, 13,* 24–30.

Heffernan, K., & Cloitre, M. (2000). A comparison of posttraumatic stress disorder with and without borderline personality disorder among women with a history of childhood sexual abuse: Etiological and clinical characteristics. *Journal of Nervous and Mental Disease, 188,* 589–595.

Heltzer, J. K., Robins, L. N., & McEnvoy, L. (1987). Posttraumatic stress disorder in the general population. *New England Journal of Medicine, 317,* 1630–1634.

Henderson, J. L., & Moore, M. (1944). The psychoneuroses of war. *New England Journal of Medicine, 230,* 273–279.

Hendrix, C. C., Anelli, L. M., Gibbs, J. P., & Fournier, D. G. (1994). Validation of the Purdue Post-traumatic Stress Scale on a sample of Vietnam veterans. *Journal of Traumatic Stress, 7,* 311–318.

Herek, G. M., Gillis, J. R., & Cogan, J. C. (1999). Psychological sequelae of hate-crime victimization among lesbian, gay, and bisexual adults. *Journal of Consulting and Clinical Psychology, 67,* 945–941.

Herman, D., Weathers, F., Litz, B., Joaquim, S., & Keane, T. (1993, Oct.). *The PK Scale of the MMPI–2. Reliability and validity of the embedded and stand-alone versions.* Paper presented at the annual meeting of the International Society for Traumatic Stress Studies, San Antonio, TX.

Herman, J. L. (1992a). Complex PTSD: A syndrome in survivors of prolonged and repeated trauma. *Journal of Traumatic Stress, 5,* 377–392.

Herman, J. L. (1992b). *Trauma and recovery: The aftermath of violence—From domestic abuse to political terror.* New York: Basic Books.

Herman, J. L., Perry, C., & van der Kolk, B. A. (1989). Childhood trauma in borderline personality disorder. *American Journal of Psychiatry, 146,* 490–494.

Herman, J. L., & Schatzow, E. (1987). Recovery and verification of memories of childhood sexual trauma. *Psychoanalytic Psychology, 4,* 1–14.

Hicklin, T. A. (2003). Methods for controlling combat stress evolving over time. *Psychiatric Annals, 33,* 720–724.

Higgins, A. B., & Follette, V. M. (2002). Frequency and impact of interpersonal trauma in older women. *Journal of Clinical Geropsychology, 8,* 215–226.

Hobfoll, S. E. (1988). *The ecology of stress.* Washington, DC: Hemisphere.

Hobfoll, S. E., Dunahoo, C. A., & Monnier, J. (1995). Conservation of resources and traumatic stress. In J. R. Freedy & S. E. Hobfoll (Eds.), *Traumatic stress: From theory to practice* (pp. 29–47). New York: Plenum Press.

Hodgkinson, P. E., & Shepherd, M. A. (1994). The impact of disaster support work. *Journal of Traumatic Stress, 7,* 587–600.

Holbrook, T. L., Hoyt, D. B., Stein, M. B., & Sieber, W. J. (2001). Perceived threat to life predicts posttraumatic stress disorder after major trauma: Risk factors and functional outcome. *Journal of Trauma: Injury, Infection, and Critical Care, 51,* 287–293.

Holeva, V., & Tarrier, N. (2001). Personality and peritraumatic dissociation in the prediction of PTSD in victims of road traffic accidents. *Journal of Psychosomatic Research, 51,* 687–692.

Horowitz, M. J., Siegel, B., Holen, A., Bonanno, G. A., Milbrath, C., & Stinson, C. H. (1997). Diagnostic criteria for complicated grief disorder. *American Journal of Psychiatry, 154,* 904–910.

Horowitz, M. J., Weiss, D. S., & Marmar, C. R. (1987). Diagnosis of posttraumatic stress disorder. *Journal of Nervous and Mental Disease, 175,* 267–268.

Horowitz, M. D., Wilner, N., & Alvarez, W. (1979). Impacts of Event Scale: A measure of subjective stress. *Psychosomatic Medicine, 41,* 209–218.

Hough, R. L., Canino, G. J., Abueg, F. R., & Gusman, F. D. (1996). PTSD and related stress disorders among Hispanics. In A. J. Marsella, M. J. Friedman,

E. T. Gerrity, & R. M. Scurfield (Eds.), *Ethnocultural aspects of posttraumatic stress disorder: Issues, research, and clinical applications* (pp. 301–338). Washington, DC: American Psychological Association.

Houskamp, B. M. (1994). Assessing and treating battered women: A clinical review of issues and approaches. In J. Briere (Ed.), *Assessing and treating victims of violence* (NDMHS #64, pp. 79–89). San Francisco: Jossey Bass.

Hsu, L. M. (2002). Diagnostic validity statistics and the MCMI–III. *Psychological Assessment, 14,* 410–422.

Hunter, J. A. (1991). A comparison of the psychosocial maladjustment of adult males and females sexually molested as children. *Journal of Interpersonal Violence, 6,* 205–217.

Hyer, L. A., Boyd, S., Stanger, E., Davis, H., & Walters, P. (1997). Validation of the MCMI–III PTSD scale among combat veterans. *Psychological Reports, 80,* 720–722.

Hyer, L. A., Davis, H., Albrecht, J. W., Boudewns, P. A., & Woods, M. G. (1994). Cluster analysis of MCMI–II on chronic PTSD victims. *Journal of Clinical Psychology, 50,* 502–515.

Hyer, L. A., Davis, H., Woods, G., Albrecht, J., & Boudewyns, P. A. (1992). Relationship between the Millon Clinical Multiaxial Inventory and the Millon–II: Value of scales for aggressive and self-defeating personalities in posttraumatic stress disorder. *Psychological Reports, 71,* 687–689.

Hyer, L. A., Woods, M. G., Boudewyns, P. A., Bruno, R. D., & O'Leary, W. C. (1988). Concurrent validation of the Millon Clinical Multiaxial Inventory among Vietnam veterans with posttraumatic stress disorder. *Psychological Reports, 63,* 271–278.

Hyer, L. A., Woods, M. G., Boudewyns, P. A., Harrison, W. R., & Tamkin, A. S. (1990). MCMI and 16–PF with Vietnam veterans: Profiles and concurrent validation of MCMI. *Journal of Personality Disorders, 4,* 391–401.

Hyer, L. A., Woods, M. G., Harrison, W., Boudewyns, P. A., & O'Leary, W. C. (1989). MMPI F–K index among hospitalized Vietnam veterans. *Journal of Clinical Psychology, 45,* 250–254.

Jackson, L., Highcrest, A., & Coates, R. A. (1992). Varied potential risks of HIV infection among prostitutes. *Social Science and Medicine, 35,* 281–286.

Jacobs, W. J., & Dalenberg, C. J. (1998). Subtle presentations of post-traumatic stress disorder: Diagnostic issues. *Psychiatric Clinics of North America, 21,* 835–845.

Jacobson, G. R. (1989). A comprehensive approach to pretreatment evaluation I: Detection, assessment, and diagnosis of alcoholism. In R. K. Hester & W. R. Miller (Eds.), *Handbook of alcoholism treatment approaches.* New York: Pergamon Press.

James, J., & Meyerding, J. (1977). Early sexual experience and prostitution. *American Journal of Psychiatry, 134,* 1381–1385.

Janet, P. (1887). L'anesthésie systématisee et la dissociation des phénomenes psychologiques. *Revue Philosophique.* Paris, Alcan.

Janoff-Bulman, R. (1989). Assumptive worlds and the stress of traumatic events: Applications of the schema construct. *Social Cognition, 7,* 113–136.

Janoff-Bulman, R. (1992). *Shattered assumptions: Towards a new psychology of trauma.* New York: Free Press.

Johnsen, B. H., Eid, J., Lovstad, T., & Michelsen, L. T. (1997). Posttraumatic stress symptoms in nonexposed, victims, and spontaneous rescuers after an avalanche. *Journal of Traumatic Stress, 10,* 133–140.

Jordan, C. E., Nietzel, M. T., Walker, R., & Logan, T. K. (in press). *Intimate partner violence: Clinical and practice issues for mental health professionals.* New York: Springer.

Jordan, R. G., Nunley, T. V., & Cook, R. R. (1992). Symptom exaggeration in a PTSD inpatient population: Response set or claim for compensation. *Journal of Traumatic Stress, 5,* 633–642.

Kaltman, S. I., & Bonanno, G. A. (2003). Trauma and bereavement: Examining the impact of sudden and violent deaths. *Journal of Anxiety Disorders, 17,* 131–147.

Kamphuis, J. H., Emmelkamp, P. M. G., & Bartak, A. (2003). Individual differences in post-traumatic stress following post-intimate stalking: Stalking severity and psychosocial variables. *British Journal of Clinical Psychology, 42,* 145–156.

Kamphuis, J. H., Kugeares, S. L., & Finn, S. E. (2000). Rorschach correlates of sexual abuse: Trauma content and aggression indexes. *Journal of Personality Assessment, 75,* 212–224.

Kangas, M., Henry, J. L., & Bryant, R. A. (2002). Posttraumatic stress disorder following cancer. A conceptual and empirical review. *Clinical Psychology Review, 22,* 499–524.

Kaser-Boyd, N. (1993). Post-traumatic stress disorder in children and adults: The legal relevance. *Western State University Law Review, 20,* 319–334.

Kaufman, A., Divasto, P., Jackson, R., Voorhees, D., & Christy, J. (1980). Male rape victims: Noninstitutionalized assault. *American Journal of Psychiatry, 137,* 221–223.

Kawana, N., Ishimatsu, S., & Kanda, K. (2001). Psycho-physiological effects of the terrorist sarin attack on the Tokyo subway system. *Military Medicine, 166,* 23–26.

Keane, T. M., Caddell, J. M., & Taylor, K. L. (1988). Mississippi scale for combat-related posttraumatic stress disorder: Three studies in reliability and validity. *Journal of Consulting and Clinical Psychology, 56,* 85–90.

Keane, T. M., Fairbank, J. A., Caddell, J. M., Zimering, R. T., Taylor, K. L., & Mora, C. A. (1989). Clinical evaluation of a measure to assess combat exposure. *Psychological Assessment, 1,* 53–55.

Keane, T. M., & Kaloupek, D. G. (2002). Diagnosis, assessment, and monitoring outcomes in PTSD. In R. Yehuda (Ed.), *Treating trauma survivors with PTSD* (pp. 21–42). Washington, DC: American Psychiatric Association.

Keane, T. M., Malloy, P. F., & Fairbank, J. A. (1984). Empirical development of an MMPI subscale for the assessment of combat-related posttraumatic stress disorder. *Journal of Consulting and Clinical Psychology, 52,* 888–891.

Keane, T. M., Weathers, F. W., & Foa, E. B. (1999). Diagnosis and assessment. In E. B. Foa, T. M. Keane, & M. J. Friedman (Eds.), *Effective treatments for PTSD: Practice guidelines from the International Society for Traumatic Stress Studies* (pp. 18–36). New York: Guilford Press.

Kellner, M., & Yehuda, R. (1999). Do panic disorder and posttraumatic stress disorder share a common psychoneuroendocrinology? *Psychoneuroendocrinology, 24,* 485–504.

Kelly, B., Raphael, B., Judd, F., Perdices, M., Kernutt, G., Burnett, P., et al. (1998). Posttraumatic stress disorder in response to HIV infection. *General Hospital Psychiatry, 20,* 345–352.

Kernberg, O. F. (1976). *Borderline conditions and pathological narcissism.* New York: Aronson.

Kessler, R. C., Sonnega, A., Bromet, E., Hughes, M., & Nelson, C. B. (1995). Posttraumatic stress disorder in the national comorbidity survey. *Archives of General Psychiatry, 52,* 1048–1060.

Khan, F. I., Welch, T. L., & Zillmer, E. A. (1993). MMPI–2 profiles of battered women in transition. *Journal of Personality Assessment, 60,* 100–111.

Kilpatrick, D. G., & Resnick, H. S. (1993). Posttraumatic stress disorder associated with exposure to criminal victimization in clinical and community populations. In J. R. T. Davidson & E. B. Foa (Eds.), *Posttraumatic stress disorder: DSM–IV and beyond.* Washington, DC: American Psychiatric Association.

Kilpatrick, D., Resnick, H., & Freedy, J. (1991). *The potential stressful events interview.* Unpublished instrument.

Kimerling, R., & Calhoun, K. S. (1994). Somatic symptoms, social support, and treatment seeking among sexual assault victims. *Journal of Consulting and Clinical Psychology, 62,* 333–340.

King, D. W., King, L. A., Foy, D. W., & Gudanowski, D. M. (1996). Prewar factors in combat-related posttraumatic stress disorder: Structural equation modeling with a national sample of female and male Vietnam veterans. *Journal of Consulting and Clinical Psychology, 64,* 520–531.

King, D. W., Leskin, G. A., King, L. A., & Weathers, F. W. (1998). Confirmatory factor analysis of the Clinician–Administered PTSD Scale: Evidence for the dimensionality of posttraumatic stress disorder. *Psychological Assessment, 10,* 90–96.

King, L. A., King, D. W., Leskin, G., & Foy, D. W. (1995). The Los Angeles Symptom Checklist: A self-report measure of posttraumatic stress disorder. *Assessment, 2,* 1–17.

Kirmayer, L. J. (1996). Confusion of the senses: Implications of ethnocultural variation in somatoform and dissociative disorders for PTSD. In A. J. Marsella, M. J. Friedman, E. T. Gerrity, & R. M. Scurfield (Eds.), *Ethnocultural aspects of posttraumatic stress disorder: Issues, research, and clinical applications* (pp. 91–122). Washington, DC: American Psychological Association.

Kissen, M. (1986). *Assessing object relations phenomena*. Madison, CT: International Universities Press.

Kleijn, W. C., Hovens, J. E. J. M., & Rodenburg, J. J. (2001). Posttraumatic stress symptoms in refugees: Assessments with the Harvard Trauma Questionnaire and the Hopkins Symptom Checklist–25 in different languages. *Psychological Reports, 88*, 527–532.

Klotz Flitter, J. M., Elhai, J. D., & Gold, S. N. (2003). MMPI–2 F Scale elevations in adult victims of child sexual abuse. *Journal of Traumatic Stress, 16*, 269–274.

Kluft, R. P. (1988). The phenomenology and treatment of extremely complex multiple personality disorder. *Dissociation, 1*, 47–58.

Kluft, R. P. (1993). Multiple personality disorder. In D. Spiegel, R. P. Kluft, R. Loewenstein, J. C. Nemiah, F. W. Putnam, & M. Steinberg (Eds.), *Dissociative disorders: A clinical review* (pp. 17–44). Lutherville, MD: Sidran Press.

Kolko, D. J. (2002). Child physical abuse. In J. E. B. Myers, L. Berliner, J. Briere, C. T. Hendrix, T. Reid, & C. Jenny (Eds.), *The APSAC handbook on child maltreatment* (2nd ed., pp. 21–54)). Thousand Oaks, CA: Sage.

Koopman, C., Classen, C. C., Cardeña, E., & Spiegel, D. (1995). When disaster strikes, acute stress disorder may follow. *Journal of Traumatic Stress, 8*, 29–46.

Koopman, C., Classen, C., & Speigel, D. (1994). Predictors of posttraumatic stress symptoms among survivors of the Oakland/Berkeley, California, firestorm. *American Journal of Psychiatry, 151*, 888–894.

Koopman, C., Classen, C., & Speigel, D. (1996). Dissociative responses in the immediate aftermath of the Oakland/Berkeley firestorm. *Journal of Traumatic Stress, 9*, 521–540.

Koren, D., Arnon, I., & Klein, E. (2001). Long term course of chronic posttraumatic stress disorder in traffic accident victims: A three-year prospective follow-up study. *Behaviour Research and Therapy, 39*, 1449–1458.

Koretzky, M. B., & Peck, A. H. (1990). Validation and cross-validation of the PTSD subscale of the MMPI with civilian trauma victims. *Journal of Clinical Psychology, 45*, 72–76.

Koss, M. P. (1983). The scope of rape: Implications for the clinical treatment of victims. *Clinical Psychologist, 53*, 88–91.

Koss, M. P. (1993). Detecting the scope of rape: A review of prevalence research methods. *Journal of Interpersonal Violence, 8*, 198–222.

Koss, M. P., & Gidycz, C. A. (1985). Sexual experiences survey: Reliability and validity. *Journal of Consulting and Clinical Psychology, 53*, 422–423.

Koss, M. P., Goodman, L. A., Browne, A., Fitzgerald, L. F., Keita, G. P., & Russo, N. F. (1994). *Male violence against women at home, at work, and in the community.* Washington, DC: American Psychological Press.

Kramer, L. A. (in press). Emotional experiences of performing prostitution. In M. Farley (Ed.), *Prostitution, trafficking, and traumatic stress.* Binghamton, NY: Hayworth.

Kramer, T. L., & Green, B. L. (1991). Posttraumatic stress disorder as an early response to sexual assault. *Journal of Interpersonal Violence, 6,* 160–173.

Kroll, J. (1993). *PTSD/borderlines in therapy: Finding the balance.* New York: Norton.

Kroll, J., Habenicht, M., Mackenzie, T., Yang, M., Chan, S., Vang, T., et al. (1989). Depression and posttraumatic stress disorder in Southeast Asian refugees. *American Journal of Psychiatry, 146,* 1592–1597.

Kubany, E. S., Haynes, S. N., Leisen, M. B., Owens, J. A., Kaplan, A. S., Watson, S. B., et al. (2000). Development and preliminary validation of a brief broad-spectrum measure of trauma exposure: The Traumatic Life Events Questionnaire. *Psychological Assessment, 12,* 210–224.

Kubany, E. S., & Watson, S. B. (2002). Cognitive trauma therapy for formerly battered women with PTSD: Conceptual bases and treatment outlines. *Cognitive and Behavioral Practice, 9,* 111–127.

Kudler, H., & Davidson, R. T. (1995). General principles of biological intervention following trauma. In J. R. Freedy & S. E. Hobfoll (Eds.), *Traumatic stress: From theory to practice* (pp. 73–98). New York: Plenum Press.

Kulka, R. A., Schlenger, W. E., Fairbank, J. A., Hough, R. L., Jordan, B. K., Marmar, C. R., et al. (1988). *The National Vietnam Veterans Readjustment Study (NVVRS): Description, current status, and initial PTSD prevalence estimates.* Washington, DC: Veterans Administration.

Kulka, R. A., Schlenger, W. E., Fairbank, J. A., Hough, R. L., Jordan, B. K., Marmar, C. R., et al. (1990). *Trauma and the Vietnam War generation.* New York: Brunner/Mazel.

Kuyk, J., Spinhoven, P., Van Emde Boas, W., & Van Dyck, R. (1999). Dissociation in temporal lobe epilepsy and pseudo-epileptic seizure patients. *Journal of Nervous and Mental Disease, 187,* 713–720.

Kwawer, J., Lerner, H., Lerner, P., & Sugarman, A. (Eds.). (1985). *Borderline phenomena and the Rorschach test.* New York: International University Press.

Lang, A. J., Kennedy, C. M., & Stein, M. B. (2002). Anxiety sensitivity and PTSD among female victims of intimate partner violence. *Depression and Anxiety, 16,* 77–83.

Lanktree, C. B., Briere, J., & Zaidi, L. Y. (1991). Incidence and impacts of sexual abuse in a child outpatient sample: The role of direct inquiry. *Child Abuse and Neglect, 15,* 447–453.

Lating, J. M., Zeichner, A., & Keane, T. M. (1995). Psychological assessment of PTSD. In G. S. Everly & J. M. Lating (Eds.), *Psychotraumatology* (pp. 104–127). New York: Plenum Press.

Lauterbach, D., & Vrana, S. R. (2001). The relationship between personality variables, exposure to traumatic events, and severity of posttraumatic stress symptoms. *Journal of Traumatic Stress, 14,* 29–45.

Lauterbach, D., Vrana, S. R., King, D. W., & King, L. A. (1997). Psychometric qualities of the civilian version of the Mississippi PTSD scale. *Journal of Traumatic Stress, 10,* 499–513.

Leavitt, F. (2000). Texture response patterns associated with sexual trauma of childhood and adult onset: Developmental and recovered memory implications. *Child Abuse and Neglect, 24,* 251–257.

Leavitt, F. (2001). The development of the Somatoform Dissociation Index (SDI): A screening measure of dissociation using MMPI–2 items. *Journal of Trauma and Dissociation, 2,* 69–80.

Leavitt, F., & Labott, S. M. (1996). Authenticity of recovered sexual abuse memories: A Rorschach study. *Journal of Traumatic Stress, 9,* 483–496.

Lee, A., Isaac, M. K., & Janca, A. (2002). Post-traumatic stress disorder and terrorism. *Current Opinion in Psychiatry, 15,* 633–637.

Lees-Haley, P. R. (1992). Efficacy of MMPI–2 validity scales and MCMI–II modifier scales for detecting spurious PTSD claims: F, F–K, fake bad scale, ego strength, subtle-obvious subscales, DIS, and DEB. *Journal of Clinical Psychology, 48,* 681–689.

Lefley, H. P. (1999). Transcultural aspects of sexual victimization. In J. A. Shaw (Ed.), *Sexual aggression* (pp. 129–166). Washington, DC: American Psychiatric Association.

Leskela, J., Dieperink, M. E., & Thuras, P. (2002). Shame and posttraumatic stress disorder. *Journal of Traumatic Stress, 15,* 223–226.

Leskin, G. A., & Sheikh, J. I. (2002). Lifetime trauma history and panic disorder: Findings from the National Comorbidity Survey. *Journal of Anxiety Disorders, 16,* 599–603.

Levin, P. (1993). Assessing PTSD with the Rorschach projective technique. In J. Wilson & B. Raphael (Eds.), *The international handbook of traumatic stress syndromes* (pp. 189–200). New York: Plenum Press.

Lewis-Fernandez, R., Garrido-Castillo, P., Bennasar, M. C., Parrilla, E. M., Laria, A. J., Ma, G., et al. (2002). Dissociation, childhood trauma, and ataque de nervios among Puerto Rican psychiatric outpatients. *American Journal of Psychiatry, 159,* 1603–1605.

Liljequist, L., Kinder, B. N., & Schinka, J. A. (1998). An investigation of malingering posttraumatic stress disorder on the Personality Assessment Inventory. *Journal of Personality Assessment, 71,* 322–336.

Lindsay, D. S. (1994). Contextualizing and clarifying criticisms of memory work. Special Issue: The recovered memory/false memory debate. *Consciousness and Cognition: An International Journal, 3,* 426–437.

Lindsay, D. S. (1995). Beyond the backlash: Comments on Enns, McNeilly, Corkery, and Gilbert (1995). *The Counseling Psychologist, 23,* 280–289.

Lindsay, D. S., & Briere, J. (1997). The controversy regarding recovered memories of childhood sexual abuse: Pitfalls, bridges, and future directions. *Journal of Interpersonal Violence, 12*, 631–647.

Linehan, M. M. (1993). *Cognitive–behavioral treatment of borderline personality disorder*. New York: Guilford Press.

Lisak, D. (1994). The psychological impact of sexual abuse: Content analysis of interviews with male survivors. *Journal of Traumatic Stress, 7*, 525–548.

Lisak, D., & Miller, P. M. (2003). Childhood trauma, posttraumatic stress disorder, substance abuse, and violence. In P. C. Ouimette & P. J. Brown (Eds.), *Trauma and substance abuse: Causes, consequences, and treatment of comorbid disorders* (pp. 73–88). Washington, DC: American Psychological Association.

Litz, B. T., Penk, W. F., Gerardi, R. J., & Keane, T. M. (1992). Assessment of posttraumatic stress disorder. In P. A. Saigh (Ed.), *Posttraumatic stress disorder: A behavioral approach to assessment and treatment* (pp. 54–80). Boston: Allyn & Bacon.

Litz, B. T., Penk, W. E., Walsh, S., Hyer, L., Blake, D. D., Marx, B., et al. (1991). Similarities and differences between MMPI and MMPI–2 applications to the assessment of post-traumatic stress disorder. *Journal of Personality Assessment, 57*, 238–254.

Loewenstein, R. J. (1993). Psychogenic amnesia and psychogenic fugue: A comprehensive review. In D. Spiegel (Ed.), *Dissociative disorders: A clinical review*. Lutherville, MD: Sidran Press.

Loftus, E. F., & Ketcham, K. (1994). *The myth of repressed memory: False memories and allegations of sexual abuse*. New York: St. Martin's Press.

Loo, C. M., Fairbank, J. A., Scurfield, R. M., Ruch, L. O., King, D. W., Adams, L. J., et al. (2001). Measuring exposure to racism: Development and validation of a Race-Related Stressor Scale (RRSS) for Asian American Vietnam veterans. *Psychological Assessment, 13*, 503–520.

Lovitt, R., & Lefkoff, G. (1985). Understanding multiple personality disorder with the comprehensive Rorschach system. *Journal of Personality Assessment, 58*, 289–294.

Lundberg-Love, P. K., Marmion, S., Ford, K., Geffner, R., & Peacock, L. (1992). The long-term consequences of childhood incestuous victimization upon adult women's psychological symptomatology. *Journal of Child Sexual Abuse, 1*, 81–102.

Lundin, T., & Bodegard, M. (1993). The psychological impact of an earthquake on rescue workers: A follow-up study of the Swedish group of rescue workers in Armenia, 1988. *Journal of Traumatic Stress, 6*, 129–139.

Luxenberg, T., & Levin, P. (in press). The utility of the Rorschach in the assessment and treatment of trauma. In J. P. Wilson & T. M. Keane (Eds.), *Assessing psychological trauma and PTSD: A practitioner's handbook* (2nd ed.). New York: Guilford Press.

Lyons, J. A., & Keane, T. M. (1992). Keane PTSD scale: MMPI and MMPI–2 update. *Journal of Traumatic Stress, 5,* 111–117.

MacAndrew, C. (1965). The differentiation of male alcoholic outpatients from nonalcoholic psychiatric outpatients by means of the MMPI. *Quarterly Journal of Studies on Alcohol, 26,* 238–246.

Malta, L. S., Blanchard, E. B., Taylor, A. E., Hickling, E. J., & Freidenberg, B. M. (2002). Personality disorders and posttraumatic stress disorder in motor vehicle accident survivors. *Journal of Nervous and Mental Disease, 190,* 767–774.

Mann, B. J. (1995). The North Carolina Dissociation Index: A measure of dissociation using items from the MMPI–2. *Journal of Personality Assessment, 64,* 349–359.

March, J. S. (1993). What constitutes a stressor? The "criterion A" issue. In J. R. T. Davidson & E. B. Foa (Eds.), *Posttraumatic Stress Disorder: DSM–IV and beyond.* Washington, DC: American Psychiatric Association.

Marmar, C. R., Weiss, D. S., & Metzler, T. (1996). The Peritraumatic Dissociative Experiences Questionnaire. In J. P. Wilson & T. M. Keane (Eds.), *Assessing psychological trauma and PTSD: A practitioner's handbook* (pp. 412–428). New York: Guilford Press.

Marmar, C. R., Weiss, D. S., Metzler, T. J., Ronfeldt, H. M., & Foreman, C. (1996). Stress responses of emergency services personnel to the Loma Prieta earthquake Interstate 880 freeway collapse and control traumatic incidents. *Journal of Traumatic Stress, 9,* 63–85.

Marmar, C. R., Weiss, D. S., Schlenger, W. E., Fairbank, J. A., Jordan, K., Kulka, R. A., et al. (1994). Peritraumatic dissociation and posttraumatic stress in male Vietnam theater veterans. *American Journal of Psychiatry, 151,* 902–907.

Marsella, A. J. (2001). Measurement issues. In E. T. Gerrity, T. M. Keane, & F. Tuma (Eds.), *The mental health consequences of torture* (pp. 277–290). New York: Kluwer.

Marsella, A. J., Friedman, M. J., Gerrity, E. T., & Scurfield, R. M. (Eds.). (1996). *Ethnocultural aspects of posttraumatic stress disorder: Issues, research, and clinical applications.* Washington, DC: American Psychological Association.

Marshall, G. N., Orlando, M., Jaycox, L. H., Foy, D. W., & Belzberg, H. (2002). Development and validation of a modified version of the Peritraumatic Dissociative Experiences Questionnaire. *Psychological Assessment, 14,* 123–134.

Marshall, G. N., & Schell, T. L. (2002). Reappraising the link between peritraumatic dissociation and PTSD symptom severity: Evidence from a longitudinal study of community violence survivors. *Journal of Abnormal Psychology, 111,* 626–636.

Marshall, R. D., Schneier, F. R., Lin, S., Simpson, H. B., Vermes, D., & Liebowitz, M. R. (2000). Childhood trauma and dissociative symptoms in panic disorder. *American Journal of Psychiatry, 157,* 451–453.

Marshall, R. D., Spitzer, R. L., & Liebowitz, M. R. (1999). Review and critique of the new DSM–IV diagnosis of acute stress disorder. *American Journal of Psychiatry, 156,* 1677–1685.

Masterson, J. F. (1976). *Psychotherapy of the borderline adult: A developmental approach.* New York: Brunner/Mazel.

Mayou, R. A. (2002). Psychiatric consequences of motor vehicle accidents. *Psychiatric Clinics of North America, 25,* 27–41.

Mayou, R. A., Bryant, B., & Ehlers, A. (2001). Prediction of psychological outcomes one year after a motor vehicle accident. *American Journal of Psychiatry, 158,* 1231–1238.

McCann, I. L., & Pearlman, L. A. (1990). *Psychological trauma and the adult survivor: Theory, therapy, and transformation.* New York: Brunner/Mazel.

McCarroll, J. E., Ursano, R. J., Fullerton, C. S., Liu, X., & Lundy, A. (2001). Effects of exposure to death in a war mortuary on posttraumatic stress disorder symptoms of intrusion and avoidance. *Journal of Nervous and Mental Disease, 189,* 44–48.

McClanahan, S. F., McClelland, G. M., Abram, K. M., & Teplin, L. A. (1999). Pathways into prostitution among female jail detainees and their implications for mental health services. *Psychiatric Services, 50,* 1606–1613.

McFall, M. E., Smith, D. E., McKay, P. W., & Tarver, D. J. (1990). Reliability and validity of Mississippi Scale for Combat-Related Posttraumatic Stress Disorder. *Psychological Assessment, 2,* 114–121.

McFall, M. E., Smith, D. E., Roszell, D. K., Tarver, D. J., & Malas, K. L., (1990). Convergent validity of measures of PTSD in Vietnam combat veterans. *American Journal of Psychiatry, 147,* 645–648.

McFarlane, A. C. (1988). Relationship between psychiatric impairment and a natural disaster: The role of distress. *Psychological Medicine, 18,* 129–139.

McFarlane, A. C., Clayer, J. R., & Bookless, C. L. (1997). Psychiatric morbidity following a natural disaster: An Australian bushfire. *Social Psychiatry and Psychiatric Epidemiology, 32,* 261–268.

McMillen, J. C., Zuravin, S. J., & Rideout, G. (1995). Perceived benefit from child sexual abuse. *Journal of Consulting and Clinical Psychology, 63,* 1037–1043.

McNally, R. J. (2003). Progress and controversy in the study of posttraumatic stress disorder. *Annual Review of Psychology, 54,* 229–252.

Mechanic, M. B., Uhlmansiek, M. H., Weaver, T. L., & Resick, P. A. (2000). The impact of severe stalking experienced by acutely battered women: An examination of violence, psychological symptoms and strategic responding. *Violence and Victims, 15,* 443–458.

Meichenbaum, D. (1994). *A clinical handbook/practical therapist manual for assessing and treating adults with post-traumatic stress disorder (PTSD).* Waterloo, Canada: Institute Press.

Mellman, T. A., David, D., Bustamante, V., Fins, A. I., & Esposito, K. (2001). Predictors of post-traumatic stress disorder following severe injury. *Depression and Anxiety, 14,* 226–231.

Merskey, H. (1993). Professional and lay opinions on multiple personality disorder [letter]. *British Journal of Psychiatry, 162,* 271.

Mertin, P., & Mohr, P. B. (2001). A follow-up study of posttraumatic stress disorder, anxiety, and depression in Australian victims of domestic violence. *Violence and Victims, 16,* 645–654.

Messman-Moore, T. L., & Long, P. J. (2003). The role of childhood sexual abuse sequelae in the sexual revictimization of women: An empirical review and theoretical reformulation. *Clinical Psychology Review, 23,* 537–571.

Meyers, J. (1988). The Rorschach as a tool for understanding the dynamics of women with histories of incest. In H. D. Lerner & P. M. Lerner (Eds.), *Primitive mental states and the Rorschach* (pp. 203–228). Madison, CT: International Universities Press.

Meyers, J. E. B. (1996). Expert testimony. In J. Briere, L. Berliner, J. A. Bulkley, C. Jenny, & T. Reid (Eds.), *The APSAC handbook on child maltreatment* (pp. 319–340). Thousand Oaks, CA: Sage.

Meyers, J. E. B. (1998). *Legal issues in child abuse and neglect practice.* Thousand Oaks, CA: Sage.

MICHIGAN STAT. ANN. §28.788 (1)(h). (1980). Callaghan cum. supp.

Miller, J., & Schwartz, M. D. (1995). Rape myths and violence against street prostitutes. *Deviant Behavior, 16,* 1–23.

Miller, K. E., Weine, S. M., Ramic, A., Brkic, N., Djuric-Bijedic, Z., Smajkic, A., et al. (2002). The relative contribution of war experiences and exile-related stressors to levels of psychological distress among Bosnian refugees. *Journal of Traumatic Stress, 15,* 377–387.

Millon, T. (1983). *Millon Clinical Multiaxial Inventory Manual.* Minneapolis, MN: Interpretive Scoring System.

Millon, T. (1987). *Manual for the MCMI–II* (2nd ed.). Minneapolis, MN: National Computer Systems.

Millon, T. (1994). *Manual for the MCMI–III.* Minneapolis, MN: National Computer Systems.

Millon, T., Davis, R., & Millon, C. (1997). *MCMI–III manual* (2nd ed.). Minneapolis, MN: National Computer Systems.

Mohta, M., Sethi, A. K., Tyagi, A., & Mohta, A. (2003). Psychological care in trauma patients. *Injury, 34,* 17–25.

Mollica, R., Caspi-Yavin, Y., Bollini, P., Truong, T., Tor, S., & Lavelle, J. (1992). Harvard Trauma Questionnaire: Validating a cross-cultural instrument for measuring torture, trauma, and posttraumatic stress disorder in Indochinese refugees. *Journal of Nervous and Mental Disease, 180,* 111–116.

Mollica, R., Caspi-Yavin, Y., Lavelle, J., Tor, S., Yang, T., Chan, S., et al. (1995). *Manual for the Harvard Trauma Questionnaire.* Brighton, MA: Indochinese Psychiatry Clinic.

Moore, L. J., Sager, D., Keopraseuth, K., Chao, L. H., Riley, C., & Robinson, E. (2001). Rheumatological disorders and somatization in U.S. Mien and Lao refugees with depression and post-traumatic stress disorder: A cross-cultural comparison. *Transcultural Psychiatry, 38*, 481–505.

Moran, C. (1986). Depersonalization and agoraphobia associated with marijuana use. *British Journal of Medical Psychology, 59*, 187–196.

Morey, L. C. (1991). *Personality Assessment Inventory: Professional manual.* Odessa, FL: Psychological Assessment Resources.

Mueser, K. T., Salyers, M. P., Rosenberg, S. D., Ford, J. D., Fox, L., & Carty, P. (2001). Psychometric evaluation of trauma and posttraumatic stress disorder assessments in persons with severe mental illness. *Psychological Assessment, 13*, 110–117.

Munley, P. H., Bains, D. S., Bloem, W. D., Busby, R. M., & Pendziszewski, S. (1995). Post-traumatic stress disorder and the MMPI–2. *Journal of Traumatic Stress, 8*, 171–178.

Nader, K. (in press). Assessing traumatic experiences in children. In J. P. Wilson & T. M. Keane (Eds.), *Assessing psychological trauma and PTSD: A practitioner's handbook* (2nd ed.). New York: Guilford Press.

Najarian, B., Goenjian, A. K., Pelcovitz, D., Mandel, F. S., & Najarian, B. (2001). The effect of relocation after a natural disaster. *Journal of Traumatic Stress, 14*, 511–526.

Nash, M. R., Hulsey, T. L., Sexton, M. C., Harralson, T. L., & Lambert, W. (1993). Long-term sequelae of childhood sexual abuse: Perceived family environment, psychopathology, and dissociation. *Journal of Consulting and Clinical Psychology, 61*, 276–283.

Neal, L. A., & Rose, M. C. (1995). Factitious post traumatic stress disorder: A case report. *Medicine, Science and the Law, 35*, 352–354.

Neill, J. R. (1993). How psychiatric symptoms varied in World War I and II. *Military Medicine, 158*, 149–151.

Nemiah, J. C. (1993). Dissociation, conversion, and somatization. In D. Spiegel (Ed.), *Dissociative disorders: A clinical revie* (pp. 104–116). Lutherville, MD: Sidran Press.

Neria, Y., Bromet, E. J., Sievers, S., Lavelle, J., & Fochtmann, L. J. (2002). Trauma exposure and posttraumatic stress disorder in psychosis: Findings from a first-admission cohort. *Journal of Consulting and Clinical Psychology, 70*, 246–251.

Neumann, D. A., Houskamp, B. M., Pollock, V. E., & Briere, J. (1996). The long-term sequelae of childhood sexual abuse in women: A meta-analytic review. *Child Maltreatment, 1*, 6–16.

Newman, E., Kaloupek, D. G., & Keane, T. M. (1996). Assessment of posttraumatic stress disorder in clinical and research settings. In B. A. van der Kolk, A. C. McFarlane, & L. Weisaeth (Eds.), *Traumatic stress: The effects of overwhelming experience on mind, body, and society* (pp. 242–275). New York: Guilford Press.

Nichter, M. (1981). Idioms of distress: Alternatives in the expression of psychological distress: A case study from India. *Culture, Medicine, and Psychiatry, 5*, 379–408.

Nijenhuis, E. R. S., Spinhoven, P., Van Dyck, R., Van der Hart, O., & Vanderlinden, J. (1996). The development and psychometric characteristics of the Somatoform Dissociation Questionnaire (SDQ–20). *Journal of Nervous and Mental Disease, 184*, 688–694.

Nijenhuis, E. R. S., Spinhoven, P., Van Dyck, R., Van der Hart, O., & Vanderlinden, J. (1997). The development of the Somatoform Dissociation Questionnaire (SDQ–5) as a screening instrument for dissociative disorders. *Acta Psychiatrica Scandinavica, 96*, 311–318.

Nijenhuis, E. R. S., Spinhoven, P., Van Dyck, R., Van der Hart, O., & Vanderlinden, J. (1998). Psychometric characteristics of the Somatoform Dissociation Questionnaire: A replication study. *Psychotherapy and Psychosomatics, 67*, 17–23.

Nishith, P., Mechanic, M. B., & Resick, P. A. (2000). Prior interpersonal trauma: The contribution to current PTSD symptoms in female rape victims. *Journal of Abnormal Psychology, 109*, 20–25.

Nixon, K., Tutty, L., Downe, P., Gorkoff, K., & Ursel, J. (2002). The everyday occurrence: Violence in the lives of girls exploited through prostitution. *Violence Against Women, 8*, 1016–1043.

Norris, F. (1990). Screening for traumatic stress: A scale for use in the general population. *Journal of Applied Social Psychology, 20*, 1704–1718.

Norris, F. (1992). Epidemiology of trauma: Frequency and impact of different potentially traumatic events on different demographic groups. *Journal of Consulting and Clinical Psychology, 60*, 409–418.

Norris, F., & Thompson, M. P. (1995). Applying community psychology to the prevention of trauma and traumatic life events. In J. R. Freedy & S. E. Hobfoll (Eds.), *Traumatic stress: From theory to practice* (pp. 49–71). New York: Plenum Press.

Norris, F. H., Friedman, M. J., Watson, P. J., Byrne, C. M., Diaz, E., & Kaniasty, K. Z. (2002). 60,000 disaster victims speak: Part I, an empirical review of the empirical literature, 1981–2001. *Psychiatry, 65*, 207–239.

Norris, F. H., & Hamblen, J. (in press). Standardized self-report measures for PTSD. In J. P. Wilson & T. M. Keane (Eds.), *Assessing psychological trauma and PTSD: A practitioner's handbook.* New York: Guilford Press.

Norris, F. H., Kaniasty, K. Z., Conrad, M. L., Inman, G. L., & Murphy, A. D. (2002). Placing age differences in cultural context: A comparison of the effects of age on PTSD after disasters in the United States, Mexico, and Poland. *Journal of Clinical Geropsychology, 8*, 153–173.

Norris, F. H., & Perilla, J. (1996). Reliability, validity, and cross-language stability of the Revised Civilian Mississippi Scale for PTSD. *Journal of Traumatic Stress, 9*, 285–298.

Norris, F. H., Phifer, J. F., & Kaniasty, K. (1994). Individual and community reactions to the Kentucky floods: Findings from a longitudinal study of older adults. In R. J. Ursano, C. S. Fullerton, & B. G. McCaughey (Eds.), *Individual and community response to trauma and disaster: The structure of human chaos* (pp. 378–400). Cambridge: Cambridge University Press.

Norris, F. H., Weisshaar, D. L., Conrad, M. L., Diaz, E. M., Murphy, A. D., Ibanez, G. E. (2001). A qualitative analysis of posttraumatic stress among Mexican victims of disaster. *Journal of Traumatic Stress, 14,* 741–756.

North, C. S., McCutcheon, V., Spitznagel, E. L., & Smith, E. M. (2002). Three-year follow-up of survivors of a mass shooting episode. *Journal of Urban Health: Bulletin of the New York Academy of Medicine, 79,* 383–391.

North, C. S., Smith, E. M., McCool, R. E., & Lightcap, P. E. (1989). Acute post-disaster coping and adjustment. *Journal of Traumatic Stress, 2,* 353–360.

Ogata, S. N., Silk, K. R., Goodrich, S., Lohr, N. E., Western, D., Hill, E. (1990). Childhood sexual and physical abuse in adult patients with borderline personality disorder. *American Journal of Psychiatry, 147,* 1008–1013.

Ogawa, J. R., Sroufe, L. A., Weinfield, N. S., Carlson, E. A., & Egeland, B. (1997). Development and the fragmented self: Longitudinal study of dissociative symptomatology in a nonclinical sample. *Development and Psychopathology, 9,* 855–879.

Okawa, J. B., Gaby, L., & Griffith, J. L. (2003, Nov.). *Dissociation and auditory hallucinations in survivors of torture.* Paper presented at the annual meeting of the International Society for Traumatic Stress Studies, Chicago.

O'Leary, K. D. (1999). Psychological abuse: A variable deserving critical attention in domestic violence. *Violence and Victims (Special Issue: Psychological Abuse in Domestically Violent Relationships), 14,* 3–23.

Orlando, M., & Marshall, G. N. (2002). Differential item functioning in a Spanish translation of the PTSD Checklist: Detection and evaluation of impact. *Psychological Assessment, 14,* 50–59.

Orr, S. P., Claiborn, J. M., Altman, B., Forgue, D. F., de Jong, J. B., Pitman, R. K., et al. (1990). Psychometric profile of post-traumatic stress disorder, anxious, and healthy Vietnam veterans: Correlations with psychophysiological responses. *Journal of Consulting and Clinical Psychology, 58,* 329–335.

Osterman, J. E., Hopper, J. W., Heran, W. J., Keane, T. M., & van der Kolk, B. A. (2001). Awareness under anesthesia and the development of posttraumatic stress disorder, *General Hospital Psychiatry, 23,* 198–204.

O'Toole, B. I., Marshall, R. P., Schureck, R. J., & Dobson, M. (1999). Combat, dissociation, and posttraumatic stress disorder in Australian Vietnam veterans. *Journal of Traumatic Stress, 12,* 625–640.

Ouimette, P. C., & Brown, P. J. (Eds.). (2003). *Trauma and substance abuse: Causes, consequences, and treatment of comorbid disorders.* Washington, DC: American Psychological Association.

Owens, T. H. (1984). Personality traits of female psychotherapy patients with a history of incest: A research note. *Journal of Personality Assessment, 48*, 606–608.

Ozer, E. J., Best, S. R., Lipsey, T. L., & Weiss, D. S. (2003). Predictors of posttraumatic stress disorder and symptoms in adults: A meta-analysis. *Psychological Bulletin, 129*, 52–73.

Pathé, M., & Mullen, P. E. (1997). The impact of stalkers on their victims. *British Journal of Psychiatry, 170*, 12–17.

Pearlman, L. A. (1996). Review of TSI Belief Scale, Revision L. In B. H. Stamm (Ed.), *Measurement of stress, trauma, and adaptation* (pp. 415–417). Lutherville, MD: Sidran Press.

Pearlman, L. A. (1998). Trauma and the self: A theoretical and clinical perspective. *Journal of Emotional Abuse, 1*, 7–25.

Pearlman, L. A. (2003). *Trauma and Attachment Belief Scale.* Los Angeles: Western Psychological Services.

Pearlman, L. A., & Saakvitne, K. W. (1995). *Trauma and the therapist: Countertransference and vicarious traumatization in psychotherapy with incest survivors.* New York: Norton.

Pelcovitz, D., van der Kolk, B. A., Roth, S., Mandel, F., Kaplan, S., & Resick, P. (1997). Development of a criteria set and a Structured Interview for Disorders of Extreme Stress (SIDES). *Journal of Traumatic Stress, 10*, 3–16.

Perrin, S. G., Van Hasselt, V. B., & Hersen, M. (1997). Validation of the Keane MMPI–PTSD Scale against DSM–III–R criteria in a sample of battered women. *Violence and Victims, 12*, 99–104.

Petrak, J. A., & Campbell, E. A. (1999). Post-traumatic stress disorder in female survivors of rape attending a genitourinary medicine clinic: A pilot study. *International Journal of STD and AIDS, 10*, 531–535.

Petrie, K. J., Booth, R. J., Pennebaker, J. W., Davison, K. P., & Thomas, M. G. (1995). Disclosure of trauma and immune response to a Hepatitis B vaccination program. *Journal of Consulting and Clinical Psychology, 63*, 787–792.

Petty, F., Brannan, S., Casada, J. H., Davis, L. L., Gajewski, V., Kramer, G. L., et al. (2001). Olanzapine treatment for post-traumatic stress disorder: An open-label study. *International Clinical Psychopharmacology, 16*, 331–337.

Pfefferbaum, B., North, C. S., Flynn, B. W., Ursano, R. J., McCoy, G., DeMartino, R., et al. (2001). The emotional impact of injury following an international terrorist incident. *Public Health Reviews, 29*, 271–280.

Phillips, D. W. (1994). Initial development and validation of the Phillips Dissociation Scale (PDS) of the MMPI. *Progress in the Dissociative Disorders, 7*, 92–100.

Pickens, J., Field, T., Prodromidis, M., Pelaez-Nogueras, M., & Hossain, Z. (1995). Posttraumatic stress, depression and social support among college students after Hurricane Andrew. *Journal of College Student Development, 36*, 152–161.

Pinto, P. A., & Gregory, R. J. (1995). Posttraumatic stress disorder with psychotic features. *American Journal of Psychiatry, 152,* 471.

Piotrowsky, C., & Lubin, B. (1990). Assessment practices of health psychologists: Survey of APA Division 38 clinicians. *Professional Psychology: Research and Practice, 21,* 99–106.

Potter, K., Martin, J. L., & Romans, S. E. (1999). Early developmental experiences of female sex workers: A comparative study. *Australian and New Zealand Journal of Psychiatry, 33,* 935–940.

Prigerson, H., Ahmed, I., Silverman, G. K., Saxena, A. K., Maciejewski, P. K., Jacobs, S. C., et al. (2002). Rates and risks of complicated grief among psychiatric clinic patients in Karachi, Pakistan. *Death Studies, 26,* 781–792.

Prigerson, H. G., Bierhals, A. J., Kasl, S. V., Reynolds, C. F., Shear, M. K., Newsom, J. T., et al. (1996). Complicated grief as a disorder distinct from bereavement-related depression and anxiety: A replication study. *American Journal of Psychiatry, 153,* 1484–1486.

Prigerson, H. G., Bridge, J., Maciejewski, P. K., Beery, L. C., Rosenheck, R. A., Jacobs, S. C., et al. (1994). Influence of traumatic grief on suicidal ideation among young adults. *American Journal of Psychiatry, 156,* 1994–1995.

Prigerson, H. G., & Jacobs, S. C. (2001). Traumatic grief as a distinct disorder: A rationale, consensus criteria, and a preliminary empirical test. In M. S. Stroebe, R. O. Hansson, W. Stroebe, & H. A. W. Schut (Eds.), *Handbook of bereavement research: Consequences, coping, and care* (pp. 613–645). Washington, DC: American Psychological Association.

Prigerson, H. G., Frank, E., Kasl, S. V., Reynolds, C. F. III, Anderson, B., Zubenko, S., et al. (1995). Complicated grief and bereavement-related depression as distinct disorders: Preliminary empirical validation in elderly bereaved spouses. *American Journal of Psychiatry, 152,* 22–30.

Prigerson, H. G., Maciejewski, P. K., Reynolds, C. F., Bierhals, A. J., Newsom, J. T., Fasiczka, A., et al. (1995). Inventory of complicated grief: A scale to measure maladaptive symptoms of loss. *Psychiatry Research, 59,* 65–79.

Prigerson, H. G., Shear, M. K., Jacobs, S. C., Reynolds, C. F., Maciejewski, P. K., Davidson, J. R. T., et al. (1999). Consensus criteria for traumatic grief: A preliminary empirical test. *British Journal of Psychiatry, 174,* 67–73.

Putnam, F. W. (1989). *Diagnosis and treatment of multiple personality disorder.* New York: Guilford Press.

Putnam, F. W., Guroff, J. J., Silberman, E. K., Barban, L., & Post, R. M. (1986). The clinical phenomenology of multiple personality disorder: Review of 100 recent cases. *Journal of Clinical Psychiatry, 47,* 285–293.

Pyevich, C. M., Newman, E., & Daleiden, E. (2003). The relationship among cognitive schemas, job-related traumatic exposure, and posttraumatic stress disorder in journalists. *Journal of Traumatic Stress, 16,* 325–328.

Raphael, B., & Minkov, C. (1999). Abnormal grief. *Current Opinion in Psychiatry, 12,* 99–102.

Rausch, K., & Knutson, J. F. (1991). The self-report of personal punitive child-hood experiences and those of siblings. *Child Abuse and Neglect, 15*, 29–36.

Riether, A. M., & Stoudemire, A. (1988). Psychogenic fugue states: A review. *Southern Medical Journal, 81*, 568–571.

Read, J., & Fraser, A. (1998). Abuse histories of psychiatric inpatients: To ask or not to ask? *Psychiatric Services, 49*, 355–359.

Read, J., Perry, B. D., Moskowitz, A., & Connolly, J. (2001). The contribution of early traumatic events to schizophrenia in some patients: A traumagenic neurodevelopmental model. *Psychiatry, 64*, 319–345.

Resick, P. A. (1993). The psychological impact of rape. *Journal of Interpersonal Violence, 8*, 223–255.

Resick, P. A., & Schnicke, M. K. (1993). *Cognitive processing therapy for rape victims: A treatment manual.* Newbury Park, CA: Sage.

Resnick, H. S., Best, C. L., Kilpatric, D. G., Freedy, J. R., & Falsetti, S. A. (1996). Trauma Assessment for Adults. In B. Hudnall Stamm (Ed.), *Measurement of stress, trauma, and adaptation* (pp. 362–365). Lutherville, MD: Sidran Press.

Resnick, H. S., Kilpatrick, D. G., Dansky, B., Saunders, B., & Best, C. (1993). Prevalence of civilian trauma and posttraumatic stress disorder in a representative national sample of women. *Journal of Consulting and Clinical Psychology, 61*, 984–991.

Resnick, H. S., Kilpatrick, D. G., & Lipovsky, J. A. (1991). Assessment of rape-related post-traumatic stress disorder: Stressor and symptom dimensions. *Psychological Assessment, 3*, 561–572.

Reynolds, W. M. (1991). Psychometric characteristics of the Adult Suicidal Ideation Questionnaire in college students. *Journal of Personality Assessment, 56*, 289–307.

Rhodes, N. R. (1992). Comparison of MMPI psychopathic deviate scores of battered and nonbattered women. *Journal of Family Violence, 7*, 297–307.

Richard, A. O. (2000). *International trafficking of women in the United States: A contemporary manifestation of slavery and organized crime.* DCI Report. Washington, DC: U.S. Department of State.

Riggs, D. S., Kilpatrick, D. G., & Resnick, H. S. (1992). Long-term psychological distress associated with marital rape and aggravated assault: A comparison to other crime victims. *Journal of Family Violence, 7*, 283–296.

Riquelme, M. J. J., & Perfetti, H. E. (2000). Rorschach in women victims of rape. *Journal of Projective Psychology and Mental Health, 7*, 133–140.

Rivard, J. M., Dietz, P., Martell, D., & Widawski, M. (2002). Acute dissociative responses in law enforcement officers involved in critical shooting incidents: The clinical and forensic implications. *Journal of Forensic Sciences, 47*, 1093–1100.

Robins, L. N., & Heltzer, J. E. (1985). *Diagnostic Interview Schedule (DIS).* Department of Psychiatry, Washington University, St. Louis, MO.

Roelofs, K., Keijsers, G. P. J., Hoogduin, K. A. L., Naring, G. W. B., & Moene, F. C. (2002). Childhood abuse in patients with conversion disorder. *American Journal of Psychiatry, 159*, 1908–1913.

Roemer, L., Orsillo, S. M., Borkovec, T. D., & Litz, B. T. (1998). Emotional response at the time of a potentially traumatizing event and PTSD symptomatology: A preliminary retrospective analysis of the DSM–IV criterion A-2. *Journal of Behavior Therapy and Experimental Psychiatry, 29*, 123–130.

Rogers, R. (Ed.). (1997). *Clinical assessment of malingering and deception* (2nd ed.). New York: Guilford Press.

Rogers, R., Bagby, R. M., & Dickens, S. E. (1992). *Structured interview of reported symptoms professional manual*. Odessa, FL: Psychological Assessment Resources.

Rogers, R., Kropp, P. R., Bagby, R. M., & Dickens, S. E. (1992). Faking specific disorders: A study of the Structured Interview of Reported Symptoms (SIRS). *Journal of Clinical Psychology, 48*, 643–648.

Roid, G. H., & Fitts, W. H. (1994). *Tennessee Self-Concept Scale* (Revised manual). Los Angeles: Western Psychological Services.

Rorschach, H. (1981). *Psychodiagnostics: A diagnostic test based upon perception.* (P. Lemkau & B. Kronemberg, Eds. & Trans., 9th ed.). New York: Grune & Stratton. (Original work published 1921)

Rosenman, S. (2002). Trauma and posttraumatic stress disorder in Australia: Findings in the population sample of the Australian National Survey of Mental Health and Wellbeing. *Australian and New Zealand Journal of Psychiatry, 36*, 515–520.

Ross, C. A. (1989). *Multiple personality disorder: Diagnosis, clinical features, and treatment*. New York: Wiley.

Ross, C. A., Duffy, C. M. M., Ellason, J. W., & Weatherbee, J. (2002). Prevalence, reliability and validity of dissociative disorders in an inpatient setting. *Journal of Trauma and Dissociation, 3*, 7–17.

Ross, C. A., Heber, S., Norton, G. R., Anderson, D., & Barchet, P. (1989). The Dissociative Disorders Interview Schedule: A structured interview. *Dissociation: Progress in the Dissociative Disorders, 2*, 169–189.

Ross, C. A., Joshi, S., & Currie, R. (1991). Dissociative experiences in the general population: A factor analysis. *Hospital and Community Psychiatry, 42*, 297–301.

Ross, C. A., Miller, S. D., Reagor, P., Bjornson, L., Fraser, G. A., & Anderson, G. (1990). Structured interview data on 102 cases of multiple personality disorder from four centers. *American Journal of Psychiatry, 147*, 596–601.

Rothbaum, B. O., Foa, E. B., Riggs, D. S., Murdock, T., & Walsh, W. (1992). A prospective examination of post-traumatic stress disorder in rape victims. *Journal of Traumatic Stress, 5*, 455–475.

Ruch, L. O., & Chandler, S. M. (1983). Sexual assault trauma during the acute phase: An exploratory model and multivariate analysis. *Journal of Health and Social Behavior, 24*, 184–185.

Runtz, M. G., & Roche, D. N. (1999). Validation of the Trauma Symptom Inventory (TSI) in a Canadian university sample. *Child Maltreatment, 4,* 69–80.

Russell, D. E. H. (1983). The incidence and prevalence of intrafamilial and extrafamilial sexual abuse of female children. *Child Abuse and Neglect, 7,* 133–146.

Sack, W. H., Seeley, J. R., & Clarke, G. N. (1997). Does PTSD transcend cultural barriers?: A study from the Khmer adolescent refugee project. *Journal of the American Academy of Child and Adolescent Psychiatry, 36,* 49–54.

Sanders, S. (1986). The perceptual alteration scale: A scale measuring dissociation. *American Journal of Clinical Hypnosis, 29,* 95–102.

Santina, M. R. (1998). *Object relations, ego development, and affect regulation in severely addicted substance abusers.* Unpublished doctoral dissertation, Department of Psychology, Columbia University, New York.

Sargant, W., & Slater, E. (1941). Amnestic syndromes of war. *Proceedings of the Royal Society of Medicine, 34,* 757–764.

Sattler, D. N., Preston, A. J., Kaiser, C. F., Olivera, V. E., Valdez, J., & Schlueter, S. (2002). Hurricane Georges: A cross-national study examining preparedness, resource loss, and psychological distress in the U.S. Virgin Islands, Puerto Rico, Dominican Republic, and the United States. *Journal of Traumatic Stress, 15,* 339–350.

Saunders, B. E., Arata, C. M., & Kilpatrick, D. G. (1990). Development of a crime-related post-traumatic stress disorder scale for women within the Symptom Checklist–90–Revised. *Journal of Traumatic Stress, 3,* 267–277.

Saunders, E. A. (1991). Rorschach indicators of chronic childhood sexual abuse in female borderline patients. *Bulletin of the Menninger Clinic, 55,* 48–71.

Scarpa, A., Fikretoglu, D., Bowser, F., Hurley, J. D., Papert, C. A., Romero, N., & Van Voorhees, E. (2002). Community violence exposure in university students: A replication and extension. *Journal of Interpersonal Violence, 17,* 253–272.

Schechter, D. S., Marshall, R. D., Salman, E., Goetz, D., Davies, S., & Liebowitz, M. R. (2000). *Ataque de nervios* and history of childhood trauma. *Journal of Traumatic Stress, 13,* 529–534.

Scheibe, S., Bagby, R. M., Miller, L. S., & Dorian, B. J. (2001). Assessing posttraumatic stress disorder with the MMPI–2 in a sample of workplace accident victims. *Psychological Assessment, 13,* 369–374.

Scher, C. D., Stein, M. B., Asmundson, G. J. G., McCreary, D. R., & Forde, D. R. (2001). The Childhood Trauma Questionnaire in a community sample: Psychometric properties and normative data. *Journal of Traumatic Stress, 14,* 843–857.

Schlenger, W. E., Caddell, J. M., Ebert, L., Jordan, B. K., Rourke, K. M., Wilson, D., et al. (2002). Psychological reactions to terrorist attacks: Findings from the National Study of Americans' Reactions to September 11. *Journal of the American Medical Association, 288,* 581–588.

Schlenger, W., & Kulka, R. A. (1989). PTSD scale development for the MMPI–2. Research Triangle Park, NC: Research Triangle Park Institute.

Schulman, M. (1979). *A survey of spousal violence against women in Kentucky.* Washington, DC: U.S. Department of Justice, Law Enforcement.

Scotti, J. R., Sturges, L. V., & Lyons, J. A. (1996). The Keane PTSD scale extracted from the MMPI: Sensitivity and specificity with Vietnam veterans. *Journal of Traumatic Stress, 9,* 643–650.

Scragg, P., Grey, N., Lee, D., Young, K., & Turner, S. W. (2001). A brief report on the Penn Inventory for Posttraumatic Stress Disorder. *Journal of Traumatic Stress, 14,* 605–611.

Segman, R. H., Cooper-Kazaz, R., Macciardi, F., Goltser, T., Halfon, Y., Dobroborski, T., et al. (2002). Association between the dopamine transporter gene and posttraumatic stress disorder. *Molecular Psychiatry, 7,* 903–907.

Selley, C., King, E., Peveler, R., Osola, K., Martin, N., & Thompson, C. (1997). Post-traumatic stress disorder symptoms and the Clapham rail accident. *British Journal of Psychiatry, 171,* 478–482.

Selzer, M. L. (1971). The Michigan Alcoholism Screening Test: The quest for a new diagnostic instrument. *American Journal of Psychiatry, 127,* 89–94.

Sembi, S., Tarrier, N., O'Neill, P., Burns, A., & Faragher, B. (1998). Does posttraumatic stress disorder occur after stroke: A preliminary study. *International Journal of Geriatric Psychiatry, 13,* 315–322.

Sewell, J. D. (1993). Traumatic stress of multiple murder investigations. *Journal of Traumatic Stress, 6,* 103–118.

Shalev, A. Y., Peri, T., Canetti, L., & Schreiber, S. (1996). Predictors of PTSD in injured trauma survivors: A prospective study. *American Journal of Psychiatry, 153,* 219–225.

Shea, M. T. (1996). Enduring personality change after catastrophic experience. In American Psychiatric Association (Ed.), *DSM–IV sourcebook, Volume IV.* Washington, DC: American Psychiatric Association.

Shear, M. K., & Smith-Caroff, K. (2002). Traumatic loss and the syndrome of complicated grief. *PTSD Research Quarterly, 13,* 1–7.

Shedler, J., Mayman, M., & Manis, M. (1993). The illusion of mental health. *American Psychologist, 48,* 1117–1131.

Shepard, M. F., & Campbell, J. A. (1992). The Abusive Behavior Inventory: A measure of psychological and physical abuse. *Journal of Interpersonal Violence, 7,* 291–305.

Shields, N. M., Resick, P. A., & Hanneke, C. R. (1990). Victims of marital rape. In R. T. Ammerman & M. Hersen (Eds.), *Treatment of family violence* (pp. 165–182). New York: Wiley.

Shilony, E., & Grossman, F. K. (1993). Depersonalization as a defense mechanism in survivors of trauma. *Journal of Traumatic Stress, 6,* 119–128.

Silbert, M. H., & Pines, A. M. (1981). Child sexual abuse as an antecedent to prostitution. *Child Abuse and Neglect, 5,* 407–411.

Silbert, M. H., & Pines, A. M. (1982). Victimization of street prostitutes. *Victimology, 7*, 122–133.

Silove, D. M., Steel, Z., McGorry, P. D., Miles, V., & Drobny, J. (2002). The impact of torture on post-traumatic stress symptoms in war-affected Tamil refugees and immigrants. *Comprehensive Psychiatry, 43*, 49–55.

Silver, R. C., Holman, E. A., McIntosh, D. N., Poulin, M., & Gil-Rivas, V. (2002). Nationwide longitudinal study of psychological responses to September 11. *Journal of the American Medical Association, 288*, 1235–1244.

Silverton, L., & Gruber, C. P. (1998). *The Malingering Probability Scale (MPS) manual*. Los Angeles: Western Psychological Services.

Simeon, D., Guralnik, O., & Schmeidler, J. (2001). Development of a depersonalization severity scale. *Journal of Traumatic Stress, 14*, 341–349.

Simeon, D., Guralnik, O., Schmeidler, J., Sirof, B., & Knutelska, M. (2001). The role of childhood interpersonal trauma in depersonalization disorder. *American Journal of Psychiatry, 158*, 1027–1033.

Simon, R. I. (Ed.). (1995). *Posttraumatic stress disorder in litigation: Guidelines for forensic assessment*. Washington, DC: American Psychiatric Press.

Simons, R. L., & Whitbeck, L. B. (1991). Sexual abuse as a precursor to prostitution and victimization among adolescent and adult homeless women. *Journal of Family Issues, 12*, 361–379.

Skinner, H. A. (1992). The drug abuse screening test. *Addictive Behaviors, 7*, 363–371.

Smith, D. W., & Frueh, B. C. (1996). Compensation seeking, comorbidity, and apparent exaggeration of PTSD symptoms among Vietnam combat veterans. *Psychological Assessment, 8*, 3–6.

Smith, G. P. (1997). Assessment of malingering with self-report instruments. In R. Rogers (Ed.), *Clinical assessment of malingering and deception* (pp. 351–370). New York: Guilford Press.

Smith Fawzi, M. C., Murphy, E., Pham, T., Lin, L., Poole, C., & Mollica, R. F. (1997). The validity of screening for post-traumatic stress disorder and major depression among Vietnamese political prisoners. *Acta Psychiatrica Scandinavica, 95*, 87–93.

Sloan, P. (1988). Post-traumatic stress in survivors of an airplane crash-landing: A clinical and exploratory research intervention. *Journal of Traumatic Stress, 1*, 211–229.

Solomon, S. D., Keane, T. M., Newman, E., & Kaloupek, D. G. (1996). Choosing self-report measures and structured interviews. In E. B. Carlson (Ed.), *Trauma research methodology* (pp. 61–81). Lutherville, MD: Sidran Press.

Solomon, S. D., & Smith, E. M. (1994). Social support and perceived control as moderators of responses to dioxin and flood exposure. In R. J. Ursano, B. G. McCaughey, & C. S. Fullerton (Eds.), *Individual and community responses to trauma and disaster: The structure of human chaos* (pp. 179–200). Cambridge: Cambridge University Press.

Solomon, Z., Iancu, I., & Tyano, S. (1997). World assumptions following disaster. *Journal of Applied Social Psychology, 27,* 1785–1798.

Southwick, S. M., Krystal, J. H., Bremner, J. D., Morgan, C. A., Nicolaou, A. L., Nagy, L. M., et al. (1997). Noradrenergic and serotonergic function in posttraumatic stress disorder. *Archives of General Psychiatry, 54,* 749–758.

Spiegel, D., Koopman, C., Cardeña, E., & Classen, C. C. (1996). Dissociative symptoms in the diagnosis of acute stress disorder. In L. K. Michelson & W. J. Ray (Eds.), *Handbook of dissociation: Theoretical, empirical, and clinical perspectives* (pp. 367–380). New York: Plenum Press.

Spinazzola, J., Blaustein, M., & Van der Kolk, B. A., (2002). *Full versus partial DESNOS prevalence in a PTSD research sample.* Unpublished manuscript. Trauma Center, Boston.

Spitzer, R. L., Williams, J. B., Gibbon, M., & First, M. B. (1990). *User's guide for the Structured Clinical Interview for DSM–III–R.* Washington, DC: American Psychiatric Association.

Springs, F. E., & Friedrich, W. N. (1992). Health risk behaviors and medical sequelae of childhood sexual abuse. *Mayo Clinic Proceedings, 67,* 527–532.

Stamm, B. H. (Ed.). (1996). *Measurement of stress, trauma, and adaptation.* Lutherville, MD: Sidran Press.

Stein, M. B., Jang, K. L., Taylor, S., Vernon, P. A., & Livesley, W. J. (2002). Genetic and environmental influences on trauma exposure and posttraumatic stress disorder symptoms: A twin study. *American Journal of Psychiatry, 159,* 1675–1681.

Steinberg, M. (1993). The spectrum of depersonalization: Assessment and treatment. In D. Spiegel, R. P. Kluft, R. J. Lowenstein, J. C. Nemiah, F. W. Putnam, & M. Steinberg (Eds.), *Dissociative disorders: A clinical review* (pp. 79–103). Lutherville, MD: Sidran Press.

Steinberg, M. (1994a). *Structured Clinical Interview for DSM–IV Dissociative Disorders–Revised (SCID–D–R).* Washington, DC: American Psychiatric Press.

Steinberg, M. (1994b). *Interviewer's Guide to the Structured Clinical Interview for DSM–IV Dissociative Disorders–Revised (SCID–D–R).* Washington, DC: American Psychiatric Press.

Steinberg, M., Cicchetti, D. V., Buchanan, J., Hall, P. E., & Rounsaville, B. J. (1989–1993). *NIMH field trials of the Structured Clinical Interview for DSM–IV Dissociative Disorders (SCID–D).* Unpublished manuscript, Yale University School of Medicine, New Haven, CT.

Steinberg, M., Rounsaville, B. J., & Cicchetti, D. V. (1990). The Structured Clinical Interview for DSM–III–R Dissociative Disorders: Preliminary report on a new diagnostic instrument. *American Journal of Psychiatry, 147,* 76–82.

Stermac, L., Reist, D., Addison, M., & Millar, G. M. (2002). Childhood risk factors for women's sexual victimization. *Journal of Interpersonal Violence, 17,* 647–670.

Stermac, L., Sheridan, P. M., Davidson, A., & Dunn, S. (1996). Sexual assault of males. *Journal of Interpersonal Violence, 11,* 52–64.

Stets, J. E., & Straus, M. A. (1990). Gender differences in reporting marital violence and its consequences. In M. A. Straus & R. J. Gelles (Eds.), *Physical violence in American families: Risk factors and adaptation to violence in 8,145 families.* Brunswick, NJ: Transaction.

Stoddard, F. J., & Todres, I. D. (2001). A new frontier: Posttraumatic stress and its prevention, diagnosis and treatment. *Critical Care Medicine, 29,* 687–688.

Stoll, C., Schelling, G., Goetz, A. E., Kilger, E., Bayer, A., Kapfhammar, H. P., et al. (2000). Health-related quality of life and post-traumatic stress disorder in patients after cardiac surgery and intensive care treatment. *Journal of Thoracic and Cardiovascular Surgery, 120,* 505–512.

Stordeur, R. A., & Stille, R. (1989). *Ending men's violence against their partners: One road to peace.* Newbury Park, CA: Sage.

Strain, J. J., Wolf, D., Newcorn, J., & Fulop, G. (1996). Adjustment disorder. In American Psychiatric Association (Ed.), *DSM–IV sourcebook, Volume IV.* Washington, DC: American Psychiatric Association.

Straus, M. A. (1979). Measuring intrafamily conflict and violence: The Conflicts Tactics (CT) Scales. *Journal of Marriage and the Family, 41,* 75–88.

Straus, M. A., & Gelles, R. J. (1990). *Physical violence in American families: Risk factors and adaptation to violence in 8,145 families.* New Brunswick, NJ: Transaction.

Straus, M. A., Gelles, R. J., & Steinmetz, S. (1980). *Behind closed doors: Violence in the American family.* Garden City, NY: Doubleday.

Taylor, S., Kuch, K., Koch, W. J., Crockett, D. J., & Passey, G. (1998). The structure of posttraumatic stress symptoms. *Journal of Abnormal Psychology, 107,* 154–160.

Tedstone, J. E., & Tarrier, N. (2003). Posttraumatic stress disorder following medical illness and treatment. *Clinical Psychology Review, 23,* 409–448.

Tichenor, V., Marmar, C. R., Weiss, D. S., Metzler, T. J., & Ronfeldt, H. M. (1996). The relationship of peritraumatic dissociation and posttraumatic stress: Findings in female Vietnam theater veterans. *Journal of Consulting and Clinical Psychology, 64,* 1054–1059.

Tjaden, P., & Thoennes, N. (1998). *Stalking in America: Findings from the National Violence Against Women Survey.* Washington, DC: U.S. Department of Justice, National Institute of Justice.

Tjaden, P., & Thoennes, N. (2000). *Full report of the prevalence, incidence, and consequences of violence against women: Findings from the National Violence Against Women Survey* (NCJ Publication No. 183781). Washington, DC: U.S. Department of Justice, Centers for Disease Control and Prevention.

Tolman, R. M. (1989). The development of a measure of psychological maltreatment of women by their male partners. *Violence and Victims, 4,* 156–177.

Torrie, A. (1944). Psychosomatic casualties in the Middle East. *Lancet, 1,* 139–143.

Trimble, M. R. (1981). *Post-traumatic neurosis.* Chichester, England: Wiley.

Turner, S. W., Yuksel, S., & Silove, D. M. (2003). Survivors of mass violence and torture. In B. L. Green, M. J. Friedman, J. T. V. M. De Jong, S. D. Solomon, T. M. Keane, J. A. Fairbank, et al. (Eds.), *Trauma interventions in war and peace: Prevention, practice, and policy* (pp. 185–211). New York: Kluwer.

Ullman, S. E., & Brecklin, L. R. (2002). Sexual assault history, PTSD, and mental health service seeking in a national sample of women. *Journal of Community Psychology, 30,* 261–279.

Ullman, S. E., & Filipas, H. H. (2001). Predictors of PTSD symptom severity and social reactions in sexual assault victims. *Journal of Traumatic Stress, 14,* 369–389.

Ursano, R. J., Fullerton, C. S., Epstein, R. S., Crowley, B., Vance, K., Kao, T., et al. (1999). Peritraumatic dissociation and posttraumatic stress disorder following motor vehicle accidents. *American Journal of Psychiatry, 156,* 1808–1810.

Ursano, R. J., Fullerton, C., Kao, T., Bhartiya, V., & Dinneen, M. P. (April, 1992). *PTSD in community samples: Development of a self-report instrument.* Paper presented at the meeting of the International Society for Traumatic Stress Studies, World Conference, Amsterdam, Netherlands.

Ursano, R. J., Fullerton, C. S., & McCaughey, B. G. (1994). Trauma and disaster. In R. J. Ursano, C. S. Fullerton, & B. G. McCaughey (Eds.), *Individual and community response to trauma and disaster: The structure of human chaos.* Cambridge: Cambridge University Press.

Ursano, R. J., & McCarroll, J. E. (1994). Exposure to traumatic death: The nature of the stressor. In R. J. Ursano, C. S. Fullerton, & B. G. McCaughey (Eds.), *Individual and community response to trauma and disaster: The structure of human chaos.* Cambridge: Cambridge University Press.

U.S. Department of Health and Human Services, Administration on Children, Youth and Families. (2002). *Child maltreatment 2000.* Washington, DC: U.S. Government Printing Office.

Valera, R. J., Sawyer, R. G., & Schiraldi, G. R. (2000). Violence and post traumatic stress disorder in a sample of inner city street prostitutes. *American Journal of Health Studies, 16,* 149–155.

van der Kolk, B. A. (1996). The complexity of adaptation to trauma: Self-regulation, stimulus discrimination, and characterological development. In B. A. van der Kolk, A. C. McFarlane, & L. Weisaeth (Eds.), *Traumatic stress: The effects of overwhelming experience on mind, body, and society* (pp. 182–213). New York: Guilford Press.

van der Kolk, B. A., & Ducey, C. (1984). Clinical implications of the Rorschach in post-traumatic stress disorder. In B. A. van der Kolk (Ed.), *Post-traumatic stress disorder: Psychological and biological sequelae* (pp. 29–42). Washington, DC: American Psychiatric Association.

van der Kolk, B. A., & Ducey, C. (1989). The psychological processing of traumatic experience: Rorschach patterns in PTSD. *Journal of Traumatic Stress, 2*, 259–263.

van der Kolk, B. A., Roth, S., Pelcovitz, D., Mandel, F. S., & Spinazzola, J. (in press). Disorders of extreme stress: The empirical foundation of complex adaptation to trauma. *Journal of Traumatic Stress.*

Van IJzendoorn, M., & Schuengel, C. (1996). The measurement of dissociation in normal and clinical populations: Meta analytic validation of the Dissociative Experiences Scale (DES). *Clinical Psychology Review, 16*, 382.

Van Loey, N. E. E., Maas, C. J. M., Faber, A. W., & Taal, L. A. (2003). Predictors of chronic posttraumatic stress symptoms following burn injury: Results of a longitudinal study. *Journal of Traumatic Stress, 16*, 361–369.

Van Ommeren, M., DeJong, J. T. V. M., Sharma, B., Komproe, I. H., Thapa, S. B., & Cardena, E. (2001). Psychiatric disorders among tortured Bhutanese refugees in Nepal. *Archives of General Psychiatry, 58*, 475–482.

Van Ommeren, M., Sharma, B., Sharma, G. K., Komproe, I. H., Cardeña, E., & De Jong, J. T. V. M. (2002). The relationship between somatic and PTSD symptoms among Bhutanese refugee torture survivors: Examination of comorbidity with anxiety and depression. *Journal of Traumatic Stress, 15*, 415–421.

Vanwesenenbeek, I., de Graaf, R., van Zessen, G., Straver, C. J., & Visser, J. H. (1995). Professional HIV risk taking, levels of victimization, and well-being in female prostitutes in the Netherlands. *Archives of Sexual Behavior, 24*, 503–515.

Vesti, P., & Kastrup, M. (1995). Refugee status, torture, and adjustment. In J. R. Freedy & S. E. Hobfoll (Eds.), *Traumatic stress: From theory to practice* (pp. 213–235). New York: Plenum Press.

Vlahov, D. G. S., Resnick, H. S., Ahern, J., Boscarino, J. A., Bucuvalas, M. J., Gold, J., et al. (2002). Increased use of cigarettes, alcohol, and marijuana among Manhattan, New York, residents after the September 11th terrorist attacks. *American Journal of Epidemiology, 155*, 988–996.

Vrana, S., & Lauterbach, D. (1994). Prevalence of traumatic events and posttraumatic psychological symptoms in a nonclinical sample of college students. *Journal of Traumatic Stress, 7*, 289–302.

Vreven, D. L., Gudanowski, D. M., King, L. A., & King, D. W. (1995). The Civilian Version of the Mississippi PTSD Scale: A psychometric evaluation. *Journal of Traumatic Stress, 8*, 91–109.

Walker, E. A., Katon, W., Harrop-Griffiths, J., Holm, L., Russo, J., & Hickok, L. R. (1988). Relationship of chronic pelvic pain to psychiatric diagnoses and childhood sexual abuse. *American Journal of Psychiatry, 145*, 75–80.

Walker, E. A., Katon, W. J., Roy-Byrne, P. P., Jemelka, R. P., & Russo, J. (1993). Histories of sexual victimization in patients with irritable bowel syndrome or inflammatory bowel disease. *American Journal of Psychiatry, 150*, 1502–1506.

Walker, E. A., Keegan, D., Gardner, G., Sullivan, M., Bernstein, D. P., & Katon, W. J. (1997). Psychosocial factors in fibromyalgia compared with rheumatoid arthritis: II, Sexual, physical, and emotional abuse and neglect. *Psychosomatic Medicine, 56,* 572–577.

Walker, L. E. (1984). *The battered woman syndrome.* New York: Springer.

Walker, L. E. (1991). Post-traumatic stress disorder in women: Diagnosis and treatment of battered woman syndrome. *Psychotherapy, 28,* 21–29.

Waller, N. G., Putnam, F. W., & Carlson, E. B. (1996). Types of dissociation and dissociative types: A taxometric analysis of dissociative experiences. *Psychological Methods, 1,* 300–321.

Watson, C. G. (1990). Psychometric post-traumatic stress disorder measurement techniques: A review. *Psychological Assessment, 2,* 460–469.

Watson, C. G., Plemel, D., DeMotts, J., Howard, M. T., Tuorila, J., Moog, R., et al. (1994). A comparison of four PTSD measures' convergent validities in Vietnam veterans. *Journal of Traumatic Stress, 7,* 75–82.

Weathers, F. W., Blake, D. D., Krinsley, K., Haddad, W., Huska, J., & Keane, T. M. (1992, October). *The Clinician–Administered PTSD Scale–Diagnostic Version (CAPS–1).* Paper presented at the annual meeting of the International Society for Traumatic Stress Studies, Los Angeles.

Weathers, F. W., Blake, D. D., & Litz, B. T. (1991, August). *Reliability and validity of a new structured interview for PTSD.* Paper presented at the annual meeting of the American Psychological Association, San Francisco.

Weathers, F. W., Keane, T. M., & Davidson, J. R. T. (2001). The Clinician–Administered PTSD Scale: A review of the first ten years of research. *Depression and Anxiety, 13,* 132–156.

Weathers, F. W., Litz, B. T., Herman, D. S., Huska, J. A., & Keane, T. M. (1993, October). *The PTSD Checklist (PCL): Reliability, validity, and diagnostic utility.* Paper presented at the annual meeting of the International Society for Traumatic Stress Studies, San Antonio, TX.

Weathers, F. W., Litz, B. T., Herman, D. S., Keane, T. M., Steinberg, H. R., Huska, J. A., et al. (1996). The utility of the SCL–90–R for the diagnosis of war-zone–related PTSD. *Journal of Traumatic Stress, 9,* 111–128.

Weathers, F. W., Litz, B. T., & Keane, T. M. (1995). Military trauma. In J. R. Freedy & S. E. Hobfoll (Eds.), *Traumatic stress: From theory to practice* (pp. 103–128). New York: Plenum Press.

Weathers, F. W., Ruscio, A. M., & Keane, T. M. (1999). Psychometric properties of nine scoring rules for the Clinician–Administered Posttraumatic Stress Disorder Scale. *Psychological Assessment, 11,* 124–133.

Weiss, D. S., & Marmar, C. R. (1996). The Impact of Event Scale–Revised. In J. P. Wilson & T. Keane (Eds.), *Assessing psychological trauma and PTSD: A handbook for practitioners* (pp. 399–411). New York: Guilford Press.

Weiss, D. S., Marmar, C. R., Metzler, T., & Ronfeldt, H. (1995). Predicting symptomatic distress in emergency services personnel. *Journal of Consulting and Clinical Psychology, 63,* 361–368.

West, C. M. (2002). Battered, black, and blue: An overview of violence in the lives of black women. *Women and Therapy, 25,* 5–27.

Wetter, M. W., Baer, R. A., Berry, D. T. R., & Reynolds, S. K. (1994). The effect of symptom information on faking on the MMPI–2. *Assessment, 1,* 199–207.

Wetter, M. W., Baer, R. A., Berry, D. T. R., Robinson, L. H., & Sumpter, J. (1993). MMPI–2 profiles of motivated fakers given specific symptom information: A comparison to matched patients. *Psychological Assessment, 5,* 317–323.

Wetter, M. W., Baer, R. A., Berry, D. T. R., Smith, G. T., & Larson, L. (1992). Sensitivity of MMPI–2 validity scales to random responding and malingering. *Psychological Assessment, 4,* 369–374.

Wetzel, R. D., Murphy, G. E., Simons, A. D., Lustman, P., North, C. S., & Yutzy, S. H. (2003). What does the Keane PTSD scale of the MMPI measure?: Repeated measurements in a group of patients with major depression. *Psychological Reports, 92,* 781–786.

Williams, L. M. (1994). Recall of childhood trauma: A prospective study of women's memories of child sexual abuse. *Journal of Consulting and Clinical Psychology, 62,* 1167–1176.

Williams, L. M. (1995). Recovered memories of abuse in women with documented child sexual victimization histories. *Journal of Traumatic Stress, 8,* 649–673.

Williamson, C., & Cluse-Tolar, T. (2002). Pimp-controlled prostitution: Still an integral part of street life. *Violence Against Women, 8,* 1074–1092.

Wilson, J. P. (1994). The historical evolution of PTSD diagnostic criteria: From Freud to DSM–IV. *Journal of Traumatic Stress, 7,* 681–689.

Wilson, J. P., & Moran, T. A. (in press). Forensic/clinical assessment of psychological trauma and PTSD in legal settings. In J. Wilson & T. Keane (Eds.), *Assessing psychological trauma and PTSD: A practitioner's handbook* (2nd ed). New York: Guilford Press.

Wilson, J., & Keane, T. (Eds.). (in press). *Assessing psychological trauma and PTSD: A practitioner's handbook* (2nd ed.). New York: Guilford Press.

Wilson, J. P., & Walker, A. J. (1990). Toward an MMPI trauma profile. *Journal of Traumatic Stress, 3,* 151–168.

Winfield, I., George, L. K., Swartz, M., & Blazer, D. G. (1990). Sexual assault and psychiatric disorders among women in a community population. *American Journal of Psychiatry, 147,* 335–341.

Wolfe, J., Brown, P. J., & Bucsela, M. L. (1992). Symptom responses of female Vietnam veterans to Operation Desert Storm. *American Journal of Psychiatry, 149,* 676–679.

Wolfe, J., Brown, P. J., Furey, I., & Levin, K. B. (1993). Development of a wartime stressor scale for women. *Psychological Assessment, 5,* 330–335.

Wong, M. R., & Cook, D. (1992). Shame and its contribution to PTSD. *Journal of Traumatic Stress, 5,* 557–562.

World Health Organization. (1992). *International statistical classification of diseases and related health problem*. (10th rev. ed.). Geneva, Switzerland: Author.

Wyatt, G. E. (1985). The sexual abuse of Afro-American and White American women in childhood. *Child Abuse and Neglect, 9*, 231–240.

Yen, S., Shea, M. T., Battle, C. L., Johnson, D. M., Zlotnick, C., Dolan-Sewell, R., et al. (2002). Traumatic exposure and posttraumatic stress disorder in borderline, schizotypal, avoidant, and obsessive-compulsive personality disorders: Findings from the Collaborative Longitudinal Personality Disorders Study. *Journal of Nervous and Mental Disease, 190*, 510–518.

Yehuda, R., Kahana, B., Southwick, S. M., & Giller, E. L. (1994). Depressive features in Holocaust survivors with posttraumatic stress disorder. *Journal of Traumatic Stress, 7*, 699–704.

Yehuda, R., & McFarlane, A. (1995). Conflict between current knowledge about posttraumatic stress disorder and its original conceptual basis. *American Journal of Psychiatry, 152*, 1705–1713.

Yoshihama, M., & Horrocks, J. (2002). Posttraumatic stress symptoms and victimization among Japanese American women. *Journal of Consulting and Clinical Psychology, 70*, 205–215.

Yovell, Y., Bannett, Y., & Shalev, A. Y. (2003). Amnesia for traumatic events among recent survivors: A pilot study. *CNS Spectrums, 8*, 676–685.

Zaidi, L. Y., & Foy, D. W. (1994). Childhood abuse experiences and combat-related PTSD. *Journal of Traumatic Stress, 7*, 33–42.

Zimmerman, M., & Mattia, J. I. (1999). Psychotic subtyping of major depressive disorder and posttraumatic stress disorder. *Journal of Clinical Psychiatry, 60*, 311–314.

Zisook, S., Chentsova-Dutton, Y. E., & Shuchter, S. R. (1998). PTSD following bereavement. *Annals of Clinical Psychiatry, 10*, 157–163.

Zlotnick, C., Donaldson, D., Spirito, A., & Pearlstein, T. (1997). Affect regulation and suicide attempts in adolescent inpatients. *Journal of the American Academy of Child and Adolescent Psychiatry, 36*, 793–798.

Zlotnick, C., & Pearlstein, T. (1997). Validation of the Structured Interview for Disorders of Extreme Stress. *Comprehensive Psychiatry, 38*, 243–247.

# Index

# About the Author

**John Briere, PhD,** is an associate professor in the Departments of Psychiatry and Psychology at the University of Southern California and director of the Psychological Trauma Program at Los Angeles County–University of Southern California Medical Center. He is a past president of the International Society for Traumatic Stress Studies and a fellow of the American Psychological Association. He is the author of numerous books, articles, chapters, and psychological tests in the areas of child abuse, psychological trauma, and interpersonal violence. His Web site can be found at www.JohnBriere.com